INTERACTIVE REALISM

Interactive Realism

The Poetics of Cyberspace

DANIEL DOWNES

McGill-Queen's University Press
Montreal & Kingston · London · Ithaca

Legal deposit second quarter 2005
Bibliothèque nationale du Québec

Printed in Canada on acid-free paper that is 100% ancient forest free
(100% post-consumer recycled), processed chlorine free.

This book has been published with the help of grants from the University
of New Brunswick and the Office of the Dean of Arts, University of New
Brunswick at Saint John.

McGill-Queen's University Press acknowledges the support of the
Canada Council for the Arts for our publishing program. We also
acknowledge the financial support of the Government of Canada
through the Book Publishing Industry Development Program (BPIDP) for
our publishing activities.

Library and Archives Canada Cataloguing in Publication

Downes, Daniel M. (Daniel Mark), 1960–
    Interactive realism: the poetics of Cyberspace/Daniel Downes.

    Includes bibliographical references and index.
    ISBN 0-7735-2854-7 (bnd)
    ISBN 0-7735-2920-9 (pbk)

    1. Cyberspace – Social aspects. 2. Digital media – Social aspects.
    3. Human-computer interaction. I. Title.
    HM851.D69 2005   302.23'1   C2004-905886-x

Typeset in Palatino 10/13
by Caractéra inc., Quebec City

To Claire

Contents

Acknowledgments

The ideas expressed in this book have evolved and grown over an extended period. Consequently, I owe thanks to many people who have contributed to their final shape. Early explorations of the relationship between virtual reality and technologies of perspective were presented in 1994 as papers at the Screensites Conference at McGill University, the Screen Conference in Glasgow, and the annual meeting of the Canadian Communication Association in Calgary. Chapter 4, on affective communities, owes much to my MA work at Carleton University and to the encouragement and insight of Chris Dornan and Michael Dorland.

At McGill, I am indebted to a number of people. I extend my appreciation to the faculty of the Graduate Program in Communications, in particular to Will Straw, George Szanto, and Gertrude Robinson. I owe a huge debt to Charles Levin for his enthusiasm for my ideas, his encouragement to develop them at my own pace and his at times maddening persistence in making me edit, prune, and focus my argument. I would also like to thank the associated faculty of the Centre for the Study of Regulated Industries at McGill's Law Faculty, who provided a home for me during my postdoctoral research and who encouraged me to explore the implications of applying interactive realism to questions of legal pluralism. In particular, I would like to thank Richard Janda, who has been a friend, colleague, research partner, and unexpected benefactor.

At McGill-Queen's, I am indebted to Aurèle Parisien for his faith in this project from the beginning. It has been a long road and Aurèle has always offered encouragement and sage advice. Through the process of peer review several anonymous readers provided useful, thoughtful, and at times challenging comments for which I am grateful. I would also like to acknowledge the work of Ron Curtis in copyediting the manuscript and, at the University of New Brunswick, of Robin Sutherland who helped edit an early draft.

I have received generous financial support for the research that forms the basis of this book, including a joint SSHRC/NSERC Master's Scholarship for studies in science policy, an FCAR grant for the PHD research from which the present book is derived, and an SSHRC Postdoctoral Fellowship.

On a more personal note, I would like to acknowledge two people who have been influential not just in my work but in my life. Many people are lucky enough to have mentors to guide their careers. I consider myself extremely fortunate that a scholar who has helped me as a student, who has shared his insights and taught me how to be an effective academic, has also been, over the past decade, a close friend. My thanks, then, to my friend Paul Attallah. Finally, I am unable to adequately express my appreciation and gratitude to my partner Claire Titus for years of patience, encouragement, love, and support. Without her faith and tolerance this book would never have been written.

Whatever errors remain are entirely my own.

The *Inventio Fortunata*

The *Inventio Fortunata*, a fourteenth-century account of unknown lands, documented the travels of the Franciscan monk Nicholas of Lynne.[1] This apocryphal tale, which was presented to King Edward III upon Lynne's return to England, became something of an authoritative guide to travels into the unknown, despite its dubious authenticity. Columbus reportedly (and unsuccessfully) tried to obtain a copy to help guide his own explorations.

Intellectual explorers of the last decade of the twentieth century described fantastic terrains similar to the imaginary landscapes of Lynne. And like Columbus, these new explorers had few resources to guide them. The uncharted territory was the socially and technologically constructed space of *cyberspace*; the explorers were journalists, researchers, writers, and artists attempting to chronicle, chart, and shape this new digital environment.

Yet, I would argue, the final shape of cyberspace remains to be seen. Are we on the edge of a new frontier, or are we, like Nicholas, drafting narratives that embody our hopes of discovery and that will soon be forgotten, taking the status of ghost books and apocrypha? As one colleague pointed out to me, cyberspace is crowded with remainder trade books, obsolete popular exposés, and academic readers. The image of the *Inventio Fortunata* raises critical questions about the extent to which we construct, rather than discover, the social world and the importance of communications for this process.[2]

In 1996, John Perry Barlow (one of the founders of the Electronic Frontier Foundation and an advocate of Freedom of Speech on the Internet) wrote his "Declaration of Independence of Cyberspace." He proclaimed:

We are creating a world that all may enter without privilege or prejudice accorded by race, economic power, military force, or station of birth ... where anyone, anywhere may express his or her beliefs, no matter how singular, without fear of being coerced into silence or conformity. Your legal concepts of property, expression, identity, movement and context do not apply to us. They are all based on matter, and there is no matter here.[3]

In the years since Barlow wrote these words a number of important legal cases – Napster, iCraveTV.com, Mp3.com, *Eldrid vs Ashcroft*, among others – have led to an increasing transformation of digital information into property protected by copyright and to intellectual property laws that favour large corporate interests and that have shaped the Internet into a global marketplace. The antiterrorism legislation in the United States and Internet security legislation in the G8 countries (including Canada) that came after the September 11, 2001, attacks on the World Trade Center and the Pentagon would seem to challenge Barlow's claim that anyone can express their beliefs without fear of coercion. To some, my claim that the shape of cyberspace is yet to be determined might seem moot.

Indeed, Barlow himself admitted in a summer 2002 interview that his hope "that the Internet was going to be socially connected, in the old, hippie sense, has not come to be." In a telling admission, he "came to feel that [he] had been promoting a society that was not turning out to [his] satisfaction." After September 11, Barlow wrote that he expected to see "the most vigorous efforts to end what remains of freedom in America."[4]

Barlow's efforts to defend the unrestricted copying and sharing of information over the Internet through the lobbying efforts and legal challenges of the Electronic Frontier Foundation have been thwarted by transnational media corporations who define Internet copying and sharing as "theft." Indeed, Barlow blames the failure of the Internet to become a rejuvenated social realm on the very qualities he championed in the mid-1990s. He says, "I used to think that the Internet was going to be a great organizing tool. And it isn't. Because it gives everybody the right to dissent, but individually – it doesn't give any incentive to collective dissent."[5] Perhaps more important is the realization that Barlow had mistaken a short-term period of technological innovation for a long-term transformation in social relations.

I have juxtaposed the idea of the *inventio fortunata* with Barlow's disenchantment with cyberspace to illustrate the central idea of this book. The fact that Internet culture has not created the world Barlow and other cyber-philosophers may have hoped for does not negate the important insight that we create the social world through processes of communication and interaction. Further, the reason the world has not been reshaped in Barlow's image of a virtual Republic of Ideas is that he, along with many others, has mistaken the technological infrastructure we call the Internet with the imaginative space we call cyberspace.

Although the convergence of technology and industry, evident in the mergers of companies like AOL-Time Warner, Vivendi-Universal, or BCE and CTV in Canada, suggests that the age of digital communication might look a lot like the previous age of mass communication, it is the importance of narratives (the stories told about new technologies) and models (based on the metaphors that characterize technologies and that set the conditions for human interaction) that will ultimately help in our efforts to understand the lasting importance of cyberspace.

How then do we begin to investigate the specificity of cyberspace as a process of both communication and social construction? The chapters that follow will explore the ways our experience of communication changes or transforms aspects of social reality. The purpose is not to argue in favour of technological change as a cause for psychological or sociological change. Such is the concern of traditional media theory, or, as I will call it, the transformative turn. Instead, I will challenge the transformative turn in media studies with a version of media ecology that emphasizes the elements of social construction. I call this new method *interactive realism*.

Interactive realism is an approach to studying new media that emphasizes both the linguistic and the nonlinguistic importance of cultural artifacts like the computer in the construction of social reality. Interactive realism focuses not on a single source of causation (seen as changes in the mode of information, the medium of communication, or language) but on relationships between representations, systems of representation, and the shape of the social imaginary. It does so by exploring the metaphors and images used to represent and model social reality. Interactive realism also includes a material dimension, since it emphasizes the importance of the technologies we use to create, store, and transmit these representations. The technologies themselves become important parts of the realities we create.

The virtual places of cyberspace have a lasting importance, not as substitutes for reality, but as environments that provide *play spaces* for experimental interactions. These are "real" spaces, even though they are not the main environments in which a society lives. Many of the negative assessments of these spaces concern more general attitudes toward technology, including fear of powerful machines; distrust of personal experience and the evidence of the senses; distrust of the body; a reduction to, or conflation of, organism and machine; and a reification of codes, text, environment, and social order. This collection of themes constitutes what might be called a poetics of cyberspace.

A poetics of cyberspace is the collection of metaphors and representations that organize, influence, and constrain our thinking in this new communicative environment. Certain metaphors might dominate the development of new technologies, but since knowledge is based on the forward reach of our experiences (compressed and focused through metaphors), experience is, by necessity, pluralistic, complex, and contradictory.

One dominant poetic of cyberspace has already been hinted at – the new media economy that threatens to shape reality into a Time-Warner-Microsoft World. While this theme will reappear throughout the book, it will not be developed as a distinct theme, because it relates to the technology (the Internet) rather than the social processes of communication that are my object of analysis. The poetics of cyberspace takes two shapes. Where it focuses on the Internet we can discern what can be called the *poetics of "e."* The poetics of "e" contains images of disembodiment, technology as an agent of "evolution," Platonic images of the "essence" of reality. In a word, these are the images that led to Barlow's disenchantment with cyberspace and the kind of hype associated with the pre-crash dot.com world of e-commerce. The other aspect of the poetics of cyberspace can be called a *poetics of mediation*; it emphasizes the pluralistic, partial character of our relationship with technology as we engage in practices of identity formation, community building, and the experience of place.

Throughout the following chapters, a number of metaphoric themes will be described that structure discussions about cyberspace and the kinds of reality constructed through computer-mediated interactions. I will use various stories as examples to encourage the reader to think about the relationships between mediation, technology, and social construction.

In chapter 1 a clear distinction will be made between the Internet and cyberspace. This distinction will be presented in the form of a dual specificity that characterizes cyberspace as both a medium of communication and a communicative experience. The method of *interactive realism* will be situated in social constructionist theories and metaphoric analysis.

Chapter 2 will present the first theme in the poetics of cyberspace – the transformative view of media ecology. Central to this theme is the idea that technology transforms individuals and society. Underlying this view is the assumption that computers are technologies of language and that it is language that transforms the psyche and the social.

In chapter 3 the transformative view will be applied to the question of identity. The transformative view can be characterized by a poetics of e-volution where technology is an agent of evolution that will ultimately displace the human. This image of displacement will be contrasted with an interactive understanding of identity whereby our experience of the world is "calibrated" by the tools of representation we use to mediate our experience.

Chapter 4 explores the nature of social identity in cyberspace. What has the transformative view to say about virtual communities? This is the realm of "e" (e-business, e-government, e-democracy). Cyberspace teaches us important lessons about community. The poetics of mediation shows how people create and maintain communities in cyberspace by interacting with one another. It characterizes these communities as play spaces where general processes of community building, norm- and law-making, and social cohesion take place.

In chapter 5 the terrain of cyberspace will be described in terms of iconic landscapes. Building on what has been presented about the transformative view of technology, these landscapes will be characterized as platonic environments that embody utopian ideals.

In chapter 6 the temporal qualities of cyberspace will be examined. Here, the interactive spaces of virtual interaction are examined using the concept of heterotopian spaces that emphasize the multiplicity of cyber-environments and the human labour involved in transforming virtual interactions into public memory.

These themes (the transformative power of technology, displacement and mediation, community, and place) each expose a tension in our relationship with technology, a tension resulting from the tendency to overemphasize technology as the agent of change rather than to focus on the new forms of interaction that arise from new processes of communication. Interactive realism is useful as an interpretive tool because it emphasizes the notion of *making*. Applied to the social world, we can use metaphor and poetics as concepts to describe the construction of social reality within the limits of bodily experience and symbolic systems.

Technology is not a neutral social or psychological determinant, nor is it merely the ideological device used to impose monolithic ways of viewing the world upon an unsuspecting population. Devices shape our experience as we use them. Technologies are, in the end, artifacts created by people living in particular, historically situated cultures who use these devices to interact with the world, with other people, and with themselves. The world we create is, to some degree, a product of the tools we use in its construction. The extent to which we become involved with our technologies, losing sight of our participation in social construction, is both a social and a personal issue. Tools are not simply the application of knowledge to extend human capabilities. They are also material with which we build the physical and symbolic worlds we inhabit.

INTERACTIVE REALISM

1

The Dual Specificity of Cyberspace

The purpose of this chapter is to clarify some terms and to situate the method of interactive realism in the broader tradition of social constructivism. In the first part I distinguish between the Internet (a technological infrastructure built to facilitate digitized communication) and cyberspace (a particular kind of communicative environment). In the second part I present the elements of interactive realism as a method for analyzing the relationships between technology, metaphor, and social construction.

One image that has had a lasting impact on the way we both imagine and use cyberspace appeared in William Gibson's 1984 novel *Neuromancer*, where he depicted a global network comprised of computer and telecommunication systems that enabled users to experience a *consensual hallucination* of moving through space and to interact with objects.[1] He called the global network the "Matrix." Perhaps more importantly, he also constructed a name for the representation produced by the Matrix: he called it "cyberspace." The term was subsequently adopted by the popular media and the public at large to describe the mysterious territory of digitized communications. Cyberspace is the umbrella term for digitally transmitted, multimedia communication as experienced by users. In cyberspace there is a sense that information is "out there" and that what a user accesses at a given time creates an experience – the sense that when we are in cyberspace, we are doing something.

In his new word, Gibson joined two terms: "cybernetics" and "space." Individually, these terms identify two key characteristics of the digital environment. The first, "cybernetics," characterizes the technological infrastructure that makes global communication possible.

In this context, "cyberspace" emphasizes the autonomous and self-steering quality of the Internet and the World Wide Web. The second term, "space," deals with the psychological experience of communication with and through computers. As an imaginative space, cyberspace invites us to question the role of physical space in setting limits for human interaction. It does this by seeming to eliminate the distance between communicators, by seeming to eliminate the gap between simulation and reality, and by questioning the boundary between human and machine.

To what extent does our psychological sense of self (or our sociological sense of community) change as computers become an increasingly prominent communication medium; what happens to us *as we use them*?

Today, images of computers, the Internet, and web pages appear in many media, becoming part of the everyday experience of North American life. While such images are intended to create consumer markets for computers, as well as for media content, the ways in which they appear in the media – a student searching the web for information for school, a computer on the desk of an executive or a secretary, a couple doing their banking on-line, a teenager downloading a movie or music file from the Internet – reflect a level of sophistication in the lives of people who rely on computers for the most basic of tasks. Representations of computers are representations of the tools we use in contemporary life. On the Internet, media "collapse," in the sense that all media (visual, auditory, textual) are used at the same time, complicating the ways in which we process information. Individuals routinely engage in practices that were once considered sophisticated, professional, and unavailable to the general public. Such practices have become, in a profound sense, sites of convergence of business, technology, regulation, and culture. The implications of these new relationships for society and personal identity are tremendous. The more people use such media in everyday life (instead of passively consuming media content) and the more such media use is socially reinforced, the more it can affect who we see ourselves to be. Computer programs are scripts or blueprints for world- and self-construction. Because of this, they provoke thinking about the boundaries between matter, life, and mind. Through digital communication, we create new collective and individual identities, as well as new environments for human interaction.

Before we go further, some terms must be clarified. In particular, the terms "Internet," "virtual reality," and "cyberspace" must be defined in relation to one another and to the shifting discourses around cyberspace as the subject has been discussed and debated since the early 1990s. David Silver (2000) provides one such classification of cyberdiscourse, grouping the field of cyberculture studies into three periods characterized by the main participants discussing the topic, as well as by the themes that dominated the literature in each period.[2] The first stage in cyberculture studies can be called the period of *popular cyberculture*. This stage, which lasted from about 1989 to 1994, was dominated by journalistic and descriptive accounts of technology and social activity. The dominant metaphor of the popular cyberculture literature was the "Internet as frontier of civilization," which was articulated by technological futurists like John Perry Barlow. Popular cyberculture accounts engaged in a dualist debate between commentators who promoted the Internet as a utopian frontier and others who focused on the dystopian potential of cyberspace.

The second stage of cyberdiscourse falls under the heading *cyberculture studies*. This period covered the midnineties and signalled the arrival of academic researchers in the field. Cyberculture studies focused on virtual communities and the nature of on-line identities. Much of this work concentrated on the empowering nature of the technology and of cyberspace as a place of community, creativity, and social construction.

Silver's third period of cyberstudies is the period of *critical cyberculture studies*. This period, which spans the late 1990s to the present, signals (for Silver at least) the establishment of a relatively coherent discipline concerned with the relationships between technology and culture. Critical cyberculture studies views cyberculture as a series of negotiations that take place both on- and off-line. These negotiations address questions about the nature and etiquette of on-line interactions, digital discourses, Internet access, and the design characteristics of computer interfaces and cyberspace environments. The present study would, according to Silver's classification, be an example of critical cyberculture studies.

Silver's classification is useful as a mental framework to apply to the various examples that will be used throughout this book. However, such a classification makes a typical error in assuming that as discourses (and academic fields) develop, new ideas completely supplant their predecessors. For example, it might be tempting to argue that the idea of cyberspace as an embodiment of the hope that communication technology can solve social ills has been replaced by the relatively mundane reality of the Internet as a vehicle for e-commerce. Yet some of the ideas, metaphors, and debates that have described and explained facets of cyberculture have longer histories and greater robustness than the classification might suggest. Indeed, the spatial metaphor of cyberspace and the importance of socially created spaces for interaction may well have long-term implications.

Returning to the three terms "Internet," "virtual reality," and "cyberspace," the Internet is a medium of communication. It is nothing more than a delivery system through which particular kinds of messages (those that have been digitized) are created, sent, received, and stored by means of computers. "Virtual reality," which was used more in the period of popular cyberculture, has at least two meanings. First, it refers to computer simulations abstracted from some part of the "real" world – for example, the output of a flight simulator. Specifically, a virtual environment is an interactive, digitally coded representation of an environment or a place that can, to varying degrees, be controlled by a user. More broadly, virtual realities are alternative or complementary social spaces. In this sense, cyberspace is a kind of meta-virtual reality wherein people can use computer-mediated communications to interact with one another in alternate and complementary social spaces. It is this last definition of cyberspace I will explore in this book.

For some, such virtual realities are particularly exciting because in them we can code not just the image but the "essence" of reality.[3] Such a claim assumes that there is a kind of continuum, with reality at one extreme and illusion or fantasy at the other, and that representations can be judged by the extent to which they reflect reality. However, our understanding of cyberspace and virtual realities will, in the end, be hindered by such a view of representation. Instead, we must come to understand representations, metaphors, and technological devices as some of the tools with which we create much of our social reality.

How does the computer change reality? Virtual realities are simply technological simulations, but as sites of shared experiences (one of the characteristics of cyberspace) they become more interesting. They are related to social construction and imagination, and there is an element of virtuality in all instances of social construction. Critic

Kenneth Burke once argued that realities are best understood as key issues in a society. For example, Burke argued that the key issue in his time was economic and that realities, therefore, were now economic.[4] Might today's realities be understood through terms such as "digitization," or "representation?" The sense of mediated reality created by cyberspace is, in the end, one of the key realities of our society.

SPECIFICITY 1 – TECHNOLOGICAL INFRASTRUCTURE

As electronic funds cross national boundaries every minute, twenty-four hours a day, the world is, indeed, wrapped by electronic highways in an invisible net, creating the global village McLuhan wrote about over thirty years ago. In the "real" world, this conglomeration of networks has been known by various names: the Worldnet, the Information Superhighway, and, most commonly, the Internet (named after the concept of *internetting*, which simply refers to the process of transferring information from one computer platform or system to another). The Internet has expanded exponentially since its conception in the late 1960s and now connects millions of computers worldwide in a global communication system.

The development of the Internet was originally funded by the U.S. Department of Defense. Military requirements for a network that could continue to operate if part of it was destroyed by nuclear attack resulted in a system in which researchers working on one connected computer could exchange information with any other computer in the network without sending signals through a formal, hierarchical structure.[5] Its growth was primarily due to a set of technical standards for digital information transfer dictated by the American government. By the mid-1990s, the text-driven Internet had been supplemented by the World Wide Web – a graphically driven process of creating Hypertext documents using a standard system for creating documents (HyperText Markup Language) and for allowing individuals to use their own computers as nodes in the Internet. This shift expanded the potential use of the networked computer as a communications device (using a standard protocol for transferring documents – HyperText Transfer Protocol). Computer users could now communicate by picture and sound as well as by text messages.

The World Wide Web created a graphical interface that was easier to use and made the Internet accessible to nontechnical users. Since

management of the Internet was commercialized in 1994, access to it
has expanded. Personal computers have also become increasingly
more powerful and affordable, as they have included multimedia
functions such as the ability to process visual and sound files at
greater speed. In the late 1990s, Apple Computer reinvigorated the
consumer computing market with the release of powerful home
machines geared to connecting new users to the Internet. Other PC
manufacturers followed suit as cellular phones, personal data assis-
tants (PDAS), and hand-held computers offered wireless access to certain Internet functions like e-mail and web browsing. The combined
effect of such developments was an explosion of potential participants in a digital culture. While the Internet took three decades to
develop, it took less than four years to become an item of mass consumption. The year 1998 was described by electronic commerce gurus
as the first "e-Christmas," as both consumer demand and business
infrastructure recorded significant Internet-based sales. A July 1999
Nielson/Net Rating study reported that 106.3 million Americans
(39 percent of the population of the United States) regularly used the
Internet. At the same time, in Canada an Angus Reid poll conducted
for the *Globe and Mail* reported that 12.7 million Canadians (55 percent) were regular Internet users.[6] Statistics Canada provided slightly
more conservative figures based on the number of households with
Internet access. In 1999 at least one household member accessed
the Internet more than once each week in 45 percent of Canadian
households. That figure rose to 60 percent in 2000.[7]

The Internet is now becoming part of a new media economy and
incorporated into a broader landscape of communication, entertainment, and information controlled by industries whose interests are
protected by copyright and trade laws. As a result, it is already being
reduced to performing an inevitably restricted set of functions.
Indeed, most of the software and hardware developed since 1994 has
been driven by business interests. The Internet has, consequently,
been rewritten as an economic environment.[8] Questions of a digital
divide between those with access to on-line service and the skills to
use them and those excluded from on-line activity because of location, class, gender, or income are the subject of a growing literature
concerning the Internet. This literature examines the impact of the
Internet on society, on the nature of work, and on the structures of
ownership in emerging industries.[9] However, it inevitably focuses on
the impacts of the technologies themselves rather than on the social

processes that are changed or created through the use of the new communication tools. This book moves beyond these important concerns to ask not only philosophical questions but also communicational questions and to examine the persistent and various attempts to create meaning in this communicative environment.

As stated above, my concern is not so much with the Internet as with the virtual reality called cyberspace – in fact, with new realities created by new processes of communication, interaction, and social construction. For example, since its beginnings thirty years ago, the Net has been used for interpersonal communication and the establishment of discursive communities.[10] The world's first on-line community arose as a consequence of the network of researchers working for the United States Defense Department's Advanced Research Projects Agency (ARPA) in the early 1970s. Originally designed to allow ARPA researchers to share data on common projects, the network, called the ARPAnet, began to be used to exchange personal messages, which in turn helped develop a sense of community between researchers in locations scattered around the country. The optimistic forecasts about new modes of communication, new forms of social intimacy, and new experiences of identity should not be simply dismissed. The existence of cyberspace challenges us to decipher the deeper significance of mediated communication.

If the Internet is analogous to Gibson's Matrix, then cyberspace is, in effect, an unintended consequence of the social processes of working and communicating over computer networks. Such unintended consequences form an integral part of the histories of earlier forms of mass communication. For example, in the early days of radio it was widely assumed that the new medium would simply supplant the point-to-point communication first facilitated by the telegraph, then by the wireless. Instead, as a result of the development of a local audience for an electrical engineer's experimental broadcasts, combined with the willingness of his employers to capitalize on a new market for radio sets, the new medium of radio became the biggest industry in the world by 1923 – just three years after the first station went on the air in the United States. Similarly, what was never predicted in the development of the Internet was the extent to which it would become a vast electronic postal, discussion, and communication network for users who have become able to communicate with like-minded individuals and communities all over the globe.

Further, cyberspace provides a social and psychological play space, since it allows for experimentation with the very processes of social construction we engage in all the time. Reality (virtual and otherwise) is interactive, and, like the physicist whose presence changes the results of an experiment, our presence and our actions, and the ways in which these actions are expressed, change the world to some degree.

SPECIFICITY 2 – INTERACTION AND IMMERSION

Digital environments are often described as having two principal properties that distinguish them from other communicative environments: they are *interactive* and *immersive*. Janet H. Murray, in her 1999 study *Hamlet on the Holodeck: The Future of Narrative in Cyberspace*, argues that as a form of literary creation – a new medium for telling stories – digital environments have four properties that can be understood as subcategories of interaction and immersion. First, they are procedural. A digital environment comes into being as a consequence of the computer's power to execute a series of rules. Second, they have a participatory quality. Computer programs are responsive to our input. Consequently, a digital environment can change the way our experience unfolds in response to the commands we enter through the keyboard, mouse, or other device. When we say that computer environments are interactive, we mean they create participatory environments within which user choices influence what is displayed on the screen.

Third, the environments created by computer communication are spatial. They represent spaces we can move through and navigate. Earlier media portray space with words, sounds, or images, but computers add the experience of moving through a responsive environment. In fact, Murray suggests that even though the spatial qualities of digital environments are exploited in graphical applications (games, computer animation, and the like), the spatial dimension of computer-mediated communication is independent both of the computer's ability to display images and of its communicative function of connecting places separated by physical geography. Instead, we know "where we are" in the digital space on the computer screen by engaging in the interactive process of navigation. When we enter commands on the keyboard or move the mouse across a pad, a visual marker – the cursor – moves to specific locations on the screen.

Finally, digital environments are encyclopedic. Think of a digital environment as a new form of television program. When we watch television, we watch a particular episode of a specific program. In the digital environment, we could access the entire series, as well as production information, biographical details of the actors, and other viewers. More importantly, there is enough information in a digital environment for us to "forget" its constructed nature – more information than we could use in a single visit. Murray suggests that new forms of interactive media will take advantage of these properties.[11]

The interactive and immersive qualities of cyberspace emphasize a strange tension between reality and representation as the technologies become powerful enough to convincingly portray imaginative spaces. In fact, cyberspace has been described as a medium that carries worlds as its content:

Cyberspace is a medium that gives people the feeling they have been transported, bodily, from the ordinary physical world to worlds purely of imagination. Although artists can use any medium to evoke imaginary worlds, Cyberspace carries the worlds themselves ... Whereas film is used to show a reality to an audience, Cyberspace is used to give a virtual body, and a role, to everyone in an audience. Print and radio tell. Stage and film show. Cyberspace embodies.[12]

However, this is a slippery definition. In fact, cyberspace is often characterized as a new stage in media evolution – one that engulfs rather than embodies and that offers an alternative to nonmediated social interaction – an escape from embodiment. Cyberspatial interactions have been argued to eliminate the body as a mediator between communicating minds. Some argue that cyberspace and virtual reality signal a fundamental shift in human nature. The experience of immersion in a cyberenvironment distances consciousness from the body to such an extent that it becomes possible to conceive of a realm of interaction based on "pure" communication that breaks all the rules of physical reality.[13] These characteristics of cyberspace – evolutionary technology, Platonic essentialism, the escape from the body – are problematic images that will be unpacked in later chapters.

For the moment, the dual specificity of cyberspace can be defined as a material context created by a technological infrastructure within which electronic communication can occur. When we communicate in such a context, we create a sense of place and a psychological experience.[14] Cyberspace emphasizes this psychological experience in ways that are different from the psychological states created by other media.

INTERACTIVE REALISM

We construct our social world with a variety of tools, languages and material artifacts, and these tools refer back to our embodied experience of the world in a process of *interactive realism*. Interactive realism investigates the significance of new technologies not from the perspective of determining what is lost, dispersed, or destroyed by using them but by exploring the opportunities they offer for new experience.

Such concerns are not addressed if we explore digitization exclusively from an economic, a political, or a sociological perspective. Although these perspectives might offer compelling explanations of why particular technologies are developed at particular times in particular historical circumstances, they tend to undervalue questions about why we might choose to use technologies (computers, for instance) in new or unintentional ways or why we keep using them as a form of communication and expression. At a more general level we can ask what happens when we mediate out interactions in a particular way over time. Interactive realism explores the processes by which our social world is supported and threatened by the images and metaphors that set the interactive boundaries in any technologically mediated situation, and specifically in the realm of digital communication.

Technology is significant for the ways it delineates the boundaries and horizons of our *life-world*. Technology is simultaneously material and symbolic, as tools and language combine to create artifacts.[15] A tool in this broad sense could be anything made by humans, from a spade to a skyscraper to a landscape. Thus, while a wild horse is not an artifact, a trained horse is.[16] Further, language involves the communication of meaning by means of tools (systems of representation, written characters, and so on). We shape the particular contours of our social reality as soon as we operate our technologies and articulate our experience.[17]

THE MOEBIUS STRIP OF SOCIAL CONSTRUCTION

Think of communication systems and processes as components in an oscillating relationship – a moebius strip of sorts – whose components alter us as we use and alter them. Digitization and communication using new technologies may be understood using the term "convergence" – but only partially.

The extent to which we claim the social world is a construction can be mapped onto a continuum. At one extreme meaning resides in the world. Thus, epistemologically, we discover rather than produce meaning. This is the position of metaphysical realism. At the other extreme, we produce and create meaning, which we attribute to objects. This is constructivism.

Metaphysical realism argues that the world consists of objects with properties, objects that stand in various relationships independently of human understanding. For the metaphysical realist, there is one correct interpretation of what the world is like (a God's-eye-view) and there is a rational, discoverable structure to that reality. Linguistic expressions and the concepts they express acquire their meaning from a direct, unmediated correlation with things in the actual world. One fundamental problem with the metaphysical realist position is the assumption that the structure of rationality transcends structures of bodily experience. There is no mention of human beings or the nature of their experience.

Constructivism, on the other hand, sees the relation of knowledge to reality as an adaptation to the environment, as opposed to the attempt to construct a disembodied rationality (as in mathematical and logical languages).[18] Language should be seen neither as a mediator between subject and object nor as a medium in which we try to form pictures of reality.[19]

Constructivism has traditionally favoured linguistics as the tool we use to construct our realities. This lingustic preference is evident both in poststructuralism (the linguistic determination of subjectivity) and in cognitive psychology (thought is, at its most basic level, linguistic).[20] Constructivism also maintains that we can explore the operations by which we assemble our experiential world and that, by becoming aware of this process of exploration, we can learn to do it differently and, perhaps, better.[21]

But this idea reduces the fuller importance of language, particularly of how we use language as an artifact. My point of divergence with linguistic constructivism is two-fold. First, my constructivism begins with the notion of *embodiment*: we relate personal experience to the body as the basis of our cognitive and linguistic categories. Our use of language as an artifact (in conjunction with other artifacts) to explore the world is grounded in experience, and we use this experience to help construct our social world.

The second problem with constructivism lies in its overemphasis on the individual nature of experience. This is a correctable weakness. A social epistemology allows us to retain a focus on the material world of artifacts, to remain realists as well as constructionists.[22] In a *social constructionist* view, then, the experience of self exists in the ongoing interchange with others in the construction of social realities.[23]

Reality is constructed through artifacts (tools and language). We might think about computers as tools with which we construct that reality. Further, we must consider the artifact (whether the technological environment, the system of representation, or the process of communication) and how we use it to construct the social – and ourselves. To explain, I must say a few words about the importance of metaphor for social construction.

METAPHOR

Instead of approaching language as a mirror or producer of reality, consider an *instrumental attitude* towards its use. Instrumentalism, in this context, means, not that language and other constructed artifacts are value-neutral (simple tools or instruments) but that they can be understood as performative (tools that are used for particular purposes).[24]

We must determine the kinds of uses to which language is put and the attitude we take toward the power of language to define reality. The emphasis here is not on language itself but on the actions of listener and speaker. For example, psychologist George Kelly (1969) claims that language functions as an instrument for probing the future and, at the same time, as a conservation tool for maintaining our composure in the face of onrushing events.[25] He suggests that an important aspect of language is what he calls the *invitational mood*; it is a probe inviting future action. If, for example, two people were exploring a deserted building and one said, "the floor is hard," the statement would leave both the speaker and the listener, not with a conclusion on their hands, but in a posture of expectancy – suppose we do regard the floor as if it were hard, what then?

Several possibilities arise: the explorers could walk across the floor without fearing its collapse; they could sit down to rest, with the expectation that the floor would not be comfortable, and so on. Words lose the invitational mood once the invitation has been accepted and experience has left its mark. In other words, the invitational mood fades at the moment when a referential link is forged or a verbal picture is stabilized. Metaphor, involving exactly this sort of referential link, is a fundamental tool in the construction of social reality. Extrapolated to the actions of a social or societal group, this fading of the invitational mood contributes to the creation of a common public image. I call the process whereby an experience leaves its mark, along with the subsequent fading of the invitational mood, the *sedimentation* of language.

METAPHOR AND SOCIAL CONSTRUCTION

Metaphor is the application to one object of a name or description that belongs by convention to something else, because of some resemblance between the two. The classical, Aristotelian, view is that metaphor is part of poetry and can be detached from ordinary language. Metaphors can achieve certain specific psychological effects, but the higher goal of language is to reveal the "reality" of an unchangeable world.[26] Consequently, metaphor is considered a deviation, or nonessential literary figure.[27] We can apply Aristotle's notion of poetics to cyberspace, since computer games, web sites, and on-line chat rooms have certain rules or forms of etiquette. Yet to do so may arguably perpetuate a literary allusion that does not quite capture the role of technology in social construction.

More recent thinking about the function of metaphor, particularly by Max Black, Donald Davidson, George Lakoff, and Mark Johnston, suggests that metaphor plays a more foundational role in structuring thought.[28]

In human communication, objects can be either represented by a likeness or referred to by a name. These two types of communication are equivalent to the concepts of the analog and the digital, respectively.[29] Psychoanalyst Gemma Fiurama (1995) suggests that a space of interaction exists between analog and digital modes of thinking, a space of metaphoricity. She argues that there is no higher frame of logic where both analog and digital serve as components. Rather, the two are separate realms that afford momentary glimpses of one another. For Fiurama, "these two modes of knowledge (the analog and the digital) resemble the planes of a moebius strip, which logically appear as separate enterprises in different domains, but while following each plane around the strip we come to recognize that it is in fact the same unified path that we are exploring."[30] In the digital mode of thinking, thoughts can be peaceful, well-regulated, and literal. Thoughts are semantically circumscribed and can be used to maintain order (Kelly's conservation function). The digital is the realm of metaphysical realism, where the world is experienced through the application of exact rules and deductive reasoning. In the analog mode, thoughts are dynamic and exciting; they transcend linguistic norms and function as extensions of reality.[31] The analog is the realm of metaphoric language and the realm of affect.

Fiurama's concept of metaphoricity does not claim a scientific status, but it does explicate how we use the tools of our culture to make sense of our world.[32]

When mapping our position in a world of discourse, we engage in a kind of play – a fictive, virtual making of possibilities – that is a type of poetics, a link between language and making (*poeisis*). We can expand the notion of poetics to extend the sense of "making" to other forms of representation. Therefore, this poetics involves the ways technology contributes to the world we make. Cyberspace is the subject of analysis, rather than the Internet.

Interactive realism explores metaphors as a condition for knowledge. For interactive realism, metaphors are not purely linguistic – they are intimately connected to the material conditions of representation. Technology is a material condition for experience. In the next chapter interactive realism will be contrasted with another version of media ecology that foregrounds the transformative power of technology.

2

The Magic Mirror:
Technology and
the Transformative Turn

This chapter will explore the first facet of the poetics of cyberspace: the transformative turn, by which is meant the common assumption that technology dramatically restructures people and societies. Perhaps the most appropriate way to introduce the transformative view of technology in the process of social construction is with a story that is not related to cyberspace at all. Hans Christian Andersen's fairy tale "The Snow Queen" can be read as a story about the unintended and unanticipated consequences of technological development. It also illustrates the common assumption that technology is both the cause of and the solution to social problems. It is an artifact – a magic mirror – that sets the story in motion.

"The Snow Queen" begins with a wicked sorcerer who fashions a magic mirror with peculiar properties and a boy named Kay, who is a victim of the mirror's power. Anything good or beautiful reflected in the sorcerer's glass dwindles to nothing; all that that is worthless or unsightly also becomes worse after its exposure to the mirror. When the sorcerer's minions fly the mirror toward Heaven (to see what trouble they can bring), the mirror shakes violently and falls to the earth, where it shatters into pieces. Unfortunately, this does not destroy the power of the mirror; each particle of glass retains the properties of the whole. Thus, if a shard falls into a person's eye, the world seems a dismal place, and if a piece becomes lodged in someone's heart, that person's heart freezes. In the tale, the fragmentation of the mirror is the last we hear of the sorcerer, but it is not the last we hear of his magic mirror.

When shards of this mirror lodge themselves in Kay's eyes and heart, his world suddenly becomes dreary, and he soon falls under the power of the evil Snow Queen. His playmate Gerda undergoes many trials and adventures in her quest to find the Snow Queen's realm and save Kay. Finding him in the Snow Queen's palace, Gerda weeps bitterly when Kay does not recognize her. Her tears thaw the lump of ice around Kay's heart and melt the piece of glass lodged inside. Able to feel once again, Kay weeps when he sees Gerda, dislodging the shard of glass in his eye. Andersen then returns Kay and Gerda to their families, where he leaves them, "grown up and yet children; for in their hearts they were children." As such, in Andersen's fairy tale Kay and Gerda remain untouched, in a fundamental way, by their adventures. This is a crucial point for Andersen, because the Kingdom of Heaven is accessible only to those who are child-like.

I have told this story to illustrate an idea crucial to our understanding of the transformative power of technology. Technology (an artifact) causes the problems, while human emotion solves them – a theme characteristic of the romanticism of much media ecology theory. The story also demonstrates several aspects of what can be called the poetics of mediation. First, both the effects of technology and their scope are unanticipated. Second, we are changed not by technology but by experiences – unlike the fairy tale characters who are "unchanged" because they do not examine the nature of their experience.

In the discourses of modern technology we are, like the children in "The Snow Queen," subject to unintended and unanticipated consequences. But unlike Kay and Gerda, we are somehow irreversibly changed by our encounters with technology (I refrain from drawing too strong a comparison between the changes brought about by technology and the Judeo-Christian Fall from Grace, although versions of this comparison appear in critiques of technology).

That being said, technology as a transforming agent lays the ground for what we might call an *Inventio Cybernautica*; cyberspace is a mysterious world created by human effort that retains a curiously autonomous status. More generally, cyberspace reinforces the feeling that technology changes us mysteriously and irrevocably.

MEDIA ECOLOGY

The idea that technology changes societies and individuals is not new. However, since the development of the Internet the view that history can be told as the story of technological development (particularly the development of communication technology) has gained prominence.

This view is called media ecology. From the perspective of media ecology, each communications technology has had the potential to influence the relationship between the media, representations, and society. Computers, unlike earlier communications technologies, are also engines of a technological convergence.

Unquestionably, technical advances in telephony and computer technology have created the tools for communicating across distances. They provide the cogs and the wheels of interactive media systems and serve as the girders of the new communication structures – laying the infrastructure for information "super-highways."[1] While researchers have observed that all forms of communication devised since the beginning of humanity are coming together in a single electronic form driven by computers, their overemphasis on changes in the technological system of communication obscures questions about the nature of an emerging culture whose forms of communication increasingly resemble media production.

Media ecology proposes that the dominant technology of communication in a society functions as the transformative agent. Such a media-centred view of history allots an independent, causal role to the dominant communications technology of an epoch.[2] It is common in communications histories to partition history into three phases governed, respectively, by an oral tradition, the printing press, and electronic media.[3] This view is reminiscent of the political economy of communications developed by Harold Innis, who wrote that different societies were shaped to a large extent by the particular space-binding or time-binding nature of their dominant medium of communication. Space-binding technologies helped create empires that needed to exert control over great expanses, while time-binding media were dominant in traditional societies, whose control extended not over territory but through time. For Innis, the new electronic media of radio and film undermined both empire and history.

Considered as a stage in media ecology, the computer is thought to be a transformative medium affecting more than society; new technology also changes the psyche. Eric Havelock, Walter Ong, and Marshall McLuhan were precursors of this view. For example, Ong (1982) argues that electronic media transform the world, continuing a process that began with writing and printing. He suggests that criticisms of the computer as a manufactured object that cannot display consciousness miss the significance of these machines. The externalization of mind goes back, argues Ong, to Plato. By separating the knower from the known, writing makes introspection possible, "opening the psyche as never before not only to the external objective world quite distinct from itself but also to the interior self against whom the objective world is set."[4]

Electronics change the media ecology dramatically. Technological tools extend human activity and shape and control the scale of human association and action. McLuhan (1964) argued that as the world is wired, it is also contracted, becoming no more than a village.[5] The imagery of the global village implies that communication technology can collapse dispersed urban alienation into the cosy confines of a preindustrial age.

Although McLuhan later identified electronic communication with the oral tradition of dialogue and dialectic, traditional values, and philosophical speculation, Innis recognized that the speed and distance of electronic communication would likely enhance the power of centralization and imperialistic power, rather than fulfill McLuhan's hope for a new tribal society.[6] Implicit in Innis is the assumption – made explicit by later thinkers – that media are extensions of human abilities or faculties and that these extensions determine social form. Yet it seems that technology affects not just societies but the individual psyche as well. While McLuhan characterized media as the transformative engine of a new tribal form of community, he also saw technology as an extension of the body. Just as the wheel is an extension of the foot and the telescope an extension of the eye, so the communications network is an extension of the nervous system.[7] When media systems function as tools, they can be understood as extensions of the self.[8]

The media ecological approach has become a useful tool for describing the effects of digitization in global communications. For example, Eli Noam describes what I call the new media economy as a media ecology. For Noam the American media industries have passed through two stages (an era of limited media and an age of multichannel communication) and are entering a third (the age of cybermedia).[9] Political scientist Ronald Diebert characterizes media ecology using the phrases "medium theory" and "ecological holism." Diebert's version of medium theory shares many characteristics with my interactive realism, since Diebert's theory "actually synthesizes and expounds what is already implicit in the work of many medium theorists – that is, an open-ended, nonreductionist, thoroughly historicist view of human existence that emphasizes contingency over continuity both in terms of the trajectory of social evolution and the nature and character of human beings".[10] Diebert, like Innis, focuses on the sources of societal change. My concern is to explore the role of technology in our individual and interpersonal experiences, as well as broader social and institutional relations. To this extent, the present work deals with some of the concerns raised by media ecologists who explore the relationship between technology and the psyche.

THE MATERIALITY OF COMMUNICATION

Technology is often characterized on the basis of its positive or negative effects on individuals and society. Optimistic views apply computer technology to various physical and social problems, describing the results in terms of a postindustrial or information society.[11] This view assumes that technology is culturally, morally, and politically neutral and that it provides tools independent of local value-systems.[12] In this instance, technology is not a determining force in society but the primary tool in humanity's mastery of nature.[13]

The computer, as a type of transformative technology, is able to radically reconfigure culture, because it changes the ways we create, store, and distribute information. The computer also supports the view that language determines subjectivity, since the programs and machines created in a digital culture can be understood as material demonstrations or models of the ways language constructs machines, the self, and reality.[14] The computer is an evocative object that serves as a model of the mind. As such, it can also transform what we believe about ourselves. Indeed, it is often argued that precisely because new forms of media and communication have resulted in new forms of subjectivity, those very media will provide the structures for new forms of social organization.[15]

One of the great rhetorical promises of the Internet is that it signals the "death of distance," whereby geographic location no longer determines the cost of communicating, the size of markets for business, and so on. Further, communication networks will cement nations and peoples together through increased commercial and cultural bonds.[16] Communications technology is seen as a powerful civilizing force based, in part, on the development of the Internet as a global electronic information network.[17]

There are many examples in advertising that capitalize on the evolutionary potential of digital technology. One has only to think of the notion of McLuhan's global village implicit in IBM's "solutions for a small planet" or the invocation of community implied by Nortel Network's use of the Beatle's "Come Together" as a slogan. At the launch of Microsoft's Windows 2000, actor Patrick Stewart gave symbolic credence to the Bill Gates's vision of a bold future by suggesting that Captain Picard (of *Star Trek: The Next Generation*) is waiting for us in the future – a future, shareholders might hope, created in large part by Microsoft.

Not everyone is optimistic about the idea of immersive media. Media ecology presents, most often, a critical view of the impact of technology on society. Indeed, many argue that the idea of an information revolution overstates the case. The death of distance is the result of a slow, complicated process that began with the optical telegraph two centuries ago.[18] The shift from biological rhythms to the mechanical rhythms of life that accompany a shift from a cycle of time characteristic of agrarian society to the market time of industrial society are seen as contributing to the general alienation of the individual.[19] The expansion of a global telecommunications infrastructure will not inevitably create a harmonious global culture. Instead, the creation of a virtual culture compulsively fixated on digital technology will only emphasize what one writer describes as "the reality of a lonely culture and radical social disconnection from everyday life."[20] This is an understandable but overly simplistic attitude towards the enormous effects computers have on society.

Pessimists argue that humans cannot control the basic thrust of technological development, which appears as a mysterious force with its own imperative.[21] This alienating power of the machine is also an important element in Marxist theory. While Marx himself remained optimistic about the uses of technology under a communist order, his concept of alienation under the impersonal forces of an industrial order has influenced pessimistic views of technology. At the heart of many technological critiques lies the metaphysical realist's opposition of illusion and reality, which appears in ideological, gender-based, and culturalist critiques of technology.

The first criticism of technology argues that in technological development and advancement there lurks a hidden ideological purpose.[22] There is a kind of confidence trick in the notion of technology as a panacea for social problems. British sociologist Kevin Robins (1995) challenges the utopian promise of new technologies and new communication contexts like cyberspace. For Robins, cyberspace reflects a common "feverish belief in transcendence," a faith that a new technology will finally "deliver us from the limitations and frustrations of this imperfect world."[23] Robins condemns such utopian aspirations as the last remnants of a Romantic sensibility in which the imagination is dead and only the technology is new (139). The use of technology to quiet or undermine class revolt dates from the nineteenth century. However, like the industrial revolution, the fruits of the information revolution did not pacify class conflict. According to one researcher, the information revolution has simply displaced the internal struggles of capitalism to the global stage.[24]

Another powerful critique of technology concerns the gendered nature of technology as a male production. From this perspective, the ideological purpose that underlies technological development is patriarchal. Zillah Eisenstein makes the compelling argument that the new cybermedia undermine the notion of a public realm of communication. They perpetuate the values of transnational capital and create a world where merely the illusion of reality substitutes for reality itself. In particular, Eisenstein shows how the democratic possibilities of new media cannot be separated from the reality that people of colour, white women, and girls around the world have less access to technology, reproductive health care, and decent living wages than men.[25]

Although the commercialization of the Internet supports the view that the ways in which we use digital communications will be increasingly restricted and appropriated by existing power structures, many of the critics I have mentioned admit that things could be different: a kind of information commons could develop or a new public realm of interaction. Indeed, Eisenstein does not dismiss the democratic possibilities of a virtual public sphere. She reminds us that more is needed than a discourse of disembodied democracy to create an actively and socially constructed public realm.[26] Thus, the social imagination is far from dead. In fact, the concepts of cyberspace, virtual reality, and virtual community are useful as imaginative spaces where we can try out various forms of social experimentation with a view to changing the increasingly global, formal, and abstract characteristics of the world we live in.

A third critique of new media can be characterized as "culturalist." This view traces its roots to early-twentieth-century critiques of mass media and is common in much of the media ecology literature. This perspective sets virtual culture in opposition to "authentic" culture.

The immediate gratification we experience on-line is opposed to the kind of political or social "freedom" inculcated through an informed citizenry who participate in democratic processes aimed at long-term social benefit. The masses, argue the culturalists, give up freedom for escapism.[27] This view is common to writers like Donald Wood and Neil Postman, who describe the debasing of culture as part of an evolutionary transition from oral, through literate, to electronic society. Postman, for example, describes television as "absurd" in relation to the rational, serious, and coherent culture characterized by print culture.[28] Wood claims the postintellectual environment of web culture is characterized by shifting relationships, nonpermanence, technological domination, and diminished responsibilities.

My critique of the transformative assumptions of ideological, feminist, and culturalist works in the media ecology literature is a critique of those underlying assumptions alone, rather than a critique of those approaches to media study in general. However, common to all pessimistic theories is the tendency to present communications technology as a totalizing force. Thus, computers are determining agents that stand against the individual. In discussions of computers in relation to writing and to cyberspace, the view that computers are transformative technologies takes a further twist. They become disjunctive (the changes to psyche and society engendered by computers are unlike earlier transformations). The change is more like an abrupt, evolutionary shift than a stage in an unfolding of history. Thus, the transformative perspective requires a view of technology as an agent of class, of power, or of some blind evolutionary process.

One of the most concise and influential critiques of modern technology appears in Martin Heidegger's essay "The Question concerning Technology," which argues that modern technology is a form of alienation. Heidegger's view of technology is important for influencing the *transformative theory of technology*. The world of technology is a Lapsarian world where human subjectivity will ultimately be destroyed. For Heidegger, knowledge is a way of revealing the world. Modern technology is, by contrast, less a mode of revealing nature through human craft than a challenge to nature.[29] Technology is not simply a collection of tools used neutrally by people but more a way of seeing and a way of enframing the world (*Gestell*). Technology mediates culture, outlines a unique style of experiencing reality, and stipulates the parameters of what can be designated as *real*. Modern technology becomes the structuring force of reality.

The power of Heidegger's argument led philosopher George Grant to conclude that the only moral choice was to retreat from technology and to take refuge in a premodern metaphysics based on human values.[30] Both technological determinist arguments and weaker arguments that explain cultural transformation as a result of new technologies contend that a people undergoes complete reconstitution as a result of some dramatic change in their situation.[31] This is a prominent subtext in various attitudes towards technology and selfhood.

Many current theorists writing about the significance of computers share the view that computers are disjunctive; computers alter subjectivity. The computer is transformative because it provides a new form of symbolic storage and transmission; it is related to changes in language. Michael Heim (1987, 1993) continues this tradition of cultural transformation, arguing that electronic writing changes cognition. Mark Poster (1990, 1995) applies the theory to subjectivity.[32] For Heim, the transformative power of the computer is based on a distinction between the medium of communication (which aims for transparency between sender and receiver) and the element of writing (the historically particular shape of language). Poster, on the other hand, accepts mediation and concentrates instead on the wrapping of language or the mode of information. Both Heim and Poster construct media ecologies, but they reach different conclusions because they concentrate on different levels of analysis. It is important to distinguish in each author's work the object of transformation. For Poster it is the societal citizen-subject but for Heim it is the psyche itself that is transformed by new writing technologies.

THE ELEMENT OF WRITING

In his 1987 study, *Electric Language: A Philosophical Study of Word-Processing*, Michael Heim analyzes the importance of computers for the practice of writing and the constitution of self. He builds on Ong's theory of the transformative power of media and suggests that each new method of preserving thought reconfigures the human psyche. Cultures survive, he argues, by means of the different ways they cultivate the capacities of the psyche. The habitual organization of sensory awareness results in a hierarchy of the senses, and the predominant sense serves as a paradigm for grasping reality. Each new configuration of the senses, each new sensorium, fosters distinctive personality structures. Consequently, Heim argues – in accordance with Ong's version of the transformation theory – the entire human personality is configured anew with every shift in the dominant medium for preserving thought.[33]

Heim argues that changes in the human psyche are the result of changes in the technology of writing – a shift from writing to word processing. The effects of word processing, then, are traceable not so much to the computer as they are to the transcendental intimacy between language and reality (31). With digitization, the significance of the written word is changed. Digitization does not necessarily compel us to pay more attention to the medium but merely requires us to speak and write under different conditions. Heim calls a set of new conditions for expressing thought *a new element*, a concept that is not to be confused with a medium. Whether media are primarily audio or visual, they are based on the exchange between humans and some pre-given material in a context that is, ideally, transparent. By contrast, argues Heim, the element of language is the concretely historical way in which, through the transcendental nature of language, symbolized thought becomes placeless (43). Therefore, digital writing, or electric language, is a form of expression that abstracts communication from embodied experience. This notion is Platonic in the sense that the realm of ideas is given a new autonomy, if not, in fact, preferential consideration over the sensory experience of the everyday world.

Heim grants the plausibility of the transformation theory – that basic intellectual changes accompany widespread innovation in symbol manipulation – and he concurs with the Heideggerian assumption that human existence today is enframed in a fundamental way by technology. However, Heim argues that electronic writing is not simply another layer in the cumulative development of history; instead, electric language "may bring with it an abrupt shift into an altogether different psychic framework for human thought" (69).

Heim's view of electronic language raises two problematic aspects of media ecology: its nostalgia for premodern culture and its romanticism. Media ecology often carries with it an implicit preference for a premodern form of culture; oral culture is assumed to be unified, not diverse or pluralistic. As critic Judith Stamps writes, the purpose of reconstructing a notion of oral and literate cultures (the project of media ecologists like Innis and McLuhan) is to create a critique of modernity. Although Stamps realizes that Innis and McLuhan view modernity as a reduced form of cultural life, she criticizes these media ecologists for their inadequate diagnosis of the poverty of modern culture: they do not go far enough in their condemnation. For Stamps, the remedy is to strengthen the media ecological analysis with critical theory such as that expressed in the culture critiques of the Frankfurt School.[34]

A second aspect of media ecology appearing in Heim's work is an implicit Romanticism, which privileges unity over multiplicity. From Neoplatonism to McLuhan, the unity of tribal culture is given preference over modernity. From this position language is not used to describe reality, as in metaphysical realism. Rather, language creates illusion, and the real is that which resists the illusory power of language.[35] For Heim, digital language repairs the illusion by coding the essence of the Platonic realm of ideas.

THE MODE OF INFORMATION

Unlike Heim, Mark Poster believes that it *is* the medium or, more broadly, the materiality of language that is the key issue in understanding the societal impacts of digitization. Poster develops the concept of the *mode of information* to periodize history after the dominant medium of communication and to build a theoretical bridge between Marxist critical analysis and poststructuralist, linguistic-based analysis. For Poster, an adequate account of electronic communication requires a theory that can decode the linguistic dimension of the new forms of social interaction afforded by new technologies. His view of media is ecological, a grand view of history periodized not by the mode of production, as in Marx, but by the means of symbolic exchange. Whereas the mode of production refers to material production, the mode of information, with its emphasis on symbolic exchange, explains subjectivity without reference to the body. Poster's view has become more complex since he first introduced the concept of the mode of information in the early 1980s, and the teleological tone of his argument has softened with time. However, by placing his arguments in terms of critical theory, Poster leaves himself open to charges of oversimplification – one of the perpetual dangers in social analysis of technology.

Poster's interpretation of computerized communication illustrates two points: a shift from an antitechnology position to an affirmation of technology emphasizing the possibilities of the media and, in spite of his wariness of technological determinism, a shift from an evolutionary Marxism to a view of media as a transformative agent. His postmodern position involves the appropriation of a panlinguistic, poststructural philosophical position for a discussion of the importance of computers as a communications medium.[36] For Poster, communications media are vital for understanding our historical period. He posits a relationship between media and society that can be simply stated in terms consistent with the media ecologies presented thus far. The dominant communication medium of a particular historical period creates a particular language form, or "wrapping" of language – a materiality of communication. This language form, in turn, determines the nature of subjectivity for those living in that period. Throughout his work Poster has moved from a view of technology as a form of alienation to a view of media as a disjunctive, transformative force.

The twentieth century has witnessed the introduction of communications systems that allow a wide distribution of messages from one point to another, conquering space and time, first through the electrification of analog information, then through digitization. The "first media age" was determined by the broadcast model of media, in which a few producers distributed information to many consumers. This model has been replaced in the "second media age" by a model of integrated technology structured by means of two-way, decentred information exchange. Many producers communicate with many consumers. In the second media age, the boundaries between producers, distributors, and consumers collapse.[37] For Poster, cyberspace signals a shift from a model of one-to-one communication in a pre-mediated age to mass media's one-to-many model in the first media age and then, in the second media age, a shift to many-to-many or all-to-all communication.

Each method of preserving and transmitting information, Poster argues, intervenes in the network of relationships that constitute a society. In particular, the extent to which communication is restricted by time and space governs the shape society may take.[38] Poster takes this idea even further by arguing that media, by determining social order, determine subjectivity. He outlines a history of the self, from the face-to-face "enunciated self" of the oral stage of communication, to the print-age self "constructed as an agent centred in rational/imaginary autonomy," and then to the electronic stage, in which the self is "decentered, dispersed, and multiplied in continuous instability."[39] It is a common strategy to appropriate terms from poststructuralist analysis in discussions of computers and subjectivity. Unfortunately, such a move perpetuates the confusion between the social self and the societal subject and reinforces the assumption that the linguistic dimension constitutes subjectivity.

Take, for instance, Poster's description of the significance of the computer as a writing technology. The process of writing affects subjectivity in ways similar to those described by Michael Heim. Poster writes:

Compared to the pen, the typewriter or the printing press, the computer dematerializes the written trace ... the writer encounters his or her words in a form that is evanescent, instantly transformable, in short, immaterial. By comparison, the inertial trace of ink scratched by hand or pounded by typewriter keys onto a page is difficult to change or erase. Once transformed from a mental image into a graphic representation, words become in a new way a defiant enemy of their own author, resisting his or her efforts to reshape or redistribute them. To a considerable degree, writing on a computer avoids the transformation of idea into graph while achieving the same purpose. The writer thus confronts a representation that is similar in its spatial fragility and temporal simultaneity to the contents of the mind or to the spoken word. Writer and writing, subject and object, have a similarity that approaches identity, a simulation of identity that subverts the expectation of the Cartesian subject that the world is composed of *res extensa*, beings completely different from the mind.[40]

For over a decade, Poster's general thesis has been that the mode of information enacts a radical reconfiguration of language, one that constitutes subjects outside the pattern of the autonomous, rational subject.[41] Poster argues that the modern nation-state requires an autonomous subject and that the medium of print supports it. While the modern age created the ideological, rational self, the postmodern (or second media) age creates a new, decentred subjectivity. Subjectivity, in this sense, is like positioning within a discursive order.

Two points are of interest. First, Poster has simply replaced one construction (the modern rational self, as required by the modern nation-state and supported by print technology) with another (the postmodern decentred subject constructed in a global media culture and supported by the Internet). Second, he shifts his attitude towards

computers from considering them pessimistically as repositories of
dead memories to considering them affirmatively as transformative
agents. In his early work, the radical reconfiguration of language
forms has a negative effect of technological alienation. He writes that
the computer stands against the living worker like an alien essence,
dominating the work process. According to Poster, the reversal of
priorities Marx saw in the factory, whereby machines (as stores of
dead labour) dominated the living (workers), is extended by the computer (as a store of dead memory) to the realm of knowledge. The
line dividing subject and object is blurred far more than it was in
Marx's analysis of labour, leading Poster to question which is the
subject, computer or individual.[42]

Poster's early conception of the mode of information is developed
in the context of an antitechnological pessimism consistent with
Marxist cultural theory. First, analysis begins with social reality.
Next, language, as practical consciousness, provides the foundation
for social intercourse and, by extension, for interiority, to the extent
that an inner life occurs at all.[43] Such a view supports the behav-
iourist avoidance of the mind and the sceptical postmodernist fear
of the body. Yet Poster is writing not at the level of the social but
at the societal level. His analysis of the mode of information per-
tains to the distal structures of society that affect only indirectly the
proximal order of the body in which the interactive social self is
largely grounded.

In his later work, Poster valorizes the foregrounding of communications, in contrast with the traditional Marxist view in which communication falls in the category of determined superstructure
reflecting the relations of production occurring in the determining
base. To this end, Poster argues that the configuration of communications in any given society is an "analytically autonomous realm of
experience" that is worthy of study in its own right. At stake, he
contends, are new language formations that alter significantly the network of social relations, that restructure both those relations and the
subjects they constitute.[44]

For Poster, the emphasis on language allows an investigation into
the ways in which communication (understood as symbolic exchange)
determines social relations and subjectivity. Poster follows the post-
Saussurian emphasis on language as the central organizing factor of
subjectivity. Thus, for Poster the structure of cultural space is essentially the structure of linguistic space. Our subjective experience is

causally and concretely determined by the language we learn and use. Again, Poster's mode of information is built on familiar theoretical ground. For example, Lévi-Strauss's structuralism, with its appropriation of the linguistic paradigm, offered a method for analysing culture as being structured like a language. In Althusser's work, Marxist themes were "read" – and reconstituted – through the terms of the linguistic paradigm. Althusser makes the case that the mode of production can best be understood as if "structured like a language."[45] Here is the crux of Poster's discussion of the materiality of communication – his theory of the mode of information. It is an awkward position, given its heavy emphasis on language as the determining force in social reality. Technological determinism is too strong an accusation to level at Poster, yet his media ecology is limiting. The perspective tends to overlook the individual's ability to make choices within the constraining and liberating boundaries of her or his culture. The categories of a particular culture are more than determinants. They are tools with which members and institutions construct that culture.

To understand Poster's marriage of poststructuralism and critical theory, we can trace his use of a particular element of Marx's conception of ideology – that it represents a false consciousness. This conception is the basis of his attack on the so-called "unified self." There was once a false belief in a unified self, Poster claims, but that is no longer the case. The key point is that ideology is a kind of veil pulled over our eyes. Because the centred self is an illusion, we have to remove the veil, which presupposes that in doing so we can get to the truth of the matter. It is consistent with both the Marxist and the poststructuralist view that ideology creates the centred self not as a concept but as a deception. Such a position also echoes the Platonic distrust of language and image, a distrust of what we experience, what we know, and what we believe. Poster's argument is predicated on a separation of the ideological (as a realm of ideas, thought, and so on) and the material world of the body. On the one hand, through the linguistic ontology of the social, a separation of mind and body is perpetuated. On the other hand, Poster describes a kind of cybernetic subjectivity predicated on dissolving the separation between human and machine. The computer not only alienates the human, as in Marx's view of automation, it also challenges the distinction between the machine and the human. Poster likens computer networks to living bodies.[46] But what does it mean for the boundaries between the human and the mechanical to blur? This question he does not ask.

He does suggest that subject constitution in the second media age occurs through the mechanism of interactivity with other people and with machines. The familiar modern subject is displaced by the mode of information in favour of one that is multiplied, disseminated, and decentred. Poster argues that interfaces of high quality allow seamless crossings between the world of the human and the world of the machine, thereby facilitating the disappearance of the difference between them.

For Poster, the Internet is disjunctive, since Internet communities function as places of difference from and resistance to modern society.[47] The Internet tends to be understood as an "extension or substitution" for existing institutions. In particular, the Internet is a substitution for the public sphere, defined as an arena of exchange, like the Greek agora or the town hall. But in Poster's media ecology, the age of a face-to-face public sphere is over. He claims that the question of democracy must take into account new forms of electronically mediated discourse and the relations and subjects they constitute.[48]

Poster is concerned not with the psyche as transformed by language (as is Heim) but with the shifting citizen-subject in a new technologically mediated culture. One can readily accept the argument that a new political order demands new definitions of its participants. However, using media ecology as the ground for this assumption creates difficulties. Whereas Heim claimed that new conditions for expressing thought changed the psyche, Poster claims that a change in the materiality of communication requires new subject positions. Although it is possible to clarify Poster's argument by emphasizing that his "subject positions" refer to the societal subject, rather than to the psyche, the two authors' arguments appear more similar than different. Poster's concern with the linguistic determination of the societal subject is based not on an acknowledgement of the social but on the privileging of the societal realm over the personal. The distinction Poster makes is based on his debt to the Marxian emphasis on social, rather than individual, consciousness. In a sense his arguments are excessively influenced (if not determined) by the "language forms" of critical theory.

To his credit, Poster astutely observes how in the second media age the media often change the things they treat, transforming the identity of originals and images. At the level of culture, Poster claims, this multiplicity and subjective instability challenges existing categories of social reality, which may lead to fundamental challenges to modern social institutions and structures. In the second media age "reality" becomes multiple.[49]

In his assessment of the importance of communication technologies for challenging the shape of contemporary cultures, Poster is not alone. The spread of a world of "generalized communication" can be linked to the demise of the central rationality of history: the narrative of European progress since the Enlightenment. The globalization of media does not inevitably result in the homogenization of world culture.[50] Instead, the contemporary world is characterized by multiple realities. Only in the past two decades or so have media and migration become so massively globalized that the public spheres created by encounters between local cultures and global media images are no longer small, marginal, or exceptional but are, rather, part of the everyday experience of an increasing number of people across the globe.[51]

Poster's social theory offers pertinent insights into this new social organization: society has become increasingly simulational, communicative practices affect psychology and social organization, and virtual realities emphasize our participation in multiple realities. However, problems arise in Poster's tendency to explain the effects of new technologies within the confines of Marxian and Althusserian models of base and superstructure in the modes of information. He perpetuates a deterministic, substantive, and evolutionary model of technological, historical, and psychological progress or evolution. His shift from a suspicion of computers as repositories of "dead" knowledge to an acceptance of the inevitable effects of computerized communication on subjectivity remains pessimistic, the object of his pessimism having shifted from the machine to the human ability to resist the inevitable effects of computerization. Third, he reduces subjectivity to the result of a system of symbolic exchange, problematizing neither the economic model of exchange as applied to consciousness nor the validity of a solely linguistic or structural model of the self. Further, the question of how the societal relates back to the social and interaction is not explored.

Poster's concept of the mode of information is linked to the Marxian critique of technology as a manifestation or materialization of an ideological project (transnational capitalism). Views of technology as a manifestation of ideology share the assumption that technology represents a kind of trick or veil pulled over our eyes. Technology is the material embodiment of a dominant ideology that imposes its technical rationality upon the unconsciousness of us all. This is a powerful cultural assumption. The rational bias of our culture presents consistency and coherency as natural, but a paradox arises. Feelings of fragmentation have also been said to characterize contemporary psychological life. And so, theories that speak to the experience of a divided self have particular power. Here is the lure of postmodern attacks on the rational, unified subject as characterized in Poster's mode of information.

A common thread in Poster and Heim is the idea that computers are disjunctive to our relationship with the world. Each writer uses the terms "poststructuralism" and "postmodernism" at varying points in his work. Their use of "postmodernism" emphasizes the importance of computers as a communication medium in contemporary society and their commitment to the application of poststructuralist notions of simultaneity, spectacle, and the dispersal of a unified human subject to describe aspects of the contemporary human condition. The convergence of technology, information, words, and images in a global communication system emphasizes the paradox of poststructuralist or postmodern views of new communications technology. On the one hand, the Internet as a network of networks supports assumptions about decentralized, universally accessible technology. The monopolies of knowledge described by Innis are challenged by the proliferation of media, information, and channels of communication. To phrase it differently, it would seem impossible to assume that we can encounter the magic mirror of global, generalized communication and yet remain untouched or unchanged by the encounter.

The technological convergence that allows messages to be coded and transmitted into an electronic public sphere also threatens our conception of self by arguing that language *is* reality. Our messages are split first from the mind and then from the physical body. Technological enframing seems to be accompanied by a fragmentation or dispersal of the subject that supports a dualist separation of mind and body, machine and human. This suspicion of technology is related to a theological and philosophical suspicion of the body and a desire to "escape the flesh" through technological means.[52] The computer-age cult of information is often condemned for choosing the alienating power of the machine over human values.[53] Critics of technology like Innis and Grant also draw a boundary between the human and the technological realms, expressing an antimodern long-ing for face-to-face community or an equally antimodern rejection of the universalizing and homogenizing force of modern technological societies. I would characterize this position as involving the construc-tion of "fences" behind which a notion of the human can be preserved against a constantly encroaching technological manifest destiny. From this perspective, the more we bring only the logical and rational ele-ments of ourselves to the technological environment, the more we are in danger of losing other aspects of our humanity. If we accept the position of technological enframing, the self will wither and only the reduction will remain.[54]

One might say that the global world of digital communication, of which cyberspace is one component, illustrates the unintended con-sequences of the magic mirror of technology. However, this is not to suggest that I subscribe to the antimodern critique of technology. My project is subtler. In different contexts the validity and usefulness of our conceptual models and strategies are often transformed. For example, where Heidegger supports a substantive view of technology as a totalizing force; there is, in his view of technology as a mode of revealing, a useful element for understanding the social construction of cyberspace.

As stated in the last chapter, understanding the poetics of cyberspace helps us understand the role of technology in social construction. The roots of "technology" (*techné*) refer not simply to the skills of craft but also to the skills of art and mind (*poiësis*). Since *techné* belongs to *poiësis*, the technological is related to the poetic. While "poetics" gen-erally refers to the rules of writing or of analysing poetry, the concept of poetics can be more broadly understood in its relation to *poiësis* – the making of the world in language and creative activity. Using this as a starting point, we can emphasize the development of interpretive and cognitive skills that link the concept of *poiësis* to constructionist epistemology. Thus, we can underscore the creative co-construction and re-construction of the social world and suggest an approach for studying how we construct ourselves and find ourselves constructed in communicative behaviour.[55]

It is not the technology but the process of communication created by the use of particular technologies that both takes advantage of social construction and laments the narrowing of choices afforded to users of that technology. This chapter has outlined the transformative turn by which both optimistic and pessimistic approaches to the effects of modern technology assume that new modes of communication have a powerful ability to alter the psyche (Heim) and the structure of social reality (Poster). The transformative turn also reinforces a perception of technology as "other," based on the argument that technology is ideological. This perception of technology as a veil pulled over the eyes is linked to a deeper suspicion of the body as the medium by which we experience the world. Finally, we can investigate how generalized communication shifts the context for our encounter with others not as a universalizing or homogenizing force but as a site providing various opportunities to emerge. The question that must be explored is the role of communication and technology in creating and maintaining these opportunities. Theories of technology as a transformative agent posit that we stand poised at a stage of evolution. We can respond either with nostalgic longing for a pre-mediated age when we were more human, or we can look forward hopefully or fearfully towards a day when we will become more or other than human.

3

Media Ecology, the Prosthetic Other, and the Artifactual Self

To call a man a wolf is to put him in a special light, we must not forget that the metaphor makes the wolf seem more human than he otherwise would.

Max Black[1]

If we are, as the media transformationists argue, at the dawn of a new stage in cultural evolution, how will the computer change our understanding of the psyche? To think metaphorically of the machine as human or to think of the human as machine is one way our culture attempts to come to terms with the computer as the predominant tool with which we both communicate and construct social reality. As machines become like us, so too do we become like machines, according to this line of reasoning.

Two metaphors are particularly useful in exploring the relationship between the human and technology in this context. The first is the metaphor of the *Prosthetic Other,* an image that disembodies human characteristics like intelligence and argues that the human is simply a biological mechanism that may eventually be replaced by a more adaptive species of intelligent machines. The Prosthetic Other is a metaphor that displaces the human, a view appearing in the work of writers who fear the displacement. It underlies the work of writers who favour the displacement of the human by technology as well.

The metaphor of the Prosthetic Other is supported by two arguments. First, from the cybernetic tradition of cognitive science comes the assumption that intelligence can be coded in computer programs. The second argument presents the computer as the agent of human displacement in evolution. Yet the relationship between machines and human cognition can best be illustrated by looking at one cognitive faculty – perception. It is here that we see how interactive realism helps us understand processes of communication and representation.

Either representations offer a transparent access to reality (the metaphysical realist view of coded representations of aspects of reality), or they represent a veil between the perceiver and the object perceived, denying us direct access to the world. This view is expressed in both the Platonism of Michael Heim and the distrust of images in much critical theory. To move beyond this dichotomous impasse, we need a more complex theory of perception that attempts to explain how we deal with representations of the world. An embodied view of perception allows us to link perception to metaphor and models as the building blocks of social reality. The skills involved in learning the cultural boundaries of perception also illustrate the kinds of skills we use in the construction of selfhood. Computer simulations, virtual realities, and on-line environents concern perspectives, specifically, the continuation of the Renaissance tradition of representation – based on a system of linear perspective we have incorporated and reified over a period of five hundred years.

This leads us to the second metaphor to be explored in this chapter: the *Cyborg*, which attempts to incorporate the power of technology into the human, as we try to avoid our eventual replacement by powerful machines. The self is not something reduced or displaced by technology. It is, by its nature, *artifactual*. Human existence is embodied and interactive, constructed and social. We exist in an extra-human sense in the world, but we also exist in culture.

THE PROSTHETIC OTHER

There are live people and then there are people who need tubes.

                                                                        Joey

Bruno Bettelheim (1959, 1960, 1967) argues that in the machine age, humans fear the loss of their humanity to their own handiwork, the machine.[2] A more insidious fear of technological society is not only that we will be replaced by technology but that we will become machines. We invariably tend to anthropomorphize the world in order to understand it in human terms.[3] Sherry Turkle, in her 1984 study *The Second Self*, describes how children, computer programmers, and others tend to attribute human characteristics to computers.

When they played with computerized games, Turkle's subjects insisted that because the machines seemed smart, it felt to the subjects as if they were playing with other people. The children believed that the computers cheated to win. Turkle concluded that computers were now a special type of technology because they modelled or mimicked a particular human characteristic – intelligence – and because they therefore enabled (or perhaps even forced) us to rethink what it means to be human.[4]

Bettelheim argues that we have always anthropomorphized the forces of power in the world, conjuring up images that are bigger than but not radically different from humanity, like images of angels or devils. In modern industrial societies, we no longer think in terms of powerful daemonic entities but of machines capable of controlling human destiny. In the machine age the source of our salvation and of our destruction loses its human qualities.[5]

My interest in Joey's case is not in the diagnosis of his condition nor in his treatment and subsequent "cure" but in the way Joey's story (as recounted by Bettelheim) demonstrates the fear of humans succumbing to technology. It also depicts the relationship between human and machine as more than one of simple alienation. This relationship can be seen as a form of illness. Bettelheim's fascination with Joey reveals a fear that the human being can become machine-like to the point of utter dehumanization.[6]

Joey, observes Bettelheim, retreated into a delusional world fashioned from pieces of the world at hand. Joey chose the world of the machine and froze himself in its image.[7] In this sense, Joey's story might (like the story of Andersen's magic mirror) be viewed as a cautionary tale. For Joey, a process of incorporation occurred whereby he became immersed in the cybernetic machinery of his fantasies.

For Bettelheim, autism (the condition he diagnosed in Joey) was not seen as determined physiologically. In fact, Bettelheim explicitly rejected the view that autism could have been the result of a chemical imbalance in the brain. Instead, he favoured the view that an environmental trauma and subsequent reaction by the infant was the cause. Bettelheim's use of the term "autism" must be placed in historical context. During the 1950s "autism," was a broad term used to describe a collection of symptoms and to distinguish the condition from mental retardation. It was used broadly to cover severe forms of infantile psychosis then grouped together under the heading schizophrenia.[8] For Bettelheim the source of autism is the existential conviction that one's efforts have no power to influence the world, a conviction caused by the earlier conviction that the world is insensitive to one's reactions.[9] Simply acting on the environment will not develop a personality; rather, the development of a sense of self is the result of learning to communicate and to interact with others.[10] The ego expands from one that only acts into one that interacts, that responds to others and slowly learns that it can modify their responses. In this sense, the more we act and interact, the more of a self we have.[11] The development of the self is a process of engagement and social interaction that is based on the particular set of social relations within which the infant finds himself or herself. The self as described by Bettelheim is a product of communicative mastery, of the development of a skill set.[12]

Joey's was not a reduced human existence or an animal-like one. According to Bettelheim, the boy's reality was that of machines.[13] Joey's everyday life consisted of an elaborate set of mechanical rituals; he externalized in symbolic form the internal workings of his bodily functions. On his bed Joey assembled toilet paper rolls, light bulbs, paper, and string that he maintained as the machinery he plugged into before he could sleep. His drawings showed schematic views of his digestive tract as a furnace and his conception of the ideal family as a group of automobiles.

In retrospect, it was Joey's identification with machines and his sense of alienation from other people that was so upsetting to those who tried to come close to him. It was difficult at times for his counsellors to remember that he was a child, because Joey's success in acting out his delusions froze their ability to respond as human beings.[14] This reciprocal dehumanization is what makes Joey's case significant as a metaphor for our own fears of the machine. Describing Joey's condition, Bettelheim writes:

All of us had feelings about how powerful our machines have become: in this nuclear age we have reason to fear that our creations may destroy us. In Joey it was so blatant that this *had already happened*. Joey had lost command of himself to machines; he was living proof that our fears were not groundless. This is why, however strange his talk, his behaviour, and later his drawings, they cannot compare in shock quality with what we experienced in his presence ... watching him interfered to such a serious degree with our ability to experience and relate to him as human beings.[15]

Joey's treatment required him to reject (symbolically) his under-standing of himself as a component in a large cybernetic system in favour of a view of himself as a human being characterized by inter-actions with other people. After he had built enough trust in his coun-sellors, they staged a "rebirth" from an egg (providing an organic rather than a mechanical origin), and he began life again as a human boy. Joey's ultimate solution to his mechanical identification was to transfer his attentions from his cybernetic gear to one, then to several, of his counsellors. He was "cured" when he developed enough "humanity" to want to be reborn as a boy. Only by rejecting the mechanical in favour of human interactions could he learn to affect (and control) his environment.

Joey was the mechanized Other who needed to be humanized, not only for his own sake but also for those who feared the machine. In one sense, Joey's "cure" was a small victory for the human against the encroaching machine. The same theme has been a staple in sci-ence fiction representations of the robot who wants to be human, like Mr Data in *Star Trek, the Next Generation* and David in Steven Spielberg's *AI*.

For Bettelheim technology represents a demonized Other; Joey makes the literal move to become a machine – to be incorporated by technology. Bettelheim raises an existential fear: what if Joey is right? If we are like machines is our sense of ourselves somehow less than it once was? This is not a new or isolated view. For example, a robot model of human behaviour, which originated in the culture of physical and technological science, is taken for granted by otherwise antagonis-tic theories such as behaviourism, cognitive science, psychoanalysis, and even existentialism.[16]

For my purposes here, there are two reasons why Bettleheim's account of Joey continues to resonate. First, cognitive science has modelled the mind as an information processor. Second, the com-puter has been described as the agent of evolution from the human-based information processor to something else.

METAPHYSICAL REALISM
AND DISEMBODIED INTELLIGENCE

Each metaphoric connection between the machine and the human poses a challenge to our sense of who and what we are. Heim argues that changes in the dominant system of writing change the psyche.

In particular, he argues that digitization abstracts thought from the body and reveals a transcendental link between language and reality. In Heim's transformative view, computers reveal Plato's autonomous realm of ideas, returning us to a premodern world where the alienation Joey experienced has been healed through the intimacy created by digital communication.

Cybernetics is a powerful science based on the metaphysical assumption that everything in the knowable universe can be modelled in a system of information. Indeed, it seeks those laws of communication that apply equally to living beings and machines. This process involves a particular use of language, representation, and modelling.[17] As a language, mathematics attempts to reduce ambiguity and vagueness through the use of precise signs and fixed rules to create meaning in equilibrium. In the words of mathematician Rudy Rucker, "Mathematics tries to replace reality with a dream of order." Rucker argues that to "devote oneself to mathematics is to turn away from the physical world and meditate about an ideal world of thoughts."[18] The computer gave new materiality to such rationality, making it possible to derive the consequences of precisely specified rules, even when huge amounts of calculation are required. This dream of mathematical order exists in cyberspace, even though it coexists with notions of dispersed subjectivity – the idea that the self (like intelligence) can be disembodied.

One of the key assumptions in the cybernetic tradition is a particular notion of representation. According to this view, thought was, throughout history, intangible and ineffable until it was possible to *represent* it. Thought "seemed still to inhabit mainly the heaven of Platonic ideals, or the equally obscure spaces of the human mind, until computers taught us how symbols could be processed by machines."[19] Here, thought functions as an ability to manipulate symbols that represent features of the world or that represent the world as existing in a certain way. In this sense, representation is based on a correspondence between symbols and reality, as well as between computers and the mind.

The key is translation from one symbolic representation to another, in order to find one that is computationally efficient in solving problems.[20] Representation here is similar to the nonmetaphoric correspondence of language to reality characteristic of metaphysical realism (see chapter 1). From this perspective, the correspondence between symbols and reality exists independently of the body. This assumption reinforces Heim's notion of the transcendental intimacy between a particular language (mathematics) and reality.

It is an important revelation that some problems can be represented formally and solved by the manipulation of formal tokens. However, cognitive scientists in this tradition make two further assumptions: that all cognition can be described as problem solving and that all problems or states that cannot be so coded are irrelevant. Consequently, cognitive science makes another assumption about its mechanisms: if problems can be solved using simple mechanisms, it follows that at some threshold these mechanisms will become complex; they will become intelligent.

In asserting the primacy of program, cybernetics and cognitive science make a big claim – as psychoanalysis and Marxism have done – to discover a new way of understanding almost everything. In each case a central concept restructures understanding: for the Freudian, the unconscious unlocks intellectual mysteries; for the Marxist, the relationship to the means of production; for the AI researcher, the idea of program.[21]

The fact that programs can be divorced from physical embodiment also supports a kind of dualism: the mind is isolated from the body; the program is mind without embodiment. Further, the concept of representation as an encoding process provides a dodge in terms of the power of representations to deceive. Since at a sufficient level of abstraction, different objects or processes can be shown to be equivalent, representation is no longer at issue. There is no metaphoric association involved. Rather, this specialized understanding of representation involves the substitution of one pattern for a more appropriately computational pattern.

For Newell, in particular, the computer metaphor of mind must not be confused with a theory of mind. He argues that a metaphor distances the object, so to speak. If the computer is a metaphor for mind, it is by the same token no more about mind than a metaphor. Metaphors leave the objects themselves untouched, or touched in only a literary way that does not change the topic itself, because it is only commentary.[22] For Newell, the metaphor can be explained away by assuming that metaphor is purely ornamental.

There are dangers in assuming that a set of "likenesses" between (say) computation and thinking provide adequate grounds for an inference of complete, or at least essential, identity.[23] In computation one actively searches for such identities. However, like straight lines, such identities are extremely hard to find in nature. Mathematical rationalists presume that their representations stand unproblematically for reality. But, more importantly, the computer as a model of the mind reinforces and encourages a dualistic separation of mental events (programs) and their environment.

The human body is clearly problematic for this perspective. In fact, the body is removed from consideration altogether in the "theory" of mind as a symbol system. As Deborah Lupton puts it, "In computer culture, embodiment is often represented as an unfortunate barrier to interaction with the pleasures of computing."[24] She suggests that in this way of thinking, the "human as computer metaphor is drawn upon as a rhetorical device to emphasize the irrationality of embodiment, with an end to denying the body altogether."[25] From the perspective of computation, we reduce the human to a kind of machine. Journalist John Hockenberry, writing about new technological interfaces for the disabled (Hockenberry himself has used a wheelchair for a quarter of a century) states boldly that "bodies are perhaps an arbitrary evolutionary solution to issues of mobility and communication ... the brain has no particular preference for any physical configuration."[26] However, this move incites a reaction on the part of critics of technology; the machine, characterized as a goal-oriented information processor, becomes a demonized human – a Prosthetic Other. This is clearly a problematic association, particularly when we consider that when a computer was a person with a particular job, that person tended to be female.[27] A number of oppositions are embedded in this move (human-machine, male-female).

A mechanized view of humanity assumes the alienating and dehumanizing nature of technology in a pathological way. The robotic view of the human (Joey) and the substitution of a mechanism for an organism (mathematical rationalism) produce, in the tradition of technological alienation, a widening split from reality, intensifying the schizophrenia of removing ourselves from the system, getting the human out of the loop, eliminating the soft, mushy factors that mess up the computations. The transition from a robotic view of the human to awareness of the presence of a Prosthetic Other implies a process of appropriation either of machines into the human or of the human into the machine. In this view, setting the computer in the role of Prosthetic Other weakens the sense of what it means to be human in the face of powerful technological extensions. Some have gone so far as to wonder whether technology has become so powerful that it somehow deserves its place on the evolutionary ladder.

POETICS OF "E" – THE COMPUTER
AS EVOLUTIONARY AGENT

Philosophical musing about the integration and evolution of human and machine (particularly in the early 1990s) has become part of the everyday practice of writing about cyberspace and virtual reality. Many writers wish to believe in the ability of new technologies to jump-start a new phase in human evolution.[28] Jaron Lanier, the computer hacker turned entrepreneur who coined the phrase "virtual reality," celebrates the new dissolution of the boundaries between the human and the environmental made possible by virtual reality technology. What Lanier describes as the virtual is simply a computer simulation of sufficient fidelity that a user can operate in the simulation. Recall Janet Murray's discussion of the procedural, participatory, spatial, and encyclopaedic qualities of cyberspace (see chapter 1). Lanier's virtual reality depends on what I described in chapter 1 as the interactive and immersive qualities of digital environments. According to Lanier, "One of the striking things about a virtual world system in which you have the pliancy, the ability to change the contents of the world easily, is that the distinction between your body and the rest of the world is slippery."[29] Such a thought experiment seems to support arguments about the postmodern fragmentation of the self. The self is completely dispersed in the virtual environment. Lanier acknowledges an intimate relationship between the virtual world system and the user. Virtual reality is a kind of prosthetic – a view that is by no means exclusive to discussions of computers. For example, however intent Freud was on de-centring the ego from its perceived role in the construction of identity, his view of technology was as something that extended the human, perhaps altering it, without the result being beyond recognition. "Man has," writes Freud, "become a kind of prosthetic god. When he puts on all his auxiliary organs he is truly magnificent; but these organs have not grown on him and they still give him trouble at times."[30] Such perceived intimacy between technology and humans reinforces the view of media as extensions of the human sensorium popularized by McLuhan and taken for granted by many current writers.[31]

The tools we use have the potential to change our interactions and, to some extent, the kind of people we are and the kinds of culture we create. The early hype surrounding cyberspace encouraged writers to suggest that a fundamental, evolutionary transformation was under way, with cyberspace providing a transitional space, not

between two places (the on-line and off-line worlds) but between
stages in human evolution or, more radically, between two life-forms
(the human and the digital/silicate).[32] The notion of a collectivized
sensorium, with the Internet understood as a kind of world brain
containing the contents of Western culture illustrates a shift from a
concern with the individual psyche to a concern with a kind of group
consciousness based on the assumption that technology extends the
reach of the human mind.[33]

Do computer archives and databases extend our ownership of
reality, or do they facilitate the loss of self in the vastness of the digital
domain? Some commentators, like anthropologist Weston La Barre,
have argued that technological extensions increase our ownership of
reality by increasing our sense of mastery over nature. Technological
artifacts are part of a larger kinaesthetic and functional self. La Barre
has pointed out that humans have shifted evolution from the body
to the extensions and in so doing have tremendously accelerated the
evolutionary process (in terms of cultural evolution).[34] Others, like
Edward T. Hall, worry that our extensions cause us to forget our
rootedness in nature.[35] Accepting the notion of the weak human, in
contrast with the strong machine, means accepting that there are optimum conditions for subjectivity. Thus, from this perspective an over-
dependence on technology erodes subjectivity. While technology
functions as an extension of human capacities, such functioning is
influenced by the way we characterize technological devices, our
place in the world, and our relationships with those extensions. The
metaphors that characterize such relationships are deep-seated, and
it is worth investigating the relevant metaphors in order to understand and use them.

In their most extreme, as in the work of astrophysicist Robert
Jastrow, arguments about technological evolution make the case for
a biological evolution as well. Jastrow writes, "The era of carbon-
chemistry life is drawing to a close on the earth and a new era of
silicon-based life – indestructible, immortal, infinitely expandable –
is beginning."[36] Is human life but the wet nurse of new silicon-based
life forms that, because they will be better suited to life in the frigid
vacuum of space, will ultimately supplant carbon life in the evolutionary cycle? While La Barre argues that it is our extensions that
evolve, such cyber-hysteria claims that the evolution of our tools is
evolution of ourselves. Moreover, once the threshold between the
human and the artificial is crossed, it is an evolution that leaves us

behind. Displacement of the subject becomes a call for the human to step aside from the evolutionary process. To illustrate, O.B. Hardison calls for the human to step aside for a silicon-based, parasitic form of life. Silicon devices draw their understanding predigested from their hosts, and their feeding, healing, and reproductive functions are all supplied for them. Hardison claims that "it is as though carbon creatures had developed brains and sense organs before they began to grow bodies."[37] Here is an example of anthropomorphism in an antihuman rhetoric. Now we are encouraged to step aside for our technological progeny.

If the simple machine becomes a complex life form, or organism, why is there no room left for the complex organism (us) once the simple (the mechanism) arrives? The blurring of the distinction between computers and animate beings is complemented, writes Hardison, by a weakening of the human sense of what reality is. This weakening is the direct result of technology, although not just the computer. Others have argued that movies and television create an illusion of presence at the unfolding of events that is detrimental to our sense that we have the power to control the world around us.[38]

To challenge the deep-rooted image of the Prosthetic Other, we need to challenge its two supporting arguments. The view that cognition is understood as information processing can be challenged by an embodied theory of cognition based on an embodied view of perception. The evolutionary relationship between technology and humans can be challenged by looking at the way technologies of representation calibrate human experience.

POETICS OF "E" – PERCEPTION AS ESSENCE OF REALITY

Where the metaphysical realist tradition attempts to codify thinking and aspects of reality in computer code, the *representationalist* tradition of perception treats ideas as resemblances, pictures, copies, or likenesses of reality. As foundations of the virtual, metaphysical realism and representationalism assume that a simulation can provide the opportunity for "pure" (as in unbodied) experience.

The desire for such pure communication is a manifestation of a platonic distrust of any form of mediation between the individual and the "true" structure of reality. Plato condemns art and poetry as deceptive imitations that interpose a screen between the mind and the reality or truth that should be the objects of its attention. Plato's legacy in the culture of simulation comprises a distrust of language and images and a preference for ideal forms over sensorial experience. This bias is reflected in the privilege accorded to mathematical models and algorithms. For the mathematical rationalist, Plato provides the eternal, fixed form of reality, and digital programs code the essence, not just the appearance, of reality.

In many cognitive theories, ideas or mental phenomena are regarded as presentations set before the inner perception of thoughts, just as a work of art is set before an interpreter. This view has its origins in the eighteenth century, when John Locke described the mind as a dark room or closet, understanding as seeing, and the idea as "some immediate object of the mind, which it perceives and has before it."[39] This is the origin of the doctrine of internal representations. Within this tradition it is easy to disregard parts of the body that are beyond the optical system and the brain. For Locke, the mind perceives nothing but its own ideas, and knowledge exists only when a correspondence or conformity occurs between its ideas and the reality of things in the world.[40] "Locke and Hume, and to a considerable extent the later empiricists, all assume an atomistic theory of perception in which simple sensory components were assembled, by reason of their co-occurrence in experience, into complex wholes. The atomistic view of perception has been dominant in cognitive science with its attempt to operationalize cognition in terms of solving problems."[41] Variations on this theme are all based on explicit representations of the problem, a formal enumeration of all possible actions taken by the program, and the rules for operating within the program until it solves the problem.[42] Newell's brand of cognitive science appropriates the classical, mechanistic model of perception and formalizes it into a model of how the information processor (organic or technological) works.

THE POETICS OF MEDIATION
AND EMBODIED PERCEPTION

By contrast, theories of *embodied perception* argue that the mind does not function on the basis of internal representations. Embodied perception supports the idea of *body knowledge* to offer an explanation of how we are perceptually oriented in both mediated situations and situations that are not technologically mediated and how this perceptual orientation contributes to our constructed selfhood. The idea of body-knowledge draws on three traditions: the phenomenology of perception, ecological perception, and theories of the embodied mind.

The *phenomenology of perception* claims that perception is neither static nor permanent but that, like the experience of the poetic image, it involves a dynamic and ever-changing process. "Perception," writes philosopher Maurice Merleau-Ponty, "is the background from which all acts stand out, and is presupposed by them. The world is not an object such that I have in my possession the law of its making; it is the natural setting of, and field for, all my thoughts and my explicit perceptions."[43] The body affords us a particular perspective on the world, a perspective determined by our own individual dispositions,[44] by the physiological characteristics of our species, and by the generally accepted codes and conventions of our particular, historically situated society. Our existence as embodied beings within the world is the natural and necessary condition of all human knowledge.[45]

As the basis of our interactions with the world, it is reasonable to assume that perceptual skills set parameters for our experiences.[46] Perception, understood not as a faculty but as an activity, emphasizes that knowledge is not simply rule-governed or linguistic but is set in the embodied experience of human interaction and by the intrinsic capacity of the body to centre, to position itself, to take hold of things.[47]

The acknowledgment that the body is central to perception and knowledge is not limited to the phenomenological tradition. *Ecological perception* theory, associated with psychologists James J. Gibson and, later, Ulric Neisser, explains perception in relation to the movements of a body in an environment. Perception is first and foremost a bodily skill – a matter of navigation through an environment. From this ecological perspective, knowing is an extension of perceiving, since the extracting and abstracting of invariants are what happens in both activities. Gibson argues that we do not reconstruct internal representations from primary sensory stimuli but that we possess enough information to perceive the environment directly without conceptual ordering. He treats perception as a noninferred, nonconstructed, direct "read off" of information from the immediate patterning of an ambient ecological array. In Gibson's ecological perception, nothing needs to be reassembled deep "inside" anything (Locke's dark room), because there was no disassembling to begin with.[48]

Information available in the ambient optical array specifies not just the positions and movements of objects but also the relationships between surfaces and points of observation; perception necessarily involves environment and self.[49] The optical information for specifying the self, including the head, body, arms, and hands, accompanies the optical information for specifying aspects of the environment. Therefore, argues Gibson, to adopt the point of view of another person is not simply a figure of speech or an advanced achievement of conceptual thought. He writes: "It means, *I can perceive surfaces hidden at my point of view but unhidden at yours*. This means, *I can perceive a surface that is behind another*. And if so, *we can both perceive the same world*."[50]

Ulric Neisser builds upon Gibson's ambient optic array to develop an ecological approach to perception as the basis of knowledge. For Neisser, the perceiver constructs anticipations of certain kinds of information that enable him or her to accept that information as it becomes available. Significantly, what is constructed is not a mental image appearing in consciousness, where it is admired by an inner observer. The perceiver must often actively explore the optic array to make such information available, by moving his or her eyes, head, or body. Such explorations are directed by an anticipatory schema that allows us to plan for perceptual action and to prepare for particular kinds of optical structure.[51]

Neisser calls perception more immediate or direct than other cognitive activities: this is his debt to James Gibson. Neisser argues that Gibson was right about the orienting aspect of direct perception, which "provides the ground to which more abstract forms of cognition ultimately refer."[52] It is through the embodied interaction with the world that an environment begins to "make sense" to the human.[53] The mechanisms underlying orientation, whatever they might turn out to be, put us in direct and realistic contact with our surroundings: we can see where we are, what we are doing, and what possibilities for action the environment affords.[54]

Neisser also attempts to address the criticisms levelled at Gibsonian direct perception in his own ecological approach to perception. First, the anticipatory schema allow for the intentionality of meaningful perception more readily than Gibson's direct read-off of the environment. Second, he reminds us that the visual system also has functions other than navigation. He claims that sight is based on two distinct functions, each depending on anatomically separate neural systems that are combined smoothly and invisibly in normal vision. The first function, geared toward *orientation* (Gibson's direct perception), enables us to see how the environment is laid out, our place in it, and what we are doing or might possibly do. The second function involves *recognition*, in which objects or symbols are matched to something like internal representations and are thus identified.[55]

Crucial to the idea of mediation is the extent to which theories of ecological perception show the body to be central to perception and, by extension, to knowledge. Others go further, to explore the indispensability of the body to consciousness.[56]

Further, the body and representation are also closely linked. For example, Israel Rosenfield (1993) describes consciousness in relation to body image.[57] Gerald Edelman (1992) also implicates bodily actions in the development of the brain, suggesting that the selective strengthening of neural connections creates different regional maps, which then interact by means of a parallel and reciprocal re-entrant signalling. He extends this model of neural differentiation into a theory of the emergence of consciousness in sufficiently complex neural networks. This means that the core of consciousness is, from the beginning, a kind of self – reference and positioning. He suggests that primary consciousness is the capacity to image an immediate past and anticipate an immediate future. This extension of the perceptual present is the root of consciousness for Edelman.[58] He reinforces my argument that we must avoid the tendency to claim that language creates reality: "Language is acquired by interacting with others in learning events, which initiate the formation of connections between semantics and phonology. It depends on having conceptual systems already in place."[59]

Language, then, follows bodily interaction with the environment and with others. It serves to detach metaphoric connections from immediate experience. Indeed, many of our abstract ideas begin as metaphorical extensions of embodied experience. For example, the God's-eye perspective, from which we observe, understand, and judge the world, illustrates how an embodied metaphor (drawn from experience) becomes an unconscious assumption about the world. At every moment we see that our surroundings are quite independent of us. This experience gives rise to a metaphoric extension in which the relation of thinkers to what they are thinking about resembles the relation of individuals to their environment. Just as the environment exists independently of the perceiver, so too the truth exists independently of the thinker. It is because of this metaphor that we so naturally use the word "see" for both visual and intellectual apprehension.[60]

There are two issues here: the directness or indirectness of sensory perception and the status of representations and language. Regarding the nature of our sensory access to things in the world, we might ask whether certain objects of perception (for example, colour, the third dimension) are added to sensory perception by the mind. Both Locke and Kant would agree with this assumption. However, pscyhologists like J.J. Gibson and Neisser reject it, along with the objectivist assumptions that the brain adds instructions to sensory imput. They also set an empirical limit on constructivist claims that the world is only a discursive construction.

One can group attitudes toward the status of representations and language into three categories. Some commentators, like the meta-physical realists (see chapter 1) and the mathematical rationalists, regard representations as reflections of reality. Others, like the con-structivists, argue that representations and language create reality. Finally, following the lead of the psychologists of embodied percep-tion, representations can be regarded as constructed objects that allow us to gain access to aspects of experience. In this sense, representa-tions are abstractions that enhance and focus consciousness but that do not absolutely determine it. This is the main assumption of the various doctrines of the "embodied mind." Embodied perception is less concerned with the nature of the appearance of things than with demonstrating how perception is a body skill-set embedded in representation, discourse, and technique.

POETICS OF MEDIATION – SKILLS AND SEDIMENTATION

How do we learn the skills of selfhood? For the interactive approach to cognition, experience is shaped by repeated action, and cognition is based on the experience of the body. Cognitive structures emerge from the recurrent sensorimotor patterns that enable action to be per-ceptually guided.[61] As basic a bodily action as balance is learned as an activity and not as the result of a set of instructions or rules. The meaning of balancing emerges through acts of balancing and the experience of systemic processes and states within our bodies.[62] The explanation of cognition as problem solving works where tasks can be explicitly specified. But for other kinds of activity, like driving, this approach is less successful. Indeed, movement such as that involved in driving depends upon acquired motor skills and the continuous use of common sense or background know-how.[63] Context-dependent know-how is the very essence of creative cognition – not something to be eliminated by the discovery of more sophisticated rules.[64] Creative cognition does not emerge by establishing and following explicit rules. Instead, it develops through interaction; it emerges by proximating knowledge and making it body-knowledge. Further, we use a variety of tools to interact with the environment. These too, as they become transparent and their use becomes automatic, become part of our body knowledge.

For example, the blind person who runs his or her hand along a cane will realize its position and its objective characteristics such as weight, hardness, smoothness, and so forth. When that person uses a cane, however, s/he is unaware of its objective position, physical traits, and the varying pressure of it in the palm of the hand. The cane now offers, like the body, transparent access to the objects he or she touches with it.[65]

Seymour Papert uses the term *bricolage* to describe a style of organizing work in terms of interaction between people and their tools, rather than in terms of advanced planning. He uses the example of teaching children the conceptual relationship between gears and power (small gears are weaker because they move faster, while larger gears move more slowly but have more power). This practical problem serves to introduce another characteristic displayed by negotiational programmers, which Papert calls *proximality*, or closeness to the object.

To facilitate the absorption of cybernetics into education, Papert collaborated with LEGO in the mid-1980s to develop a construction set and to "give up trying to entice children into my cybernetic world ... and instead to put cybernetics into their world."[66] His goal was to make the relationship between children and programming more "real" by moving the activity from the school to the home; once computers are integrated into the daily lives of children, they can become part of the sedimented background of the life-world. Papert characterizes this hope as follows: "Looking forward to the future, it seems obvious that children will grow up building cybernetic constructs as fluently as they now build cars and houses and train-track circuits. Only then will cybernetic thinking really become part of their culture."[67] Papert observes that those children who were more successful in building this kind of construct did not have better rules, but they did have a tendency to see things in terms of relationships, rather than properties. They used a style of reasoning that allowed them to imagine themselves "inside the system."[68] For Papert, "better" performance was characterized by an ability to play, to engage in interaction, and to be able to incorporate the metaphor-models of the building situation.

In virtual reality, as the hardware (gloves, helmets, visual displays, and so forth) becomes transparent, we experience exactly this sense of what Turkle and Papert call *proximality* (or closeness) to the objects in the virtual world. The controlling movements of the body become habitual and automatic, and part of our physical, sensorimotor repertoire, and the environment becomes opaque. By this I mean that we are not concerned with the relationship between the virtual display and any objects they might stand for in the "real" world. Rather, we are concerned with the relationship between our bodily actions and the changes or responses they might trigger in the virtual environment. Such relationships are also part of our more mundane interactions with computers.

When we learn a new task our mistakes prevent us from focussing on the task at hand. Until we master the new task, our attention is drawn again and again to the tool as we internalise new metaphors and learn new skills. Body knowledge develops as the metaphors become sedimented, the skills become habitualized, and the tools become transparent.

TECHNOLOGY CALIBRATES PERCEPTION

Just how do devices shape perception? How do we explain the intimate relationship between our devices of representation and our sense of selfhood? One clue lies in the sense of proximality mentioned in the previous section. Once we reject representations as a transparent reflection of reality or as barriers to reality, they become the material with which we construct our metaphors, models, and experiments with the world.

For example, as the process of linear perspective takes on the transparency of a natural state of cognition, we tend to forget its origins as a method for pictorial representation and its relationship to devices that required particular postures and attitudes. In turn, modes of perception become sedimented and naturalized in a given culture. Further, the devices that a culture uses to create images have a relationship to the underlying assumptions about perception and cognition they support.

THE VIEW THROUGH ALBERTI'S WINDOW

Filippo Brunelleschi (1377–1446) has been traditionally credited with the invention of the first mathematical procedure for codifying rules for perspective. Leon Battista Alberti (1402–72) produced a less scientifically accurate but more visually convincing and aesthetically pleasing system of perspective. Alberti's perspective provided the artist with a single, harmonious system for the relative proportions of every figure, object, and spatial division within a pictorial field.

Drawing with linear perspective is artificial, and before the process was internalized by artistic practice, it required a device to enable the draughtsman to transfer what was seen through a screen to the picture plane. Linear perspective portrays an object as it is perceived from the outside (from a fixed point of view external to the represented reality). The general principle depends on two conditions: the level of the viewer's eye when viewing an object (which determines the *horizon)* and the viewer's distance from the object. A picture is drawn as a view from a window might be drawn – with a necessary spatial barrier between the artist and the world s/he represents. Indeed, Renaissance art theory refers to the painting as a "window into the open" (Alberti's *fenestra aperta* and Leonardo da Vinci's *vetro*). In the system of linear perspective, the artist's point of view arguably corresponds to that of the spectator. Even today, learning to draw in linear perspective still involves a student imagining some sort of imaginary, transparent wall onto which the object of the drawing is projected. This imaginary wall signifies the inevitable barrier between the artist and the reality represented.[69] It also reinforces the metaphoric assumption that thought is a mental image.

With the development of film, then television, then virtual reality, the viewer's distance from the visual plane decreases; the window moves closer to the body, which reinforces its illusion of invisibility. This process enables writers like Joshua Meyrowitz (1985) to claim that television makes the public private by bringing the world into the living room. In virtual reality the distance between viewer and image may decrease even further, while the distance between artist and image actually increases through the process of translating numerical information into images to be subsequently manipulated in "real time." The computer screen provides a layer of mediation between the artist and the viewer. Originally a grid of wires stretched across a wooden frame, the invisible plane between the artist and object is a window: an open faucet for sensory input. However, the screen processes all sensory information that passes through it, establishing the artist's distance from the world of "natural" sensory phenomena. Through the screen, the artist translates and mediates experience in order to create images. This process foreshortens and transposes three-dimensional phenomena onto a two-dimensional plane. Linear perspective and the image of the draughtsman's screen serve both as a social code for representation and as an epistemological stance.[70]

The invention and subsequent dominance of linear perspective had broad consequences for the way people perceived their relationship with the world.[71] According to Robert Romanyshyn, the self becomes a spectator within the landscape of linear perspectival vision, separated from the world by his or her window on the world. The body becomes a specimen, divorced from the self, and the world becomes a spectacle for this detached and observing eye.[72] This visual bias has been described as the degradation of what was, for Alberti and his contemporaries, a metaphor. For me, our culture's so-called visual bias is not the result of a process of degradation but of sedimentation. We have not simply debased unmediated experience through its inadequate representation in linear perspective. We have, instead, learned to represent aspects of the world in particular ways and now accept representations at face (or interface) value. Alberti's window is virtual reality *in potentia*. It is a technique for abstracting visual experience: the device allows an artist to lift an aspect of the world out of its natural context, to render it more malleable.

PERCEPTION AND BUILDING MACHINES

Technological innovations in the nineteenth century had radical implications for how people perceived the world. Jonathan Crary (1982) argued that devices such as the camera obscura shaped nineteenth-century understanding of how perception worked. For Crary, such devices influenced not just attitudes towards the world but attitudes towards the self as well.[73] Anne Friedberg describes the panorama, diorama, and panopticon as technologies that train observers. However, perceptual devices also foster a dualism, in that they train the body to assume that vision (and the visible) are separable from the rest of the body.

The popularity of panoramas should not be underestimated. There were almost as many houses showing entertainments of this kind in

Victorian London as there are cinemas today.[74] Panoramas and dioramas were massive paintings displayed in specially constructed buildings. These theatres were generally made of wood and were lit by candles or gas. Consequently, most of the buildings and canvasses were eventually destroyed by fire, leaving little trace of their popularity and influence on the perceptions of contemporary viewers.

The invention of the panorama is usually attributed to Robert Barker, an Edinburgh painter, in about 1785. The panoramic illusion was created by a combination of effects. The paintings combined realist techniques of perspective and massive scale. The mode of viewing these paintings involved placing the spectator in the centre of a darkened room surrounded by a scene lit from above. Sophisticated lighting effects enhanced the astonishing illusion of reality.[75]

An important aspect of the panorama and other visual entertainments was the fact that they were not simply modes of visual representation but were also the forms of presentation or exhibition – they were buildings in which audiences saw pictures.

The success of the panorama inspired a crop of inventions of similar entertainments. Daguerre opened a 350-seat theatre for his invention, the diorama, in Paris in 1822 and later built an amphitheatre at Regents Park in London. The images were seen through a 2800-square-foot screen of calico, half of which was opaque and half painted in translucent colour. The diorama's translucent image was lit from behind, while the opaque image was lit from the front, creating the illusion that the painting exuded brilliant light. The images often portrayed a landscape in daylight that, as the lighting shifted, showed the same scene at night. The intensity, placing, and colour of the light were varied by an elaborate system of pulleys, cords, slides and shutters. The diorama was a multisensory experience in which motion, sound, and the environment were all crucial to the experience.

Another dominant "machine of the visible," the panopticon (1791), can be contrasted with the panorama (1792) and diorama (1823). The panopticon was a model of prison proposed by Jeremy Bentham in 1791; it was designed to control the relationship between the seer and the seen. All the inmates in the panopticon would occupy cells that faced a central guard tower with windows all round it. The prisoners would not be able to see into the tower, but the guards would be able to observe any cell. Consequently, the prisoners would never know when they were being observed. In such a prison, the seer experiences a sense of omnipotent voyeurism, while the seen incorporates a sense

of disciplined surveillance.[76] Foucault made much of the power relationship between the panopticon and surveillance.[77] By contrast, the
panorama and the diorama were building-machines with a different
objective. Whereas the panopticon was designed to *confine* the
spectator-subject, these visual entertainments of the nineteenth century were designed to transport the spectator. Friedberg explains:
"The panorama offered a spectacle in which all sense of time and
space was lost, produced by the combination of the observer in a
darkened room (where there were no markers of place and time) and
presentation of 'realistic views of other places and times.'"[78] The panoramic and dioramic observers were, for Friedberg, given an imaginary illusion of mobility. The panorama was the bourgeois public's
substitute for the Grand Tour.

The significance of the panorama and the diorama is not so much
the technique of creating the image that creates a magical sense of
reality but the technique of experiencing the image. Unlike the panopticon, which has influenced contemporary thinking about surveillance, power, and the intrusive nature of the Internet, the idea of
building machines as tools for experiencing the world has been
neglected. These entertainments provided the experience of the
process, rather than the product, of sight.

IMAGES AS RECORDINGS OR CONSTRUCTIONS

The assumption that media exert a powerful influence on our sense
of identity is persistent: cinematic and electronic media have not only
historically symbolized but also historically constituted a radical
alteration of the forms of our culture's previous temporal and spatial
consciousness. Just as the photograph did in the last century, so in
this one, cinematic and electronic screens differently demand and
shape our "presence" to the world and our representation in it. "Presence" refers to the positioned awareness of being in an environment.
This becomes a marker for subjectivity, because postmodernism challenges the assumption that with no "place" there can be no presence.
Electronic communication is experienced not as a discrete, intentional, and bodily centred projection in space but rather as simulta-
neous, dispersed, insubstantial transmission of information across a
network. Thus, the "presence" of the electronic mode of communication is at one remove from previous representational connections
between signification and referentiality.[79]

The image is a transcription that brings to mind, with varying degrees of success, some original thing. For some, the image is a pale reflection of that original thing, and they strive to invoke the original object, the "real," without mediation. This is the dilemma of the transformative view; on the one hand, computers offer access to a Platonic essence of reality – the code – while at the same time, they draw attention to the medium of representation that is the agent of transformation. The issue of primary importance in discussions of representations as they apply to cyberspace is the issue of proximality: what or who is close to what? Photography, in particular, has been discussed in terms of the extent to which the photograph does or does not provide a direct correspondence to external reality. When it has seemed that the photograph could easily demonstrate the kind of metaphoric relationship between image and reality characteristic of the poetics of mediation, theorists of photography have often attached ontological status to the image, in a kind of making manifest of the internal representation, reinforcing the Cartesian model of mind.

For example, it has been argued that photography provides the technology to record the world and capture its integral realism.[80] When a photograph is taken, an image of the world is formed automatically, without the creative intervention of a human agent.[81] Thus, the photographic image is somehow more "objective," capturing more than a likeness.[82] This is a powerful argument. The artist is the mediator between world and image, and photography allows one to bypass the mediation. This attitude is consistent with the desire for a pre-mediated state of social interaction that surfaces in discussions of the nature of virtual communities. The photograph, particularly, as a witness to reality, proves the existence of the external world. As a consequence, the human agent becomes a barrier situated between the world and its images, a position consistent with the technological pessimism discussed in chapter 2.

The photograph claims a more direct correspondence to reality than earlier images because of the "automatic" nature of the camera. This is an erroneous, though powerful, assumption. In reference to proxy, we are encouraged to assume that the photograph is a conduit to reality. To take a photograph or to gaze at a photographic image is often compared to adopting the epistemological perspective of the detached observer. The picture may distort, but a photograph passes for incontrovertible proof that a given thing happened.[83] As a consequence of thinking that reality can be captured through photography in a fixed form, by removing the agent altogether from the task of reproduction, one puts oneself into a certain relation to the world that feels like knowledge and power.[84] For many, photography resolves the epistemological question of the reality of the physical world, since the photographic image is assumed to refer to an object in the physical world. Photography embodies an epistemological stance in which the observer is detached from events and devices objectively record aspects of the world. However, this amounts to a naive and problematic view of reality.

The nature of the proximality of the photographic image to the world it represents becomes less rigid when we consider moving pictures. For example, the indexicality of film (the link between the image and its referent, as in the case of lightning serving as an index of an oncoming storm) is less important in cinema than in photography. Film theorist Christian Metz argues that "the initially indexical power of the cinema (turns) frequently into a realist guarantee for the unreal. Photography, on the other hand, remains closer to the pure index, stubbornly pointing to the print of what *was* but no longer *is*."[85]

The indexical power of the cinema to draw our attention to what is portrayed (rather than what is represented) changes the relationship between the recorded image and the viewer. In cinema, the task is convincing the viewer, as a willing participant in the experience of viewing, of the plausibility (not the actuality) of events displayed on the screen. To say that images are presented realistically is a very different claim than to say that we have apprehended or appropriated the subject photographed. The process of creating images in digitized form complicates the proximality of image to reality even further.

Digitization works by reducing images to picture elements called *pixels*. Any aspect of the image can be altered mathematically, since the brightness, contrast, or sharpness of any pixel exists as a numerical value in computer code. The very ease of altering digital images means that digitized imagery allows much greater potential for manipulation than does traditional photography. Even the indexical claim of photography is now questionable. Traditionally, the truth status of photography has rested on two claims: empiricist assumptions about the optical system and about the understanding of photography's operation (as an objective tool for recording reality as it is) and claims about the authority of the institutions that employ it. While earlier writers assumed an indexical relation between the camera and the image imprinted on the film, with digitization the viewer will no longer be sure of this relationship. The index will be erased and the photo will become "pure iconicity."[86] The concept of pure iconicity has two implications. First, whereas photography separates the viewer from the represented world, digitization separates the camera from the image. In terms of proximity, the image-maker now has closer access to the basic components of the image (pixels and the binary code), which, in terms of cognitivism, are also the building blocks of reality. Thus, in one sense the digital image-maker might consider herself closer to the essence of reality than the photographer. In another sense, the process of image-making is detached even further from the human agent. The perceptual system is displaced by the rational, cognitive abilities of the programmer to create patterns in code.

Digitization offers the possibility of removing any intervening mediation between the idea and the viewer (the same claim was once made about photography). The codification of reality into digital form substitutes one set of "objects" for another. A second implication may reinforce both traditional fears of the power of images and the hopeful potential of changing our assumptions about the connections between image and reality. Let me explain. Pure iconicity means that the image points to a referent, but this referent either does not exist, or it retreats from our perceptual or intellectual grasp to become inaccessible and leaves us with only the act of pointing. This can be clarified with an example.

Digitized images in cinema offer us an "is" that never "was." For example, the 1994 film *The Crow* was almost shelved only days from completion when star Brandon Lee was killed in a shooting accident on the set.[87] The production was salvaged when special effects artists were able to create a five-second sequence of crucial importance to the narrative using a body double, computer-generated images, and outtakes of Lee. Using computers to control a process similar to the television technique of chroma-key (in which an actor filmed against a blue screen is edited against a previously filmed background), the special effects team stamped the star's visage into a composite scene in which he never appeared. In the words of special-effects producer Mark Galvin, "If we've done our job well people won't know that we've worked on the film ... and I think that's what we're proudest of."[88]

This process of creating scenes with an absent actor was by no means automatic. The task required over six hundred hours of human and computer labour. The creation of composite digital images is less like the process of photography than like painting, since it involves a complex set of artistic, as well as technical, decisions. Digital imagery is constructed imagery that encourages a viewer to deal with the image in a direct manner. Digital images are, at their most successful, opaque objects in their own right, side-stepping the relationship between object and world. Instead, digital images function as if the objects they portray existed. In a sense, the objects in a digital image function like the impossible drawings and prints of M.C. Escher and serve to remind us of the possibility of the impossible.

Twenty years after *Star Wars* was released, director George Lucas used digital technology to restore and add to his *Star Wars* trilogy. In *The Phantom Menace,* according to Lucas, "A lot of what we did – like shooting a new set of lips to glue onto an actor, putting an extra here or there, or things like that – was shot digitally, which was certainly more cost effective."[89] In fact, Lucas uses digital technology to make movies in an old-fashioned way, by shooting reaction shots: actors walking, rising from chairs, leaving rooms, and so on. This stock footage is compiled into the same kind of library of motion that a computer animator builds of his or her characters. From this library of sequences, specific scenes can be constructed in the editing room (the computer desktop). Similarly, television shows that incorporate computer animation (*Babylon 5*, the *Star Trek* shows) and newer computer-animated series (*Roughnecks: The Starship Trooper Chronicles*) blur the lines between animation and special effects. Further, films like Peter Jackson's *Lord of the Rings* trilogy present digital landscapes more compelling than many computer games. This blurring happens because the same process of digitization occurs more commonly as the most cost-effective manner of producing special effects. The lure of digitization is also evident in Tim Burton's *Mars Attacks!* Burton chose computer-generated imagery (CGI) over the techniques of motion animation he had previously used in *Beetlejuice and A Nightmare before Christmas* because digital effects were a third of the cost of stop-motion animation.

A process of sedimentation occurs with images, whether they are categorized as real, irreal, or simulational. Images become naturalized. If the digital program can achieve a level of operational, functional isomorphism to an aspect of reality, it does not seem a stretch to assume the same between image and reality. Reproductions are considered natural as they are invested, through familiarity, with "the authority of the obvious, commonsensical, and self-evident to the point that their status as *reproduction* is occluded."[90] Sedimentation allows us to shift our attention from the power of an image to accurately reflect some part of reality to the processes by which an image is invested with authority.

The screen of the Renaissance artist disappeared over time, and yet it still appears in discussions of linear perspective. The artist could "get closer" to the subject, first, by learning to ignore the perspective device and, later, by ignoring the abstract rules for drawing in linear perspective. With photography, the viewer can learn to ignore the role of the artist and get closer to the image. With virtual reality, the viewer steps through the window as realism is increasingly defined by our ability as viewers to identify with and to enter into active participation with the image. The desire for interaction is not a new phenomenon. Yet the authenticity of an image is always socially constructed and reinforced. A representation of the real owes its objective appearance not to its agreement with the very reality of things but rather "to conformity with rules which define its syntax within its social use."[91] How literal or realistic the picture is depends upon how standard the system is. If representation is a matter of choice and correctness a matter of information, realism is a matter of habit.[92]

The development inherent in computerized simulations is not simply that they are taken as valid but that they are endowed with the legitimacy of other images. The virtual image, as a challenge to earlier forms of representation, gains importance when the image takes on such a level of fidelity that it can function for the real in such a way that we forget the quality of unreality that reminds us of the nature of the image as artifice.

Watching motion pictures, we actually perceive entities and events, but this involves a more or less distorted reality belonging (psychologically speaking) to a world not entirely our own but to one that seems distant.[93] The "virtual," as a realm of objects, tempts us to a similar understanding. There is no artificial experience, since experience is a quality of she or he who experiences. There is only experience of the artificial.

Traditional assumptions about the privileged relationship between the photographic image and its referent have supported a kind of naive realism and a perpetuation of psychological models based on the notion of internal representations. Discussions about digitalized images generally take this assumption for granted, replacing it with an equally naive idealism premised on the simulational power of the digitalized image. The photograph is afforded a relationship to reality based on its proximality to the source of the image. The relationship of the digital image to its source is that of an operative image based on a formal equivalence and a functional similarity. Each assumption is simplistic. The photograph is not automatic but involves the selective intention of framing. The digital image, too, involves creation and filtering.

THE CYBORG AS ARTIFACTUAL SELF

Thinking of the computer as a communications medium and as an artifact emphasizes how the technology has effects as we use it. We can reconsider the self constructed through interactions with the world as mediated by the material conditions of life and representation. A number of feminists have taken up exactly this kind of social constructionist position, arguing that the power of language to set the parameters of identity, class, race, and gender is most dangerous when it creates the kind of universal categories I have described in relation to claims about the representational power of symbolic systems to codify reality. The temptation to reify social constructions into universals does not require us to reject social construction altogether – just to recognize the inherent dangers.[94] Subjectivity is constructed through a continuous process and ongoing constant renewal based on an interaction with the world, "by one's personal, subjective engagement in the practices, discourses, and institutions that lend significance (value, meaning, and affect) to the events of the world."[95] Interactive realism offers a way to characterize the mediating role of communication technology (a materiality of communication) that may be useful in thinking about the creation of female and male subjectivities emphasizing the sense of presence (self and environment) necessary to any mediated interaction.

This chapter began with the metaphoric relationship between the wolf and the human. Similarly, by incorporating the technological into our definitions of selfhood, we become like technology. We do not need, however, to be appropriated by machines or to become mechanistic in our self-definitions. We become cyborgs. The term "cyborg" was first used in 1960 to describe a self-regulating system in which drugs could be administered to an astronaut to adjust automatic responses during space travel.[96] Like the Prosthetic Other, the cyborg has been characterized as a kind of illness metaphor.

For example, the term *cyborg subjectivity* has been used to describe a symptom of the military information society. Cyborg subjectivity involves a paranoic rationality expressed in the machine-like self. It combines an omnipotent fantasy of self-control with fear and aggression directed against the emotional and bodily limitations of the human being. For cyborg subjectivity, information technology is associated with a narcissistic illusion of controlling the external world characteristic of optimistic views of technology as an instrument for the mastery of Nature. Critics of cyborg subjectivity disdain the presumptions that with technology we can either remake the world in our own image or merge the human and technological environment in a blissful union.[97] In fact, one of the most telling features of cyborg subjectivity is that it reflects a fear of losing control to the technological, rather than confidence that technology can be controlled or that it can be used to control the world around us.

The image of the cyborg has also been invoked as an idealized virtual body that offers at least a temporary solution to the Enlightenment view of the body as irrational, weak, and passive; this view is characteristic of much cyberculture writing. In the evolutionary view of technology, computers replace body as well as mind.[98] Indeed, the same hierarchy of spirit over flesh is present – this time the operative narrative is a psychotic descent into the realm of body as mechanism. The cyborg metaphor in each of these cases is reductive.

However, the cyborg metaphor is appealing because this construction mediates, in that it creates a bridge between a human body and a mind confronted with the computational power of machines. It is a hopeful metaphor precisely because it emphasizes our intimate relationship with technological artifacts. We change, but the changes occur as we create, use, and think through and about our technology. Both the Prosthetic Other and the cyborg metaphors attempt to deal with the recognition that technology has become an evolutionary agent and that this process creates a situation in which the human is ill-equipped for survival.

Donna Haraway provides one demonstration of the ways media representations can challenge the assumption that concepts associated with the Enlightenment are in any way "natural" or gender-specific, although technology as a social construction exemplifies maleness in its expression of a rationalistic, universal, and utopian vision of technology and computing. Writers like Cameron Bailey (1996) and Sherry Turkle (1996) have demonstrated the difficulties of representing race and gender in cyberspace.[99] The politicization of concepts as seemingly "natural" as gender or race is a powerful and strategic act of symbolic construction. Furthermore, according to Donna Haraway, communication sciences and modern biologies are constructed by a common move – *"the translation of the world into a problem of coding*, a search for a common language in which all resistance to instrumental control disappears and all heterogeneity can be submitted to disassembly, reassembly, investment, and exchange."[100] She writes that "cyborg politics is the struggle for language and the struggle against perfect communication, against the one code that translates all meaning perfectly, the central dogma of phallogocentrism."[101] Mark Poster (2001) continues this line of argument in his evaluation of the new politics of cyberspace. He argues that on the Internet we are continually invited to engage in the communicative practice of self-construction. The resulting social figure of the cyborg thus reconfigures political practice.[102]

For these writers the metaphor of the cyborg serves not to demonstrate the general malaise of technological society but to suggest ways for people to define themselves as powerful agents within that same technological order. Further, use of the cyborg emphasizes translation, playfulness, and analogy. For Haraway, translation is always interpretive, critical, and partial. Her use of the cyborg as metaphor can be linked to Melanie Klein's conceptualization of play as an acting out of roles and positions that develop our sense of identity.[103] For Klein play is crucial to the child's development of ego. As the ego develops, a true relation to reality is gradually established out of this unreal reality.[104] In this, Klein recalls what I have called the skill set of selfhood. The truth of the sense of reality is based on a child's ability to cope with events in the external world influenced by biology and social normativity. The cyborg metaphor first rejects the view that people (particularly women) are excluded from the world of science, defining all people as objects and agents embedded in a technological system.

Haraway celebrates the possibilities of breaking down traditional notions of identity by appropriating metaphors from technology. She argues that technology allows us to question the grand narratives of science and what it is to be human, gendered, natural, or constructed. She creates what she calls boundary creatures – simians, cyborgs, and women – all of whom have destabilized Western evolutionary, technological, and biological narratives. She challenges an artificial distinction between the association of science as a male realm and nature as a female domain.[105] Her attempts to create metaphors for the place of women in a technologically dominated society are provocative and valuable. They are offered as more appropriate to a technological order than references to women as "goddess." As useful as metaphors for gender can be, it is unfortunate that the metaphor of the cyborg has become less a site of interaction or dialogue about our place in a technological society than just an image of the human and prosthetic. Haraway's aggressive tactic takes the language of the beast – the technological order – and applies terms from "Big Science" to the feminist project.

Haraway also demonstrates the poststructuralist attitude to language that argues that essentialist definitions are wrong, whether they are misogynist or feminist in origin. Haraway provides a place for interactive realism in her cyborg world of boundary creatures, simians, and monsters. She writes that "the recent history for much of the u.s. left and u.s. feminism has been a response to this kind of crisis by endless splitting and searches for a new essential identity. But there has also been a growing recognition of another response through coalition – affinity, not identity."[106] She argues, without so calling it, for a kind of pluralism by suggesting that the theoretical and practical struggle against unity through domination and incorporation "ironically not only undermines the justifications for patriarchy, colonialism, humanism, positivism, essentialism, scientism, and other unlamented -isms, but *all* claims for an organic or natural standpoint" (24–5).

What do we make of the metaphor of the cyborg? Haraway and those who continue her use of the metaphor emphasize the relationship between language and identity formation. Others take the concept more literally. Naturalizing concepts like reason insulates them from reconsideration. For example, writers like cyberpunk Bruce Sterling appropriate Haraway's concept of signifying monsters, arguing that cyberpunk is "posthumanist" science fiction that believes "technological destruction of the human condition leads not to future shocked zombies but to hopeful monsters."[107] The creative potential of the metaphors is transformed into an attempt to develop a posthumanist ideology, as if the evolutionary change had already occurred. This rhetorical move also delegitimizes the political potential of a metaphor like the cyborg by denying its metaphorical creativity. By reducing the cyborg to a literal description of an evolutionary step, Sterling takes what was for Haraway a radical act of interpretation and appropriates it as a description of reality.[108]

The machine metaphor emphasizes a fear of the encroaching technological other. As was demonstrated by the case of Joey, cybernetics has been used as a metaphor for illness caused by a sense of dehumanization in reaction to powerful machines. The Freudianism of Bettelheim emphasizes this sense of dehumanization. Poster's dead knowledge and Marx's dead labour are characteristics of the cyborg subjectivity, which takes a different approach to the problem of the machine. Here, technology is a manifestation of a more general scientistic hubris. Haraway, in contrast to these positions, plays with the distinction between the human and the machine. Thus, she provides a partial opening for interpreting and negotiating the relationship between the two. In general, cyberculture embraces the dissolution of the categorical separation of machine and human. The fascination with the cyborg requires not a fear of the Prosthetic Other but an active embrace.

Sterling betrays a simplistic understanding of postmodern philosophy that is absent from much of this work. Even Michel Foucault, in an explicit attack against the Enlightenment assumption of a unified human subject, does not express such an overt sentiment against humanity. Foucault's antihumanism, in contrast with Sterling's, is a condemnation of the hubris of our own cultural heritage, rather than an invocation of evolution. Foucault writes:

I don't think there is actually a sovereign, founding subject. I am very sceptical and very hostile toward this conception of the subject. I think on the contrary that the subject is constituted through practices of subjection, or, in a more anonymous way, through practices of liberation, of freedom, as in Antiquity, starting of course from a certain number of rules, styles, and conventions that are found in the culture.[109]

This view is not inconsistent with the constructionist self that changes through its interactions. Foucault's attack, like Poster's, is aimed not at the psyche but at the societal citizen-subject.

The window that separated the Renaissance artist from the world he perceived has, ultimately, become a blade severing the head from the body. Cyberspace is often characterized as a realm where disembodied minds are able, so it seems, to interact. Its implicit dualism creates a "phantom border" between the "user" and the information system. Disembodied intelligence takes language (recall Heim) and argues that intelligence is virtual; it is independent of the body – the code or program is independent of the machinery. Disembodied intelligence and the view of perception as representation share a contradictory platonism and an evolutionary logic.

Perception theories that consider images as reductions of the world or that simply argue that the world is contained in the image are fantasies of control. Cyberspace challenges the fixed moment of the photograph; it is a world of images using representations as working models. The fear of cyberspace illustrated by the story of Joey is the fear that we cannot hope to fix, to secure, or to master the flux of information that distances and ultimately separates us from one another. We question even the possibility of establishing connections between images and their referents. At the same time, if the coded essence of the actual is embedded in the virtual, then cyberspace is a materially embodied mind-space that ultimately fulfils the same desire for mastery; one creates a type of *machine aesthetic* in which we mechanomorphize ourselves to adapt to a naturalized technological environment.

As an alternative, to think about perception as a skill set emphasizes its social nature. Perception can be understood as being based on the incorporation of certain tools and techniques relevant to the situation. Perception as a skill set also implies that one can get better at it. The extent to which we become adept at using representations in our cognitive dealings with the world is a measure of social competence, if not mastery, since our social lives are based upon representations endowed with legitimacy and concreteness.

Perception is also embodied in devices (panorama, camera, virtual reality). The habit or convention of perception is one of many attitudes that we use in our social engagements with the world. The opposition of image and reality, like the opposition of the virtual and the real, is misdirected. Instead, the image, understood as a denotation, a translation, a metaphor, or a model, offers less a reflection than an invitation to think about reality.

4

Virtuality and the Bit Republic

Recall the image of Feud's prosthetic god; the modern human's technological extensions sometimes gave them trouble. Implicit in this image is the assumption of a range of selfhood challenged by the technological ability to reach beyond human capabilities. Technological extensions challenge our sense of self in a variety of ways. A sense of self requires a poetic assemblage of experience. One experiences oneself not as an entity but as having a place from which one perceives and acts and where one is perceived and related to. As argued in the last chapter, the self is ecological, artifactual, and enacted. One also perceives oneself in relation to the groups to which one belongs – one has a social self. The transformationists argue that that new modes of information change the language that constitutes new subjects. Poster, for example, tells us that democracy must account for these new and dispersed subjects.

In this chapter the technological linkage that creates the context for mediated interaction (the context for new social subjects to emerge) will be discussed in terms of the transparency or opacity of the technological system. Where the linkage is assumed to be transparent, technological extensions are understood to have no adverse effects on selfhood or community. Distance is conquered through the technologically facilitated return to intimate social relations. By contrast, where the linkage is perceived to be opaque, technological extensions create a *teleproxemic* effect, which can be described as an illusory sense of intimacy. Here, distance is assumed to destroy local ties. Finally, immersion empties the self, and the human cries for critical distance. The metaphoric nature of interactive realism posits that we experience an oscillating process of proximation and distalization in our social interactions. The issue is how we learn appropriate self-skills in particular contexts.

At the level of social interaction these attitudes towards technological mediation affect our notion of community. The problem with the discursive construction of virtual communities is not the relationship between distance and the self. It is the perpetuation of dualism. Three contexts that exemplify the notion of the cybercommunity as a safety zone for social experimentation will be presented to demonstrate the various ways the social subject is constituted and protected in the virtual community. The LambdaMOO is an example of the intrusion of the bodied world into the play space of the MUD. The Electronic Frontier Foundation provides an example of the construction of protections (both on the Internet and in the outside world) to keep the societal bodies of the law away. Finally, the multiplayer computer game *Ultima Online* provides an example of how on-line gaming has incorporated many of the concepts of social construction, community maintenance, and protection.

It was Marshall Mcluhan (1964) who first attempted to reinvest modern culture with a kind of electronic tribalism based on mass communication and a new ability to feel *present* across vast distances. Presence in this context concerns the assumption of an *optimum range* for the self beyond which it fragments, dissolves, and disappears. This assumption implies that the sense of self is supported by the extent of its control over its surroundings. Bearing this in mind, consider Theodore Roszak's (1986) suspicion of the simulated reality of computerized culture. He argues that simulated worlds may not be the kinds of places we want to inhabit. For Roszak, "Simulations are a step away from the disorderly reality around us into the tidy fictions of the computer ... the 'universe' which we can create on a computer screen is a small, highly edited, simulation of reality. Moreover, it is a universe created by a small, highly edited simulation of *ourselves* ... We do not bring the full resources of the self to the computer."[1]

Virtual reality is for Roszak a reduction and an abstraction of aspects of the "real" world created not for the purposes of creative experiment but for mastery. The preference for face-to-face, over mediated, communication is, in some ways, a communicative fundamentalism. Suspicion of representations is symptomatic of a more basic distrust of the evidence of the senses. Roszak's distrust of simulations is based on an even more basic distrust – that representations produce a veil between ourselves and reality. Representations are threatening for Roszak because they are distanced from reality, because they are fantasies. Cyberspace, likewise, threatens an orderly reality, because it provides a compelling forum for the construction of new social contexts, affinities, and alliances.

VIRTUALITY

At this point, it is necessary to distinguish between virtual reality (a computer simulation constructed to emphasize the qualities of inter-action and immersion) and the concept of virtuality (based on the relative transparency of a technological system that allows a user to experience a communicative event and to ignore the technology mediating the experience). Virtuality can be understood as a person's incorporation of, or adaptation to, a new technologically mediated situation. As with the distinction between the Internet and cyberspace made in chapter 1, "virtual reality" refers to the technology, whereas "virtuality" concerns the nature of the psychological experience. To emphasize this distinction, the terms "simulation" or "simulated environment" will be used in what follows, instead of the term "virtual reality".

Virtuality relies on technological transparency and the ability to process images in various ways to permit mediation between humans and the material world. Further, social interaction in the virtual realm requires an imaginative leap. In simulated environments, the trans-parency or opacity of the mediation system (the technological linkage between the human and the world) has important effects on the nature of our mediated experience – on our sense of proximality.

The success or failure of a simulated situation depends on the degree of our awareness of the system itself: does the technology recede into the background, or does it intrude into our attempts to interact with the world? Different mediation systems can be classified by the kinds of mediation they perform. A system can transmit infor-mation, filter data into a form appropriate for human or machine processing, record information, or generate simulations. These aspects of technological mediation are hindered by several limita-tions. For example, transmission can operate only at the speed of light, and recording is limited by storage capacity. Simulations are limited by the complexity and unpredictability of reality. Rather than attempting exact duplications of reality, simulations aim for selective fidelity, which can be understood as an artistic reduction based on the functional needs of the system user.[2]

Selective fidelity refers to the dedication of system resources to particular elements of a simulation at a given moment, based on the requirements of the user. The purpose is to create and maintain an overall sense of adequacy in the simulation. For example, the visual quality might be heightened at the expense of the audio, or, conversely, simplified graphics might be accompanied by heightened audio fidelity. The system designer must establish the appropriate degree of fidelity for the system to attain transparency such that users are aware of themselves and other users more intensely than they are aware of being in a constructed environment.

Selective fidelity also represents one's perceptual posture – the intentional attitude one brings to objects in the simulation. Selective fidelity thus encourages sedimentation, which, you will recall, is the process by which representations become naturalized. For example, when one communicates with another person over the Internet, one might feel able to project one's consciousness through the system. So engaged in the experience of on-line communication, it seems that one is actually "there" in an electronic space. This feeling is what seduces Poster, and it has become so common for users of internet relay chats (IRCs) and instant messaging applications that we hardly notice the technology as we use it. This was not always the case.

The first time I communicated in "real time" over a bulletin board in the early 1990s, I experienced this sense of extended presence. I posted a message to a friend who happened to be logged on at the same time and who responded immediately. The barriers between my friend and me faded quickly into the background (barriers like the time it took for messages to travel, our typing speed, and so on). The intensity of being aware of another person communicating directly with me while I was on-line allowed me to quickly reach a state where the intervening computer terminal, time delays, and so on, disappeared. The situation became "other" than my regular modes of communication but not in any sense of the word unnatural. The time delays between the messages I typed and my friend's responses were masked by the time it took me to think of responses to his messages, to type them, and to shift my gaze from the computer keyboard back to the screen. The surrounding environment – early morning in a dimly lit study – focussed my attention on the interaction, fostering a compelling sense of intimacy. My sense of self was not, in this situation, either fragmented or disconnected from my body.

Interacting in a simulated environment raises an important issue regarding the sense of emplacement. Where do we draw the line between our sense of self and the technological linkage that allows us to communicate with another in a technological context? To use terms from the discussion of the Prosthetic Other, where do we draw the line between the prosthetic and ourselves? In particular, what does the computer display (the screen) represent in this assemblage as it transmits messages from ourselves and others? The screen is a border, a liminal site, a place of dislocation that simultaneously separates us from one another and brings us together. The screen is a permeable border that allows a cataract of experience to pass. The screen frustrates our cultural will to erase the palimpsest of subjectivity. So where do we draw the line between ourselves and the outside world when our interactions are technologically mediated?[3]

TRANSPARENT LINKAGES
AND DISTAL ATTRIBUTION

Electronic communications, like print messages, distance the addresser and the addressee by accentuating the feature of language that permits a gap between speaker and listener. This gap is often understood in terms of efficiency; the human voice can be extended by technology.[4] It can be argued that the technological systems that mediate communications have no negatively discernable effects on our ability to speak across distance. While we may be able to separate the delivery system from the message in communication, how do we develop delivery systems that extend our ability to take action in environments where we are physically absent? This is the concern of telepresence research.

Presence has been defined as the sense of being in an environment. Telepresence describes the experience of presence in an environment by means of a communication medium. For example, a doctor in Montreal who uses a virtual reality system to examine a patient in Yellowknife is engaged in a telepresence event.[5] It is generally held that a sense of telepresence occurs when manipulators at the work site have the dexterity to allow operators to perform normal human functions. In the case of our doctor, effectors in an examination room in Yellowknife must respond to his commands. At the control station the doctor must receive sufficient quality and quantity of sensory feedback to provide a feeling of actual presence at the site.[6] Telepresence also implies that one can create a sufficiently sensitive linkage in which one could feel more present there than here (similar to the shift in attention I felt on the bulletin board system).

Is there a practical difference between presence and telepresence? For the telepresence researcher the answer is no. Researcher Jack Loomis uses the concept of *distal attribution* to refer to the sense of presence extended by some device.[7] The only difference between presence and telepresence is, according to Loomis, that true presence occurs when the sensory data supports only the interpretation of being somewhere other than where the sense organs are located. Distal attribution to a remote location, by contrast, occurs when the sensory data represent both the remote location and the device or linkage connecting the observer with the remote location.[8] This creates the *double awareness* we experience when looking at a picture and in using a metaphor. Double awareness, it becomes clear, is one of the defining characteristics of our experience of communication in cyberspace.

For the purposes of telepresence research, distal attribution occurs when there is a lawful relationship between what we perceive and the responsiveness of the distance mechanism to our signal. Distal attribution occurs only after a user has become skilled.[9] The distal can be experienced only as engaging and immersive to the extent that we have learned to work with the linkage as a prosthetic. As we develop microkinetic skills – whereby the movements we make in the hardware create expected results in the simulation – we experience distal attribution. If, on the other hand, we are disappointed in our attempts to control and to forget the linkage, distal attribution will not occur. In other words, virtual communities can exist to the extent that members learn to experience communicative interactions associated with communicating across distance.

On-line, it is possible to feel somewhere between here and there, but it is impossible to identify exactly where one is "located." Similarly, it is difficult to determine at what point in the process one's locational sense shifts, or, for that matter, how long the shift will last.[10] Telepresence is not an automatic phenomenon. To experience a sense of telepresence involves a complicated process of adaptation. The system user must develop particular skills to accept the reduced input of the technologically mediated situation as sufficient to trigger the sense of presence. We learn such things with startling ease. Melanie Klein observed that the child builds a sense of reality based on its relation-ship with objects. This observation offers a useful premise in thinking about presence in simulated environments. A similar assumption is made in Bettelheim's contention that it is our ability to respond to and to alter the environment that supports ego development.

According to telepresence researcher Carrie Hector, "A sense of presence in a virtual world derives from feeling like you exist within but as a separate entity from a virtual world that also exists."[11] Hector describes three elements that combine to create a sense of presence. First, a sense of subjective personal presence can be defined as a mea-sure of the extent to which and the reasons why one feels like one is in a virtual world. Next, a sense of social presence is the extent to which other beings also exist in the world and appear to interact with you. Finally, environmental presence is the extent to which the envi-ronment itself appears to know that you are there and to react to you. To Hector a key component of presence is the ability to modify the environment.[12] The sense of self develops with the affirmation that our actions have an effect on the environment. The psychological task in designing virtual environments is to convince the user that the virtual world exists and that the person is experiencing or can expe-rience the virtual environment. In fact, for those who assume the task of creating transparent linkages, virtual worlds could be more attuned to our presence than the real world. In Hector's words, "It is quite possible that a virtual world that is more responsive than the real world could evoke a greater sense of presence than a virtual world where the environment responds exactly like the real world."[13] There are two criticisms of telepresence: that distance weakens our sense of self and, conversely, that immersion in virtual environments weakens our sense of self.

TECHNOLOGICAL OPACITY: EXTENSION TRANSFERENCE AND DISTAL DISEASE

For some, the experience of the world at one remove poses a threat to our sense of identity. By using technological extensions, we can become concerned with the linkage to such a degree that we lose sight of both its intended function and our sense of being separate from it. For example, Edward T. Hall argues that when an organ or a process becomes extended, evolution speeds up at such a rate that it is possible for the extension to take over.[14] Extensions no longer simply create a demonized Prosthetic Other; when we use extensions, the "inner" world of the self is so stretched that our basic categories are focussed outside the body. Hall's concept of *proxemics* refers to an optimum range of selfhood. Through processes of technological mediation, proxemics (the range of sensory awareness) becomes tele-proxemics (where we become absorbed in the linkage), and distance empties the self. Hall names the mechanism for the pathologies associated with extensions *extension transference*, defined as the "common intellectual manœuvre in which the extension is confused with or projective identification with our artifacts takes the place of the process extended." Extensions are reductionist – they never replace what has been left out.[15]

Teleproxemics is defined by scholar Stephen Duplantier as "being from afar": there is an illusion of being close while yet somehow distant at the same time. Part of our ability to be deceived by what Duplantier calls "phony" environments is the neurological basis of our perception. We think we perceive real things, but the perceptions are many steps from the real world.[16] We have already challenged a similar reductive attitude regarding language and images.

From this perspective, any mediation (whether technological extension, representation, or image) gets in the way of a human-scaled, interactive community – another example of the pervasiveness of Platonic and dualist assumptions. For Duplantier, the "smoke and mirrors of distance perception makes the earth seem like a single, easily grasped or conceived thing."[17] From the perspective of extension transference we lose sight of ourselves as distance is increased between us and our actions. Susan Sontag similarly suggests that an illusory sense of mastery comes from our use of distancing technology. This assumption can be challenged by the constructionist claim that we learn to operate within environments by developing appropriate skills. Our use of distal knowledge (knowledge obtained technologically, beyond the unaided human sensorium) occurs through a process of re-proximation, whereby abstract knowledge becomes cultural material and part of the fabric of reality as constituted through human interaction.

Duplantier continues a tradition of thinking that face-to-face communication creates a "better" form of community than a distance community. Neither is he alone in valorizing nonmediated forms of community as somehow being more authentic than technological society. For example, James Beniger (1987) argues that pseudocommunity represents the "reversal of a centuries-old trend from organic community – based on interpersonal relationships – to impersonal associations integrated by mass means.[18] Equally sceptical is the opinion that virtual communities cannot be considered in the same way as real-world communities because they are symbolic and representational.

I have given the idea of teleproxemics based on the notion of unmediated communication more attention than some readers might feel it deserves. Yet the idea that face-to-face interactions form the ground of a more authentic community is frustratingly persistent. Recent social science grapples with just this question – can communities be organized around communicative practices? Diana Saco (2002) critiques the idea of the face-to-face realm as the authentic realm of community in a way that resonates with many of the arguments raised here. She writes:

If we were to describe, however, what is at stake in the kind of sociality that many political theorists seem to regard as important to democracy, we could define that, minimally, as an interactive form of communication that enables attentitiveness and responsibility toward other participants in a shared *social* space, understanding by the emphasis on *social*, that such spaces do not reduce to the conventionally physical spaces within which bodies move.[19]

Before we discuss the construction of skills for operating with distance we must turn briefly to the third challenge to identity in virtual environments, one that acts as the inverse of the teleproxemic effect – immersion. From this perspective, immersion means a lack of critical distance that severs all ties between the self and reality.

TRANSPARENT SELFHOOD: IMMERSION VS CRITICAL DISTANCE

Like other forms of writing, electronic writing creates a gap between writer and reader. The individual can judge dispassionately the words of another without his overbearing presence. However, electronic culture fosters another interpretation of the space between sender and receiver. The combination of enormous distances with temporal immediacy produced by electronic communications both removes the speaker from the listener and brings them together.

These opposing tendencies reconfigure the position of the individual so drastically that the figure of the self, fixed in time and space and capable of exercising cognitive control over surrounding objects, may no longer be sustained.[20]

If distance empties the self, a completely immersive world should solve the problem by creating a virtual environment where we can experience proximal relations with simulations. If we could substitute images for sense data, the system could fade into the background, and extension transference would no longer be a problem; the new media would immerse us in a sensory experience. Immersion can be defined in this context as an experience of direct perception – of an immediate experience in a simulated environment. Immersion is not simply a matter of sophisticated systems that provide sensory input. Immersion is not a quality of the medium but of the spectator: it is a quality of experience based on one's imaginative engagement in a particular situation. For example, in viewing a film we do not move out of our real world and into an unreal one in any literal sense. We do, however, create conditions in our world "that allow us in imagination to experience a world that we know, both cognitively and emotionally, not to be real."[21] Virtual embodiment is based on immersion; the simulated environment helps create a sense of shared reality.

However, immersion can also signify a loss of mastery, a surrender of control. The reader will recall Bruno Bettelheim's fear of technology. Consider his conception of the self as challenged by mediated images: "When we watch a film we regress and lose our critical faculties. We lose awareness of our body position, we no longer orient ourselves within the world of our experience – we are being oriented by the camera, forced now to look this way and now that way ... The more I responded to a movie, the more it carried me away into its world, and the less of myself was left in the experience."[22]

Notice that this is not a description of a perceptual experience. It is an account of a moral dilemma. Bettelheim worries that the experience of immersion dissolves his sense of self because the illusion presented on the screen is more compelling than reality. Yet, as I have shown, this is precisely the goal of the telepresence system – to create a compelling "there." For Bettelheim, the dream or fantasy becomes more appealing than the "real," and we may court symptoms of psychosis by wanting to become *like* the powerful technological Other that controls the images or by preferring the immersive world of the cinematic image over our own reality.

Writers often express a fear that technology will either change us or that people will choose technologically mediated experiences of which we do not approve. In media, like computing, the body is not to be trusted. For example, Carol J. Clover, in her book *Her Body, Himself: Gender in the Slasher Film*, writes that "horror and pornography ... are the only two genres specifically devoted to the arousal of bodily sensation. They exist solely to horrify and to stimulate and their ability to do so is their measure of success."[23] Recent critics of the Internet make a similar case, arguing that networked technology reduces more and more human experience to the form of bits. While art involves representation and fabrication, there is something about digitization that threatens reality with its representations. Politics, for example, becomes "cyber" in the sense that illusion and spectacle stand in for democracy.[24]

Jay David Bolter writes about new technology as a form of literacy opposed to the image-based technology of television in an argument similar to Bettelheim's contrast between cinema and high art.[25] For Bolter the distinction is best expressed in the contrast between literate culture (with which he allies the computer) and television or image culture. Bolter and Grusin (1996) describe *re-mediation* as that function of media that both innovates in cultural practice and tries to make itself transparent. Bolter's problem with digital technology is that it tries to fool the user into thinking she "stands in the same relationship to the content as she would if she were confronting the original medium."[26]

The dichotomy rests on an assumption of critical or theoretical distance that characterizes the experience of reading a printed text as contrasted with the immediate perception of the world associated with the broadcast image. Bolter argues that the digital computer reconfirms the dichotomy between perception and semiosis as two distinct aspects of mind, and the computer comes down firmly on the side of semiosis. The immediate perception of the world is not open to the computer. Like all writing systems, the computer must work through signs in order to represent, classify, and operate on perceived experience.

Bolter assumes that the world is a text. To accept the computer as a model of the mind is to accept the view of thought as the manipulation of signs. Bolter's hypertextual utopia is the vision of bringing all these networks together into one unified whole. He works to prove that the intelligible world is a network of signs and that the external world is a reflection of the textual mind. He fears the world as characterized by the televised image because of its seductive quality and because images can deceive. Television for Bolter is primarily a perceptual, rather than a semiotic, medium. The whole purpose of television is to deny the sign and to convince the viewer that he or she is looking *through* the screen at the "real world beyond." Television seeks to foster the illusion that viewing the televised image is a situation of pure perception; the televised image provides a perfect recreation of the world. Unlike the computer, which is a technology of literacy, television therefore works against literacy in favouring image over idea, emotional response over analysis.[27]

The computer is less a species of literary technology than a species of the more generalised category of representational technologies, of which television is another. In fact, the link between computer-mediated communication and other forms of image-based media is now much stronger than when Bolter originally claimed the computer as a new form of typewriter. The main focus of the World Wide Web is not the production of content (a practice that would fulfil the Internet's democratic potential) but the viewing of already existing content. Producing individual web pages is not the dominant activity for those who use the web. The dominant activity is surfing for content.[28]

Elsewhere, I have argued that there is institutional evidence of a push on the part of the entertainment and software industries to recreate the web in the image of television.[29] But there is nothing inherent in the technology that dictates an inevitable relationship between audience and message. Each medium is constructed through the practices of production, distribution, exhibition, and use. Yet for some, television is threatening because of its very power to engage its audience.

For those fearful of immersion, television makes it difficult for the viewer to maintain a critical distance, and distancing is always a feature of reading a text. The television viewer is not a reader, precisely because she cannot easily step back from or alter the pace of the presentation. Television programs invite viewers to lose themselves, not to stand back and analyze. In any writing technology, the situation is reversed: perception is a by-product of semiosis in which readers move back and forth between confronting the signs (reading with a critical distance) and allowing themselves to be absorbed into that

imagined world (passive reading). Here Bolter argues that writing
allows for double awareness. Yet, as shown above, double awareness
is a form of cognitive activity that also applies to the mediated experience of distal attribution. There is no reason to assume that it cannot
occur when we are immersed in a mediated experience.

Bolter argues that passive reading (the desire to be surrounded by
the text) is as close as reading can come to being a perceptual experience. The goal in passive reading is to forget oneself by identifying
with the narrative world presented. In this sense passive reading is
antireading, since true reading is an encounter with signs in which
the reader continually asserts (and repeatedly loses) his or her independence of the text.[30] Again, this consciousness of the medium is
similar to that aspect of distal attribution in which one remains aware
of the technological link between the teleoperator and the object
manipulated through the prosthetic system.

Reader and text are opposed to viewer and screen in the tension
between immersion and critical distance. In perceptual experience
there is for Bolter a loss of self that is threatening. However, such a
"loss" is threatening only if you identify self with the digital, the
critical, and the rational. While Bolter does not refer to the proximal
and distal realms, his distrust of immersion could be identified as a
distrust of the extreme proximal. Stated in these terms, teleproxemics
and the extreme proximal identify mediated experiences that lie outside the range of unmediated perception. They are modes of perceiving that fall outside what might be called an optimum range for
selfhood that is common to Hall, Bettelheim, Duplantier, and Bolter
– the range of human awareness unaltered by prosthetic extension.

THE DIGITAL POLIS

A virtual community is, quite simply, a group of people who communicate regularly by technological means and who feel linked by
common purpose or interest. There have been virtual communities
for as long as people have engaged in prolonged relationships mediated through correspondence. Chess players stage matches through
the mail. Professionals maintain a sense of community through their
membership in professional associations. The difference between
these forms of association and on-line communities is that these
narrow forms of association can be used as models for managing

personal relations – that community can be disembedded in the same way that the cybernetic view argued intelligence can be disembodied.

Narrative is an important facet of social reality. Narrative helps construct the social, since it defines a coherent world within which social action occurs.[31] Narrative analysis thus becomes a powerful technique for revealing assumptions that define a particular social setting, and it looks to recurring communicative forms and patterns that indicate the evolution and presence of a shared group consciousness.[32] The basic communicative process (involving the transmission and reception of meanings, motive) also involves the creative and shared interpretation of an event that fulfils a group psychological or rhetorical need. People share experiences, thereby building group consciousness, and it is by way of this process that a group creates a social reality.

However, certain narratives, like the narrative of progress, are often condemned for being ideological manipulations of social reality or public opinion. The notion of progress is part of the modernist project that invokes grand narratives to explain society.[33] Crucial to understanding modernity is the assumption on the part of its champions that through technological advancement society will improve more than simply its standard of living.

Similarly, the Internet has been interpreted as the saviour of modernity by promising to fulfill the ends of the Enlightenment.[34] Yet one of the consequences of modernity is the creation of disembedded social institutions that no longer reflect the cultures from which they arose.[35] Virtual communities take an extreme aspect of disembeddedness – the notion that communities can be built on narrative alone – and create communities that exist only as traces of interpersonal communication. In this way, virtual communities are experiments in society building that serve as boundary tests of the viability of purely discursive forms of community.

Alfred Schutz's (1943) phenomenological sociology realizes that we inhabit multiple realities. More recently, Benedikt Anderson (1983) describes society in terms of the various intersecting imagined worlds, and anthropologist Arjun Appaudurai (1990) describes communities of sentiment that are characteristic of diasporic groups.

Such communities are not simply forms of escape but also precursors to action.[36] These affective communities are characterized by an emergent (whether conscious or unconscious) sense of belonging to a social group constructed and maintained by discussion, not defined by location or territory. This means that to understand an Internet community as a *digital polis* is to contrast it with other kinds of community. For example, Internet communities differentiate themselves from other communities by virtue of active membership based on affinity and by subject matter. They exist through social practice and are characterized by the promotion of a novel form of social organization with internal discipline.[37] They represent and emphasize in dramatic symbolic form the fact that political, social, and legal actors are subject to multiple and overlapping jurisdictions and associative allegiances. Communities based on members' participation in on-line discussion groups are distinct from other imagined communities in the external world for several reasons. Internet society is based on language, which develops alternate methods for expressing community. For example, "netiquette" helps reinforce standards of behaviour that discussants might miss from nonverbal cues.[38] These standards then become codified practices.

It is a common assumption that community arises organically through communicative interaction. Virtual communities are no different: they develop through repeated interactions; over time, personal relationships emerge in cyberspace.[39] The proliferation of virtual communities has been explained as a response to the hunger for community that has followed the disintegration of traditional communities around the world. Thus, it is argued, the Internet allows for a reemergence of community that corrects the imbalances of mass society.

For example, telepresence occurs when the linkages become transparent. For many, technology must become an unobtrusive background effect to function well. The more technology becomes transparent, the more we hope for and aim towards what Don Ihde calls the *perfectly transparent situation*. This means reducing communication to the simplest situation, the face-to-face situation that is itself not technologically mediated. However, the perfectly transparent communications situation is an ideal that cannot be practically achieved and never really existed. This ideal supports the dualism of mind and body that assumes there can be a "meeting of minds" in close proximity. A common view of virtual community argues that the networked computer provides just the kind of transparent linkage that enables unmediated community to emerge.

In this view, transparent technology creates a new form of community based on unmediated interactions in the sense that the human body is eliminated. Although technology has become so pervasive that the age of face-to-face talk is over,[40] new information forms will lead us back to new forms of social intimacy. A critical aspect of the information highway is its implicit promise of a new sense of community.[41] Discussing the early possibilities of computers as communications devices, researchers suggested that digitization would create a context in which "communication will be *more effective* and productive, and therefore more enjoyable."[42] Thus, the Internet would make community better.[43] Why? Because as digital communication overcomes time and space it allows us to communicate[44] and to create communities of common interest rather than communities of common location.[45]

Cyberspace does allow participants a rare form of freedom. As communication is detached from the intersubjective play of bodies that structures the proximal-social realm, members of virtual communities can experiment with identity. As journalist Howard Rheingold puts it: "The physical world ... is a place where the identity and position of the people you communicate with are well known, fixed, and highly visual. In cyberspace, everybody is in the dark. We can only exchange words with each other – no glares, or shrugs or ironic smiles. Even the nuances of voice and intonation are stripped away."[46]

Virtual communities allow for greater anonymity than the visual stereotyping that is possible in "real" communities. This can have beneficial effects. For example, on-line support groups offer greater anonymity than face-to-face groups. Members place and receive messages "without cues to age, gender, race and physical appearance."[47] Many people seem to prefer the anonymity of digital communication over the problems inherent in face-to-face encounters. Individuals with physical handicaps who find it difficult to establish relationships in the off-line world may find it easier to establish relationships on the Internet, where their ideas and opinions matter – not their appearance.[48] However, increased Internet use by support group members can also be associated with "retreat from family interaction, shrinking social circles, isolation, loneliness, and depression."[49]

Yet even on-line identity markers affect the nature of interpersonal communication. For example, Beth Kolko argues that to be "unmarked" in a virtual community is to be Caucasian; "to be anything else requires an explicit discursive act, one that is often taken by other members as confrontational."[50] Thus, while virtual communities may eradicate many opportunities for discrimination in interpersonal communication, it is more likely that they will result in an overall reduction of identity markers, since the only markers are conventional, discursive, and typographic.[51]

Internet communities, according to Dave Healy, "tend to perpetuate a culture of separation in the very midst of what appears to be an unprecedented opportunity for community building."[52] He identifies several limitations inherent in on-line communities that stand in the way of democratic digital culture: inequality of access, structural constraints based on the fact that Internet communities exist through voluntary participation, lack of diversity within communities that actually promote conformity and homogeneity, the impermanence and instability of virtual communities, and their innate noninstrumentality – they do not lead to action.[53]

One recent study comparing the sense of group or collective identity of participants in on-line and off-line feminist activities reinforces this last observation. According to the author of the study, collective identity requires the following elements: shared definitions of reality; clear boundary markers that emphasize similarities between group members and differences from the opposition; a heightened sense of group membership achieved through self-reevaluation of shared experiences, opportunities, and interests; and negotiations of new ways of acting in public and new ways of thinking that enable group members to "free themselves" from the dominant culture. In the study, on-line groups did not create these conditions of group membership.[54] This is particularly important for researchers who champion the utopian promise that virtual communities can emerge as new democratic forms of association.

The Internet is the first form of media that allows access to unprocessed material or information about events to be delivered to an audience with neither the time constraints of broadcast media nor the space limitations of the traditional press. The Internet could foster democratic participation, since as one writer puts it, it "will provide voters with infusions of raw, uninterpreted information, allowing them to uncover their own agendas and to provide their own insights into the meanings of surveys and other data that customarily filters [sic] first through the analysts and reporters."[55]

In other media contexts, this "infusion of raw, uninterpreted information," which is characteristic of the Internet, receives a less favourable interpretation. For example, law professor Cass Sunstein argues that the Internet actually poses a threat to democracy because of the self-selecting nature of affinity groups. According to Sunstein, democracy requires surprising encounters with opinions that are not our own, to enable discussion, debate, and decision making.[56] British communication scholar James Curran also takes a critical view of the press, arguing that media practices restrict audience choices and control by limiting the number of channels as well as the points of view expressed in these channels.[57] However, the media also abandon one of their traditional roles by abdicating responsibility to weigh and balance the viewpoints that are expressed. The role of sifting and assessing information is thus made the responsibility of the reader or viewer – much as the task of the Internet user is to interpret the flow of information that is available. For Curran, conglomerates no longer operate as independent watchdogs serving the public interest. Instead, they are self-seeking, corporate mercenaries "using their muscle to promote private interests" (87). A common criticism of mass-mediated politics is that politics becomes telespheric and spectacle.[58]

Chapter 1 referred to the antiutopian materialism of Kevin Robins. Robins challenges the idea of virtual communities (or techno-communities, as he calls them), since they represent a fundamentally antipolitical ideal of community that denies the economic and political structures of power relations. For Robins, "immediacy of communication is associated [in virtual communities] with the achievement of shared consciousness and mutual understanding. The illusion of transparency and consensus sustains the communitarian myth, now imagined at the scale of a global electronic *gemeinschaft*."[59]

The paradox of technologically mediated community is that it valorizes a pretechnological form of social grouping.[60] From Habermas comes the notion that the public sphere is a discursive construction subject to the rules of performance and debate. For Habermas, public opinion is formed by an emerging consensus that arises from rational, public discussion. He criticizes mass media for transforming public participation into consumerism and politics into spectacle.[61] Literary culture was, for Habermas, intimate in nature. This is important to proponents of Internet society.

Virtual communities are closely akin to the minority communities of the radical environmentalism (deep ecology) movement.[62] They assume a foundational form of community that, even though facilitated by communication technology, creates a spiritual community that resides in a mythic, premodern form of association.

Of course, the problem with critical views of communities that do not create consequences in the off-line world is the implicit universalizing or valorizing of one particular form of community – the political – into a normative structure for all communities. By such a measure, all virtual communities will be "less than" real communities whenever they fail to inspire activism in the social world. Further, by associating on-line interactions with immersive mediation (like television viewing) critics make an implicit distinction between political communities whose goal is some form of civic action and media audiences whose goal is the passive consumption of media content at worst and a shared experience at best. In fact, sharing common experiences is one of the ways social groups are formed and maintained.

PROTECTING THE VIRTUAL COMMUNITY
FROM INTERNAL ATTACK

Digital communities are based on multiple awareness; the constructed personae who inhabit virtual environments stand as our representatives in the virtual community. Their actions and words are our words. Yet through immersion and engagement, our personae also seem to live in their own right in the digital sphere. Therefore, when our personae are threatened, we cannot help experiencing the threat as directed at ourselves as well as our proxies. The design of our virtual proxies is important because it directly affects the nature of "real" interactions on-line. As Beth Kolko claims, there is nothing virtual about the reality of your interactions and relationships with other people in these spaces.[63] The potential for feeling threatened (or even injured) by aggressive behaviour within a digital play space was demonstrated by the "cyber rape" on the LambdaMOO. Like the story of Joey, this story has become one of the most often cited (and perhaps overused) stories in cyberlore. However, I use this example to focus not on the nature of the violation but on the nature of its resolution – a focus less common in discussions of the LambdaMOO.

The LambdaMOO is a multiuser domain (MUD) – a database designed to give users the impression of moving through a physical space, in this case "a very large and very rustic chateau built entirely of words."[64] People take on personae and communicate with others by typing dialogue, descriptions of their own appearance, and actions in much the same way that dramatic scripts are written as a combination of dialogue, description, and stage commands. The LambdaMOO is, in fact, a database on a computer at the Xerox research facility in Palo Alto, California, that is accessible to outside users through an Internet address. The MUD is constructed of a series of subprograms containing descriptions of characters, rooms, and actions or stage directions, as well as the rules of grammar and syntax for acceptable communicative behaviour. These subprograms are run by the main program (the MUD itself), which then allows users to "interact according to rules very roughly mimicking the laws of the physical world."[65]

One night in March 1993 a user logged in from a New York University computer and appeared in the main meeting area (the living room) of the MUD as a fat clown in a soiled harlequin suit who called himself Mr Bungle. Mr Bungle proceeded to enter sadistic fantasies into a program called a "voodoo doll" that served the purpose of "attributing actions to other characters that their users did not actually write."[66] Using the voodoo doll, Mr Bungle forced other characters to violate themselves and engage in various acts of explicit sex against their users' will while his laughter was "heard" to echo throughout the living room. This assault continued until a systems operator ran his own program that incapacitated the offender's voodoo doll program.

Several days later, outraged by the fact that a member of their "community" had forced them to commit acts against their will (or perhaps, more accurately, had written scripts for their characters which were beyond the original authors' control) members of the community met on-line to decide the fate of Mr Bungle. Unable to reach consensus, one systems operator took it upon himself to resolve the situation by terminating the user account, effectively killing Mr Bungle.

However, within days of the secret execution, Mr Bungle had apparently been reincarnated as Dr Jest. Journalist Julian Dibble describes the community response to Bungle's new incarnation: "Almost immediately, members of the community called for another execution or 'toading,' but their resolve waned upon the realization that Bungle/Jest could simply reincarnate again ... his execution seemed to have mellowed his demeanor. He eventually left the community voluntarily and never returned."[67] Later still, a process for deciding what actions were to be acceptable on the MUD was established. "Virtual rape" was defined as "a sexually related act of a violent or acutely debasing or profoundly humiliating nature against a character who has not explicitly consented to the interaction."[68] In the text-based world of the LambdaMOO, even the term "act" must be explicitly defined in accordance with the grammar of the programmed environment. Thus, an act is considered to be a message that uses a stage command that signals that a character is performing some action in the virtual environment.

Virtual environments like the LambdaMOO are examples of what Heim has called the ontological shift triggered by the changing relationship between words and the world since the proliferation of computer-mediated communication. People are "immersed" in the experience of interaction afforded by virtual communities, "developing concern for their character's reputation that marks the attainment of virtual adulthood."[69] What does LambdaMOO illustrate? At one level it illustrates our investment in the words that stand for us in cyberspace and an equally strong investment in the social institutions and the processes of interaction established on-line. More important, behaviour in cyberspace can be regulated through code at a structural level. In the words of legal scholar Lawrence Lessig, in cyberspace a law is defined "not through a statutes, but through the code that governs the space."[70]

During the Bungle attacks, a user's hand no longer controlled the output of the computer keyboard. The actions of the MUD users no longer had the expected effects. This situation had several effects. Psychic engagement made the victims look on in horror as the action continued on screen. The illusion of proximal social interaction on-line did not simply disappear. The cyber rape was a verbal assault, like an obscene phone call, but unlike responding to a phone call, the victims could not simply hang up. Their personae continued to operate and function in the MUD. With the failure of the transparent linkage in distal attribution, the sense of being "elsewhere" is shattered. When the linkage failed to respond to the victims' commands at Lambda it did so because control of their personae was taken from them by Mr Bungle. Rather than experiencing a failure in the telepresence effect, they felt trapped with their personae in the MUD. In terms of proximality, two things occurred. Before the Bungle attacks, users felt close to their personae; they felt close to the objects in the simulated environment. During the attack, users felt powerless. In a very real sense the victims were objectified by another user in the play space. This is the nature of the "rape" in the LambdaMOO.

An extreme example can underscore the intensity with which a person can identify with his or her on-line persona. In November 2001 a young man named Shawn Wooley committed suicide. He was an obsessive on-line gamer who spent hours at a time playing the multiplayer game *EverQuest*. In trying to explain the reasons for her son's death, Wooley's mother discovered that he had been extremely disturbed when a long-time companion in the game stole all the money from Wooley's character and refused to give it back. Psychologists suggest that such a traumatic setback in the virtual world could have traumatized an already vulnerable young man.[71]

Internet communities try to escape the top-down imposition of dominant power structures by setting themselves off as play spaces and, in part, by denying the necessity of bodies to community. This strategy is inadequate if we remember the role of play in identity and community construction. Virtual communities can be better understood as playgrounds for social experimentation.[72]

Play allows us to leave the bonds of the social order for a while. The play space is safe; we can experiment without fear of extreme consequences. Play is distinct from ordinary life not only in locality but in duration. For example, a game is "played out" within certain limits of time and place, containing its own course and meaning. However, the limits of time and space governing the game are in one sense overcome as play attains a kind of immortality; the game can be played again and again.[73] In the end, the microkinetics of virtual community participation involves learning bodily techniques appropriate to a particular cultural framework of habit and experience.

The LambdaMOO can be described as a playground or even as a consecrated spot set apart from the activities of everyday life. Players enter freely into the play world, logging in from their own computers to play, for a time, in a world with "a disposition all its own." In fact, in the text-based worlds of cyberspace these worlds are clearly delimited and organized around specialized rules of grammar and syntax that apply only to the play world.[74]

Following this line of argument, what are we to make of Mr Bungle? Bungle's attitude displays his understanding that his actions were symbolic and occurred within the confines of the play space. He did not physically commit a crime. He did, however, violate the tacit rules of engagement of the MUD. In contrast to "the cheat" (a player who acknowledges the play world's existence and works around the rules of the game), Mr Bungle represents "the spoilsport" (a player who shatters the play world, invoking the wrath of other players who cast out the offender to defend the continuation of the play community).

Richard MacKinnon advocates symbolic punishment for infractions on the Internet. Denying the persona's access is akin to capital punishment. Conforming to the rules of engagement becomes a condition of virtual existence.[75] For MacKinnon, the effectiveness of virtual punishment depends on how well its implementation brings the action of personae into accordance with the social priorities of a particular community. Virtual punishment effectively controls the behaviour of personae in virtual communities under certain conditions. The member's persona must demonstrate a stake in the community. This, in turn, secures values by emergent or formal governance and adjudication.

Mr Bungle's abuse of the living room as a meeting place for members of the Lambda community falls into the behaviour characterized by the spoilsport. Bungle's unrepentant attitude at the meeting that decided his fate as a Lambda member marked him as someone who broke the rules of the game. Most importantly, he broke the rules after playing for long enough to know the acceptable community standards, as well as the formal rules of the game. The meeting itself, occurring spontaneously, was essentially a gathering of players who desired to save the play world from an attack from within. Mr Bungle's ultimate expulsion – the heated debate among members that resulted in his "termination" – acquired the inevitability of the reaction of players to the spoilsport who must be expelled from the game to preserve the community.

Finally, amendments to the rules of the game, clearly defining "virtual rape" in the context of the Lambda community, emphasized the community desire to insure against a similar occurrence in the future. It was significant that Bungle's "crime" was rape. He gained control of other virtual bodies, thereby breaking the victims' link between outside and inside. He took away their ability to play. The issue is one of power and powerlessness, and this returns us to the importance of embodied experience.

Tensions over how to administer the LambdaMOO are illustrated by tensions between competing definitions of the MOO itself. According to legal scholar Jennifer L. Mnookin,[76] some participants view the MOO as a diversion, a virtual playground. For these people the process of determining and codifying "LambdaLaw" seems unnecessary and frustrating, constituting nothing more than an absurd bureaucratic impediment to enjoying the MOO. From this perspective, participants who advocate a formal codification of law for the MOO take themselves and LambdaMOO far more seriously than they should. Those resisting this process believe that LambdaMOO is, in the end, a game and that this virtual society ought not be mistaken for a real one. For the second group, those who take LambdaMOO seriously as a society, law has both pragmatic and symbolic significance. On the one hand, a legal system is a practical necessity, because the society requires workable mechanisms for adjudicating disputes, enacting legislation, and establishing its standards of conduct. However, law simultaneously serves a symbolic function as well: if LambdaMOO has a well-defined legal system, then it can be convincingly argued that LambdaMOO is a society. That is, the existence of LambdaLaw becomes itself proof that LambdaMOO is more than a game, that what happens there is not just recreation but the creation of a virtual community. Games have rules but, as Mnookin argues, who has ever heard of a game with a Supreme Court and a complex legislative system? In this sense, formalized law becomes a mechanism by which LambdaMOOers can prove that they are engaged in something greater than a role-playing game, that they are participants in a full-fledged virtual world. More than dispute-resolution mechanisms and legislative procedures, law also provides something more: legitimacy.

In fact, Mnookin argues that defining LambdaMOO as a role-playing game serves the desire for legitimacy characterized by those who want to establish a well-defined legal order. Defining the MOO as a role-playing game serves to ensure it retains a certain freedom or sovereignty from impositions from outside law. Indeed, such a definition increased the MOO's freedom of self-determination, self-definition, and social experimentation.

The LambdaMOO story is instructive for the way it describes a process for identifying and dealing with social transgressions as part of a social contract. Howard Rheingold, one of the earliest of the popular cyberculture writers, wrote in 2000 that just these questions of negotiation, facilitation, and rule-making have kept virtual communities as the exception, rather than the rule, in on-line interaction. Rheingold writes:

In order to succeed, a virtual community has to have an affinity – the answer to the question: what would draw these people together? It has to present a user interface that doesn't baffle the newcomer but gives a range of options to the experienced user. Building a social space online doesn't guarantee that people will inhabit it. It has to have a social infrastructure, including *simple written agreements to a social contract governing online behavior and sanctions for transgression*. It needs skilled human facilitation. And there must be some plan for bringing a continuing stream of newcomers into the community.[77]

PROTECTING THE VIRTUAL COMMUNITY FROM OUTSIDE ATTACKS

Why should the social scientist, the cultural critic, or the legal scholar care about the emergence of communities in cyberspace? Legal scholars examine previous regulatory processes and the ways groups invest resonances to create normativity. As shown in the example of the LambdaMOO, one crucial aspect of virtual communities is how they create replicas of institutional or governmental normativity in the bitsphere. In the end it is not very useful to assume that previous forms of association will simply be moved to a new realm of interaction without substantive transformation. Instead, perhaps replicas of functions, much like Wiener's notion of the operational image that fulfils the function of some original process or organism, will emerge whereby virtual communities will resemble outside communities and yet remain distinct.[78]

Virtual communities develop rules and norms to protect the play space from internal abuse. Through self-definition they also protect the play space from external influence. However, protecting the play space from external intrusion does not happen through purely discursive practice. Nor are the models for discursive, literate public cultures maintained solely though communication.

Michael Warner, in his investigation of the role of printing in the construction of the eighteenth-century American Republic, argues that the cultural constitution of a medium is the set of political conditions of discourse.[79] Warner cast his attention back to the eighteenth century to gain insight into the radical political and social changes facilitated by the use of printing to disseminate information and spur political debate in America. So too are we afforded a glimpse of the kinds of communities, institutions, and even citizenship engendered by new modes of communication like the Internet. Political discourse on the Internet resembles the publication of pamphlets and papers characteristic of Warner's "republic of letters."

Warner's analysis of the culture of letters coinciding with the American Revolution shows how a symbolic public sphere was supported through a variety of social practices other than the exchange of printed ideas. As has been stated, symbolic convergence suggests that we create a "group mind" through the sharing of common symbolic experiences. Arjun Appadurai has also shown how shared symbolic experiences like global media create imagined communities. It is important to realize that these are never entirely abstract, formal, or distal. The founding of the Electronic Frontier Foundation illustrates how the democratic play space in cyberspace must be protected from outside interference by off-line actions.

Early in November 1988 a virus (a software program that can alter data or erase a computer's memory) was unleashed over the Internet by Robert Morris, a graduate student at Cornell University. After Morris unleashed the "worm," the Internet community divided in a bitter debate over issues of freedom of expression and access to computer networks. While Morris was given a light sentence as a first-time offender, a precedent was set by the case. The u.s. government had decided that to get a conviction for computer abuse, it was necessary only to prove unauthorized access, not intent to harm.[80]

In 1990 the u.s. government initiated a series of arrests and criminal charges and the confiscation of large amounts of data and equipment in a crackdown on the computer underground. Computer hackers were labelled a deviant social class. In July 1990, in the aftermath of the crackdown, the Electronic Freedom Foundation (EFF) was formed by John Perry Barlow and Mitch Kapor. Both Kapor and Barlow had been visited by FBI agents investigating the activities of the computer underground.[81] The EFF outlined its purpose in its inaugural press release: "While well-established legal principles and cultural norms give structure and coherence to uses of conventional media like newspapers, books, and telephones, the new digital media do not so easily fit into existing frameworks. Conflicts come about as the law struggles to define its application in a context where fundamental notions of speech, property, and place take profoundly new forms."[82] The EFF used interaction outside the Internet to preserve on-line rights and activities. It wished to use the Internet to create a transformative digital community in the form of a global agora, or marketplace. However, it realized its goals could not be achieved solely through on-line discussion. Rather, the task needed lobbying, conventions, and public attention in the media to reinforce common bonds and to create a space for stakeholders like the EFF to participate in the governance of digital communications. In other words, the EFF worked to build a community of interest.

According to Barlow, individuals, not governments, must ensure cyberspace develops as a free and open communication environment. The right to privacy, like the right to expression, must be actively fought for, since governments will continually test those rights as the electronic frontier evolves. Barlow suggests that the law should not be involved until normative practices emerge in cyberspace.[83]

The task of the EFF involves "bringing civilization to Cyberspace."[84] Civilization in this context includes a libertarian view of noninterference on the part of government, radical free speech, and free markets.[85] The EFF also proclaims its role as educator, in which it can "define the appropriate metaphors and legal concepts for life in Cyberspace" by encouraging communication between the public and policymakers and corporate officials.[86]

To illustrate the importance of off-line bodies in the electronic frontier, the EFF closed offices in Cambridge, Massachusetts, and opened offices closer to the seat of power, in Washington, DC. The lobbying effort must be located in body-space as well as cyberspace to have broader social impact on government policies. Mitch Kapor has criticized the federal government with claims that the overuse of force and confiscation of private property has created a "chilling effect on a valuable social experiment" underway on America's computer networks. Ultimately, Kapor believes that a new culture is growing on the computer networks, one that may easily be smothered by excessive abuse by the risk of "being tyrannized by a majority."[87] Kapor argues that "large systems, whether the government or private, have an inhumanity that is fundamentally intolerable."[88] Kapor defends the rights of hackers as the same as the rights of all citizens in cyberspace, not because he condones their actions, but, rather, because he is even more apprehensive of an obtrusive government presence in the new communication environment.[89]

The EFF argues that the goal in legislating cyberspace is "to create a well-defined, reasonable legal environment for system operators and users."[90] However appealing the rhetoric of freedom and political choice may sound, it is imperative to remember that the interests served in the name of reason and freedom are not only those associated with personal freedom but those associated with commercial interests, as well.

Like Barlow and Kapor, Mark Poster argues that cyberspace can be more democratic than modern organizations like the u.s. government, which seeks to preserve existing institutions.[91] Perhaps such a view provides one reason for naturalized metaphors like the information highway. Cyberspace as a frontier fantasy is framed around the battle between good and evil in a mythical narrative that is sufficiently removed from everyday life to be seen as a reality but not as a direct threat to the concerns of average citizens. Increasingly, as more people use the Internet, such a view is untenable.

ULTIMA ONLINE: WHO RULES BRITTANIA?

Let us return to the idea that cyberspace can be used to create safety zones for experiments in community building. One form of cyber-community that has consciously taken advantage of the relationships between interaction, the transparency of technological linkages, and the active fostering of shared group experience is the networked game.

Cooperation and competition between multiple players have been characteristic qualities of interactive games since their early days. Kline et al. (2003) suggest that networked play (by which they mean two or more machines connected so that players can compete or cooperate in a shared game world) is one characteristic that helps create a new form of interactive mediation. Significantly, in networked play human players are connected through machines to other people. Their skills are tested against other players instead of the computer. Consequently, according to Kline et al., the communities that develop around a game are based on interactions other than game play: "As with most other forms of human-to-human contest, network gaming generates social relationships, from abusive taunting to carnival get-togethers, that extend beyond the moment of play. Most of the activities that surround physical sporting events – post game discussion and argument, formation of teams and leagues, tournaments, gamelore and gossip – also surround network gaming, making it one of the most important incubators of so-called 'virtual communities.'"[92]

Perhaps the ideal example of network gaming is *Ultima Online*, which is based on a long-running series of computer games that began in 1991. *Ultima Online* (uo) was released in 1997. Developed by Richard Garriott, the original *Ultima* games were military conquest and strategy games. We can see in some of the issues arising around

UO many of the themes discussed in this chapter, including the emergence of community through shared experience and narrative, protection of the game space from attack, and the interrelationship between on-line and off-line contexts. In the mid-nineties, a combination of criticism about the violent nature of the *Ultima* games and a developing maturity on Garriott's part led the developer to shift focus from fighting to the psychological nature of the gaming experience. With the release of *Ultima IV*, a player could no longer win the game simply by fighting his or her way to the end. Instead, a player could win the game only by upholding what Garriott called the eight Brittania virtues: compassion, valour, honour, honesty, spirituality, sacrifice, justice, and humility.[93]

Even though Garriott explored issues such as prejudice and nationalism in subsequent versions of *Ultima*, social problems emerged with the release of *Ultima Online*, problems concerning the ethics of online play and, in particular, the issue of "player-killing" (PKing). While a player could return to the game after being killed, her or his on-line personae would lose everything it had accumulated to that point in the game. As Kline et al. report, "PKing became a serious barrier to recruiting new players."[94] Garriott, who often appeared in the game as the character Lord British, appealed to the members of the gaming community to resolve the problems of on-line play as part of the game. Raph Koster, head designer on the early versions of *Ultima Online* recounts how one such incident of game conflict came to be seen as one of the key pieces of gamelore and eventually, one of the basic myths of *UO*. According to Koster,

There was this place called Kazola's tavern – a player-run bar that was out in the woods in a wild area – and for some reason, it was very popular. It was a very pacifist community. They just liked to hang out and talk. It got a lot of recognition and so one of the game administrators noticed it and, as per game policy, he "blessed" it. He designated it as important to the game. This attracted the less pacific crowd who came over, started killing people, and tried to take over the tavern. They came in and circled the tavern, and there were fights and everything … What happened was that many of the role-players gathered together to fight the bad guys. They stood out front and defended the place. And they made it! This story … became one of the key myths of *Ultima Online*.[95]

Koster is pragmatic about the process of creating myths in interactive settings. He argues that players must have a level of emotional engagement in the situation and that the environment must offer scope for actions that will significantly alter it. He points out that it took over nine months to transform the game play at Kazola's tavern into a myth, observing that it was "only on looking back on it that we shaped it into a story."[96]

Another interesting component of UO is how the game incited legal action in the off-line world. In particular, the game became a site of conflict between on-line and off-line techniques for regulating behaviour. In 1998, UO was the object of the first class-action suit aimed at a computer game. The suit, led by a player named George Schultz, was launched on the grounds that the system servers were unstable. Their frequent crashes erased character information, and hours of play were forgotten "in a sort of massive social amnesia."[97] The suit proved difficult for the plaintiffs, since the players continued to participate in on-line games, and in September 1998 a judge refused the request for a class-action suit (although individual court challenges were allowed to proceed). Eventually, Origin and Electronic Arts (the companies responsible for the game) settled these individual suits by making a donation to the San Jose Technology Museum of Innovation. According to Kline et al., Schutz claimed victory because the lawsuits served as a "wake-up call" to the gaming companies, as well as the general computing industry. In particular, Schutz claimed that the computing industry had been forced to take both issues of technological transparency and issues of customer satisfaction seriously. It is also interesting to note that in 1999, shortly before Origin released the latest version of UO, it closed down the discussion boards by which the citizens of Brittania had originally aired their grievances about the game.[98]

How we characterize the technological linkage that facilitates distance communication affects selfhood. If the linkage is transparent, communication is assumed to occur in much the same manner as in face-to-face interactions. But if we view the extensions as opaque and powerful, our sense of community becomes illusory; community becomes a pseudo-community in which we ignore the intersubjective play of bodies that provides the ground for archetypal utopias. Finally, if the linkage immerses us in perceptual experience at the level of the extreme proximal, the self can be overwhelmed by sensory experience, losing the ability to achieve a level of critical distance.

The important aspect of telepresence research is that virtuality is learned and that participation in virtual communities is voluntary; we choose to participate in on-line communities. The emerging social organisations are significant precisely because they call into question those we currently engage in. The crucial factor is that we learn to function in virtual communities just as we learn to function in communities that are not technologically situated. The question that arises is how skills, notions of transparency, technological extensions, and other components of communication affect the construction of communities. Selective fidelity shifts the range of selfhood from the extreme proximal to the abstractions of distal culture.

Social interaction, like perception, is intimately related to the technologies that enable and constrain participation. Our attitudes toward technology do not alter the importance of the interactions as fundamental elements in social construction. How we characterize the social groupings we seek through computer-mediated communication reflects our assumptions about technology and the degree to which we have incorporated them into our repertoire of basic metaphors. Virtual communities are set apart from the everyday by the nature of written communication, by their population by enacted personae, and by their definition as play spaces or safety zones where interactions take place outside the bounds of everyday society.

The process of forming social allegiances in new technological contexts inevitably raises questions about social cohesion, affinity, and order in other social contexts. Thus, the proliferation of Internet communities can be seen as a form of dramaturgical play that captures the democratic spirit of the Enlightenment social imaginary. One must, inevitably, try to understand how web communities link to theoretical and practical considerations about gender, nation, fantasy, and embodied experience. Perhaps in periods of social transition the similarities between social realities are particularly important, because to get your bearings in a new environment requires bringing your past with you. We try to act in the bitsphere as if we were acting in the world "as it was" – and we tend to criticize our failings correspondingly.

5

The Iconic Landscapes of Cyberspace

What a place subjectively appears to be predisposes behavior, although images must reflect the material world in some logical way to be appropriate as formulations of expectation.

John Jakle[1]

The topic of this chapter is the poetics of place in relation to the constructed environments within which communicative interactions take place – the character of the places we occupy when we inhabit cyberspace. From the transformative perspective cyberspace embodies utopian hopes and dystopian disappointments. The utopian realm of global communication emphasizes the realm of digital communication as a rationally organized environment, contrasted with the disorderly interactions of human bodies. Cyberspace is often assumed to be a *digitopian* construction; it is a working model of the dualist separation of mind and body that provides an example of the importance of actualizing the virtual based, once again, on the persistent metaphor of disembodiment.

REPRESENTATION AND THE CONCEPT OF PLACE

The importance of spatial construction in the study of cultural practices was greatly overlooked through most of the twentieth century. Mainstream urban geography and ecology generally viewed space as acting as a container – a featureless ground against which social interactions took place. It was what Michel Foucault described as Newtonian space, where "space was treated as the dead, the fixed, the undialectical, the immobile. Time, on the contrary, was richness, fecundity, life, dialectic."[2] By contrast, in critical theory any theory of space was a specific manifestation of a general theory of social organization as it was articulated within space. Thus, as in the case of mainstream urban geography, within the context of critical theory there was no need to study the space produced in a particular social organization separately from an analysis of social relations.[3]

In the 1980s a number of social theorists and geographers (particularly, but not exclusively, in Britain) were concerned to incorporate the spatial into any social theory attempting to make sense of what was then described as the beginnings of an interconnected world.[4] As a materialization of culture, space is more than either a neutral container or the by-product of patterns of social relations. By the 1990s some geographers sensed that although the places within which particular social interactions occurred were important, it was the nature of those interactions that helped create identities that were shaped by particular locations. For some, communication technology allowed community to be conceived as disembedded from the local space. This, it was argued, was one of the factors contributing to global interdependence. As one geographer put it, "it is possible for the world, with its vast problems and great diversity, to collapse or coalesce upon each and every individual who shares in its technologies of communication."[5] For others, particularly feminist geographers, identities were lived as an experience of place, "our body being the medium through which place is lived."[6] This consciousness of the importance of place in social theory emphasized the importance of space as a component of shared experience.

Space structures metaphorically.[7] As stated in the epigraph that begins this chapter, particular places can be identified as both expressions of localized behaviour and as environments that invite particular behaviours. Thus, the built environment does not simply reflect culture; objects of the built environment are negotiated as carriers of social meaning.[8] Places are settings configured to encourage ongoing, regularized activities. As social expectations become attached to icons of place, places come, as a function of their physical reality, to carry much of the memory load used to sustain appropriate social interaction. As physical objects continue to serve as the location for repeated social situations, those very activities come over time to be viewed as structural. The places come to stand as icons facilitating the recall and renewal of social relationships.

"Landscape" refers to an ensemble of material and social practices and their symbolic representation; it is a social product that embodies a point of view. Images of landscape are visual transcriptions of social practices within geographical boundaries. Methods of constructing the landscape reflect and reinforce a sense of place and self.

Let us take an example not restricted to the Internet. The justification of a market-based economic system assumes a natural inclination to create markets based on an "economic rationality inherent in all persons." David Williams argues that a critical examination of World Bank practices reveals that the economy is an actively constructed space, "not simply in terms of the need for 'right' economic policies or a 'good' institutional and regulatory environment, but because economic rationality itself must be constructed."[9] In the end, the World Bank example involves two constructions: the state is perceived as a barrier to economic development, and economic rationality is constructed as a natural human inclination.

Places, then, can be understood as images, as representations that structure the kinds of activities that occur within their boundaries. As such, places provide a metaphoric opening for creativity and complexity. Such a materiality of cyberplace is the subject of chapter 6, but first we must ask if there is an evolutionary or transformative view of place that parallels the transformative view of media.

Henri Lefebvre suggests that each mode of production has its own particular space and that a shift in the mode of production entails the production of a new space. By way of example he describes the Renaissance town as the production of a discourse and the production of a reality adequate to particular coded spatial practices.[10] The spatial code served to fix the alphabet and language of the town. Facades were humanized to create perspectives; entrances and exits, doors, and windows were subordinated to facades; streets and squares were arranged in concord with the public buildings and palaces of political leaders and institutions. Perhaps cyberspace is, as Mark Poster might argue, the landscape appropriate to the mode of information. Certainly the structure of a spatial code can be discerned in the building machines of representation and mediated experience described in chapter 3.

It is possible to think about cyberspace as an iconic landscape for social interaction. Further, this landscape reflects some dominant assumptions: that space is socially constructed, that technology generalizes communication, that technology is an evolutionary agent, that interactions can be detached from the proximal realm through the application of global telecommunication systems, and that through technological means a "perfect" society might be achieved. Advocates of Internet communities often assume that community can be created and sustained by messages and information (communication without meaning or symbolic interaction without material engagement). Might digitopia, then, be the imaginary space that resolves differences and embodies a hope in liberal tolerance and the fulfilment of the possibility of communication? As Raymond Williams once wrote, media messages can contribute to a sense of social anxiety by exerting pressure and establishing limits to thought rather than by direct control.[11] Would cyberspace be more likely to heal or exacerbate social anxieties through the construction of interactive places?

TECHNOLOGY AND UTOPIA

The communication network is an eternal promise symbolizing a world
that is better because it is united. From road to rail to information
highways, this belief has been revived with each technological generation
yet networks have never ceased to be at the centre of struggles for control
of the world.

                                                    Armand Mattelart[12]

Historian Langdon Winner argues that "all conceptions of utopia rest on an implicitly technological model."[13] In the context of cyberspace, virtual communities, like cybernetics, assume that communication allows for stability and order.

The utopian dream, which can be traced back to both Bacon and Hobbes, posits that "if one could fashion the conditions of reality to suit a preconceived design, both certainty and control would be assumed."[14] Utopia, like the Hobbesian political order, approaches perfection because it is deliberately fashioned and because it is grounded on rational principles. Not only can technology produce the ideal state, but it also signals an end to the illusions propagated by ideology. Sociologist Daniel Bell states that technology offers a break with ideology and the dawn of a new society "in which individuals can create their own modes of communication and their own communities."[15]

In *Ideology and Utopia* Karl Mannheim makes a stronger link between the utopian and the ideological impulse; both can be defined by their discordance with social reality. Ideologies look backward to justify the status quo and to maintain the orderly vision of a ruling class. Utopias are forward-looking models of order professed by a rising class in opposition to the status quo.[16] From a utopian perspective, the technology of cyberspace can be seen either as a technological agent of change or as a model that critiques previous utopian visions and that emphasizes the resolution of social conflict and economic disparity through digital communication. What distinguishes cyberspace technologies from earlier technological and utopian promises is the apparent desire (of both the technological optimists and the proponents of transformation theory) to accept this digital space as normative.

The utopian impulse stemmed from the Enlightenment preoccupation with reason and the discovery of natural laws in the physical sciences.[17] Behind various metaphors of technology (from the Machine Age to the Information Revolution) lies a perception that modern history is characterized by a process of continuous change and that machines and other manifestations of new technology are at the centre of the process.[18] Advocates of technology assumed that the human resembled a machine, that the environment has already to a degree been mechanized (or systematized), and that technological experts should govern society.[19] This kind of utopia thus becomes a technological project. A disjunctive view of history instigated by the transformative power of technology is consistent with technological utopianism. Each new technology can be seen both as a means for providing lasting solutions for contemporary problems and as a "radical departure from previous historical patterns."[20]

The technological utopians' confidence in the imminence of utopia distinguished them from most other contemporary utopians, whose failed schemes often caused disillusionment and occasionally produced anti-utopias. The mastery of nature through the application of technological means is regarded as the fulfilment of humankind's destiny, the beginning of a new epoch for humankind, and the elevation of the human to a status only slightly short of omnipotence.[21] The domestication of both technology and nature will resolve the tension that Leo Marx, among others, has deemed irresolvable: the tension between the industrial and the agrarian orders, between the machine and the garden. The utopians would resolve the tension by modernization rather than abandonment of the garden, by transporting the garden out of the wilderness and relocating it in the city – a city itself to be transformed from a lethal chaos into a healthy order. The Garden City may be the prime utopian spatial trope. However, the city is also portrayed in this tradition as a scene of disorder and of industrialism out of control. Thus, before turning the discussion to the dominant utopian vision of cyberspace, it is necessary to describe its converse, the image of the dystopian metropolis.

THE LABYRINTH OF NASTY DREAMS

While utopian visions may entice us with hopes of a bright new world brought about through technology, dystopians warn that utopian rhetoric can become fanatical and ideological. According to communication scholar and sociologist Vincent Mosco, the utopian optimism that the Internet will foster absolute democracy and affiliation within society is "seductive but false ... containing promises unfulfilled or unfillable."[22] Such images and myths, argues Mosco, are created by media, big business, and governments to placate the public with a hope for a positive future in the face of technological uncertainty.[23]

This media critique emphasizes the seductive power of virtual imagery in the form of a gothic fantasy of a technological other – a ghost in the machine. Films like *Lawnmower Man, The Matrix*, and *The Thirteenth Floor* or television series like the short-lived *VR 5* or *Harsh Realm* offer glimpses of a technologically invoked end time, as well as a dangerous vision of images run amok. Such films create an eschatological fear of the body that requires purification either by rejecting technology or, as in the case of the hero Neo in *The Matrix*, by using technology for one's own purposes. It is in the context of such dystopian narratives of the "near future" that we can best position the spatial descriptions that appear in the work of William Gibson.

Gibson represents a group of science fiction writers who rose to prominence in the mid-1980s and who labelled themselves *cyberpunks*. Cyberpunk translated postmodernist motifs of the dispersed self and apocalyptic visions of the future; it made the metaphors of postmodern fiction literal. The dispersed self became the android or "personality construct," and the information society was literalised into a "world." In his study of cyberpunk fiction, *Constructing Postmodernism*, Brian McHale identifies the dominant settings, or zones, in which most cyberpunk narratives unfold. For example, the Urban Zone is the source of the most characteristic cyberpunk imagery. Cyberpunk created an ideological critique of the perceived failure of the utopian project.

The most characteristic and influential example of the cyberpunk Urban Zone is the Sprawl, the cityscape of Gibson's stories. For

McHale, the Sprawl represents the chaotic melting pot of the transnational cultural economy. He writes: "The compositional principle of the Sprawl and its cognates, terrestrial and extraterrestrial, is maximally intimate juxtaposition of maximally diverse and heterogeneous cultural materials (Japanese, Western, and Third World, high-tech and low-tech, elite and popular, mainstream 'official' culture and youth or criminal subcultures, etc.)."[24] Cyberspace is nested in an environment of urban overcrowding, a global economy of such disparity between rich and poor that the rich are "no longer even remotely human."[25] This is the cyberworld of the hacker as criminal, the place where paedophiles lurk in chat rooms prowling for victims. It is the vision of cyberspace as a nightmarish urban jungle. We are familiar with such Urban Zones in contemporary science fiction films (think of the Los Angeles of *Blade Runner* (1982) or James Cameron's *Terminator* (1984), or the Gotham City of *Batman* (1989)).

Director Tim Burton's Gotham City, designed by British production designer Anton Furst, was described in the original script as "if Hell had sprung up through the pavement and kept on going."[26] Similarly, Burton's patchwork urban labyrinth provides an exaggerated view of what happens with uncontrolled development or with the technological utopia that is unchecked in a free-market zone. Thus, Gibson's novels represent an internal conflict between a utopian vision and a dystopian vision that can exist only as an oscillating reaction to one another (another example of metaphoricity). In *Neuromancer* (his first novel) Gibson describes the world as "a deranged experiment in social Darwinism designed by a bored researcher who kept one thumb permanently on the fast-forward button."[27] Gibson's Sprawl appears in the film *Johnny Mnemonic* (1995), which is based on one of his short stories, and most recently in James Cameron's television series *Dark Angel*. For Gibson, new forms of digital communication are only the latest in a long line of false utopian agents, raising the fear that the evolving world made possible by new technologies will reinforce, rather than replace, current systems of power. Bentham's panopticon is the dominant landmark of dystopian cyberspace.

The Urban Zone characterizes a number of technological fears. The realm of cybernetic subjectivity confirms Bettelheim's fear of the technological Other. It also signifies the teleproxemic cultures that Duplantier warns against. For those who fear it, the cyberspace in Gibson's fiction is a realm of total mediation and immersion and a loss of critical distance. What is even more unsettling about this vision of the future is that it does not represent a utopian break with the past but rather a continuation of present trends towards the transnational corporate state. Gibson's world is becoming, to some degree, our own; it is characterized by urban sprawl and a free-for-all market of corporate warfare based on those few who can afford access to information and those who cannot (the information rich versus the information poor).

THE HEAVENLY CITY

The fascination with new technology as the agent of utopian manifestation continues today in the view of cyberspace as a utopian configuration. In the writings of architect Michael Benedikt, we encounter an optimistic projection of cyberspace as utopian model. His work provides a conceptual underpinning for what is, in a sense, a practical problem – how do we give visual shape to this new cultural space? It is important to realize that in its desire to fashion a utopian digital sphere, a rising digital class is part of the network of power. This is another paradox in cyberspace.

Benedikt suggests that cyberspace can be understood in relation to Karl Popper's model of three interconnected conceptual spheres, which comprise the whole of the world. For Popper, the world can be divided into the material, natural world; the world of individual minds and experience comprising the subjective world of consciousness; and the objective world of public structures. Benedikt defines these public structures as abstract informational patterns of social action or communication. Cyberspace becomes, in this scheme, the latest and perhaps the final evolutionary stage of a conceptual world in which the material is finally cast away, fulfilling, as one journalistic account puts it, the long-held desire to "escape the physical world's constraints for a pure mental realm."[28] Here is one of the clearest statements I have found of the assumption that cyberspace fulfils an evolutionary dream to leave the material world behind as it becomes the place where disembodied minds go. Benedikt invokes the image of the Heavenly City giving resonance to the dream of a utopian, platonic, spiritual realm beyond the limitations of embodiment.[29] Benedikt's concern with providing a conceptual justification for building cyberspace connects his work with the earlier technological utopians.

Four threads intertwine to create Benedikt's conception of the cyberspatial world: 1 a group mind based on shared myth, 2 the now familiar view of a transformative technology as a stage in media ecology, 3 the Heavenly City as a structuring ideal, and 4 mathematical rationalism. Accepting what Michael Heim calls the "transcendental intimacy" between language and reality (see chapter 2), Benedikt perceives the existence of a "group-mind" that shapes common beliefs. Common beliefs, in turn, become myths that inform not only our stories but the ways in which we understand each other. Myths both reflect and create the human condition. Benedikt argues that cyberspace becomes a cultural stage for acting out mythic consciousness, generally by young males. One problem with this conception of myth is that the mythic realm tends to be somehow separate from mundane, everyday existence. Myth is here devalued in much the same way that the cognitivists devalued metaphor and the technological pessimists devalued the image. To understand myth as sets of group fantasies that become part of a broader cultural heritage, we must grasp the far-reaching function of myth that extends beyond the play-acting of adolescents. The narratives of any social group help constitute the reality in which they function as a collective. In contrast with this view, such narratives can be programmatic, literal, and totalizing, but they can also be open-ended, invitational, and ambiguous; the building blocks of shared experiences are the foundation of social cohesion.

The history of media technologies and the development of information technology provide the second thread of influence for the development of cyberspace. Following the works of theorists such as Harold Innis, Marshall McLuhan, and Mark Poster, Benedikt accepts the notion that dominant media of communication shape different societies. But he gives preference to McLuhan's theories of media and displays an uncritical acceptance of technological determinism. He believes that the democratization of the means of idea production and dissemination increases with new media. Similarly, the growth of scientific knowledge and cultural practices is conceived as promoting the growth of Popper's third world of ideas. Information is characterized as scattered and abundant, resisting centralized attempts to control it.

Poster's Second Media Age is also based on the premise that in earlier communication systems it was far easier to control information than in the contemporary Digital Age. Benedikt sees a significant evolutionary step in the democratization of media and the conquest of space and time with the ability to transmit messages electronically and to store information.[30] His conceptualization of cyberspace falls into what I have described as the transformative view of media as a disjunctive agent of change. However, Benedikt's vision of cyberspace can be traced to the broader tradition of technological utopias. This debt is clearly evident in his discussion of cyberspace as a fulfilment of the Heavenly City.

Historian Carl L. Becker argues that while we tend to think of the eighteenth century as the age of reason, the philosophes were nearer the Middle Ages and less emancipated from medieval Christian thought than they quite realized or than we have commonly supposed.[31] The medieval image of the Heavenly City comes from the doctrine that at God's appointed time the earth would be swallowed in flames and that on this last day, good and evil would finally be separated. For the recalcitrant, there was reserved a place of everlasting torment, while the faithful would be gathered with God in the Heavenly City, there in perfection and devotion to dwell forever.[32] The eighteenth-century philosophers demolished the Heavenly City of St Augustine only to rebuild it with more up-to-date tools. They toned down a picture of salvation in the Heavenly City to a vague notion of a "future state" and the idea of the immortality of the soul to a more generalized and social perfection.[33] For the love of God, they substituted love of humanity; for the vicarious atonement, the perfectibility of man through his own efforts; and for the hope of immortality in another world, the hope of living in the memory of future generations. The enlightenment looked forward to the future as to a promised land, a kind of utopia.[34]

For some, utopianism represents an escape from the present by taking refuge in the future, which may be the re-creation of a long-lost past. In terms of technological thought, the utopian impulse can be articulated as such: technology is the tool of the conjoined ideologies of progress and development. Technology is also the engine of perfection, in the sense that progress, utopianism, and development are intertwined in the constant drive to improve or correct the inadequacies of the present.[35]

For Michael Benedikt, the Heavenly City of the Enlightenment philosophers represents a rational space perfectly suited to the mathematical nature of computer graphics. He pulls from the history of architecture a symbolic desire to realize the image of the Heavenly City of Revelations and suggests that traditional images of the Heavenly City have common features: "weightlessness, radiance, numerological complexity … hopeful fragments … in the attempt to physically realize the cultural archetype. They represent the creation of a place where we might re-enter God's graces."[36] The task of architecture in cyberspace according to Benedikt is to make manifest the dream of a culture. Here is one source of digitopia. The cyber-architect must visualize the intrinsically nonphysical and give inhabitable, visible form to society's most intricate abstractions, processes, and organisms, a "wrapping" of spirituality.[37]

Immersion accepts the constructed reality of the social world. An interaction occurs, not between terms or between present and absent speakers, but between the embodied inquisitor and experiential traces. Such traces can be sensory, physical, or symbolic. One can identify in the desire to visually orchestrate a myth of origin an attempt to realize the Heavenly City as seen through the filters of the mathematical, rational mind. However, this attempt traces its origins less to the Book of Revelations than to the works of Bacon and Descartes. Here lies the connection between cyberspace as a utopian landscape and the rule-based computational rationalism of the metaphysical-realist epistemology.

The final thread in the context for cyberspace involves the historical refinement of mathematical modelling and visualization. Benedikt suggests that the mathematical practice of diagramming creates visualizations that "seem to exist in a geography, a space borrowed from, but not identical with, the space of the piece of paper or computer screen on which we see them."[38] Mathematical diagrams possess a reality greater than a picture of the natural, phenomenal world. This is similar to our earlier discussion of the power of formal systems to encode and model the world. Benedikt embraces the Platonic realism of mathematical rationalism, which offers a true image deeper than that provided by the senses.

Benedikt's use of the concepts of the group mind and Platonic realism is significant, because it shows that proponents of virtual community are to be found in engineering and architecture culture – the construction crew of the new Heavenly City. Implicit in his approach are several attitudes that have been discussed in earlier chapters, including the cybernetic belief in the ability to code and control information, the belief in the transformative and evolutionary power of technology, the view that as technology becomes transparent, distal communities are enabled; and the Platonic preference for disembodied community characteristic of virtual communities.

Architecturally, there is an appeal to the construction of spaces based on the technologically extended human; Freud's prosthetic God might build its Heavenly City. Benedikt is clearly a media ecologist.

He identifies an evolutionary pattern in the transformation of preliterate communities (characterized by physical action and nonmediated communication) to literate societies (characterized by symbolic action). The landscapes of cyberspace are punctuated by people interacting in computer-generated, technologically mediated environments. The weaknesses of this kind of evolutionary logic has already been discussed. Yet it remains influential in both theoretical and applied discussions of cyberspace. So does a mystical faith in the ability of technological artifacts like the Internet to correct the ills of modern society.

Cyberspace is more than hardware or software. It is for Benedikt "a place, and a mode of being." While cyberspace is defined by the interconnected computers forming its borders and highways, it also exists at the level of human perception and experience, thought and art. The tendency to naturalize cyberspace (by describing it as a landscape) and to define it as a step in human evolution reveals a problem that appears throughout the literature of technological utopias. However, that having been said, the utopian mode of thinking does influence cyberspace at a practical level. Programmers do attempt to build virtual environments that model utopian aspirations. The *mirror worlds* of computer scientist David Gelernter demonstrate this process.

MIRROR WORLDS

Computer scientist David Gelernter argues that in the near future a common computing experience will be the interaction of people in what he calls *mirror worlds*. Without reference to Gibson's fiction, Gelernter and his colleagues were working in 1991 to build the architectural foundation for cyberspace. Mirror worlds are "software models of some chunk of reality, some piece of the *real world*."[39] They are representations (in the sense that they are functional and descriptive) of an iconic landscape. In the future, according to Gelernter, software projects will assume the characteristics of civil engineering projects and represent sites of interaction in which people move about and manipulate data and share social, virtual spaces.

However, he also suggests that the common perception of software must change before complex mirror worlds can become the norm. It is generally assumed that a computer program is "a highly specialized kind of *document*."[40] Gelernter suggests that in the future, software "will metamorphose into something more like stone or steel or concrete." In this new future, "understanding software doesn't mean understanding how program texts are arranged, it means understanding what the *working infomachine itself* is like – what actually *happens* when you embody the thing and turn it on – what kind of *structure* you are creating ... the look and feel of the *actual* computational landscape."[41]

For Gelernter, the configuration of computing code into some kind of functioning machine that can be perceived as such creates a condition in which it is possible to accept the infomachine as tangible and real. In other words, Gelernter describes a shift in proximality, which is exactly the same kind of shift that is required in Papert's discussion of children and cybernetics. Both Papert and Gelernter realize that a tremendous amount of training at the conceptual level must occur before their metaphoric models become basic metaphors that orient social action in a cybernetic future. For Gelernter "running a program – an *information machine* or infomachine for short – is the *embodiment* of a *disembodied machine*."[42] Here we detect a shift from Heim's view of electronic language to the sedimented view: that a piece of software is a thing.

The infomachine is an iconic representation of both a procedure and a conceptual space. An infomachine represents a landscape that is divided into plots. "As the machine runs, the landscape changes. It evolves, like the surface of a developing photograph; the stuff inside those plots changes; eventually it's done – the process is complete, you have what you want, and the evolution stops."[43] A plot can contain three kinds of thing: an information chunk, a procedure, or more plots. An information chunk is usually a number or an alphabetic character but may also be a word or a phrase. A procedure tells you how to accomplish something. In the "command post" of the plot is an automaton Gelernter calls the Actor, which is just another name for the homonculus. The Actor is equipped at all times with the *script* (a set or list of procedures to be carried out). The disembodied information machine that the programmer lays out is called the *spec*. A complete spec includes a *map* of the information landscape and the aforementioned script, to be carried out by the Actor. A programming language is a system for writing down information machine specs, or, in other words, for creating unbodied infomachines.[44]

In Gelernter's world the distinction dissolves between the physical world of matter and the world of electrical impulses and digital codes. For all practical purposes, one world is as good as another. New software cathedrals will rise, monopolizing the energy and attention of thousands in their structures. They will broadcast an aesthetic and a worldview to millions, molding behaviour and epitomizing the age. Thus, Gelernter acknowledges the importance of social consensus based upon a widely held set of assumptions – an ideology as it were – or a sufficiently chained social fantasy that acquires the aura of truth for a particular social group. In this case, the computer programmers and the public administrators who must ultimately sanction the development of mirror-world software projects are engaged in community building and the creation of a collective consciousness.

Mirror worlds are conscious attempts to construct a spatial metaphor that can be easily sedimented in social practice: the information landscape. Information is reified into plots, chunks, and actors. Gelernter describes his informational landscapes as something very like the agricultural landscape of the American Midwest, providing a link to the tradition of technological utopias. It no longer matters if these computational subroutines prove anything about sentience, since they work as models of machines we use and as models of the symbolic environment we inhabit with greater frequency. Gelernter recognizes that to change the "fabric" of reality, we must change the language we use to describe and negotiate it. He also addresses a crucial problem with a canniness uncharacteristic of engineers; he realizes that it is not sufficient to build new technologies: one must also sell the idea of them.

A subtle shift in the goals of computing projects is apparent in the kind of "public works" Gelernter envisions. He makes two assumptions: we can conceive of infomachines created solely by coded instructions and we can conceive that by changing the metaphor we use to explain software, we can change the "reality" of what is produced. Both assumptions are entirely consistent with our earlier assertion about abstract machines and the role of language understood as the formal manipulation of symbols.

THE PLATONIC MIND AND THE FLESHY BOND

Interactive computing networks were developed in the 1960s and led to the spread of a global network of telecommunications and computers. Along with the virtual-reality interface, the networked computer facilitates the development of an environment in which images, gestures, and voices create a compelling sense of presence in cyberspace.

The promise of virtual reality is the psychological promise implicit in technological utopian thought: mind expansion by means of an extended sensorium results in the extension of human power over nature and the realization of a digitized, utopian realm of pure communication.

Virtual reality promises to expand the sensory experience of sound and images beyond the limits of the mass media, beyond even the confines of the picture frame or the television screen. As Susan Sontag suggests, in our experience of mass media we conflate real social events with our experience of them in the media. This is one of the reasons why virtual reality is engaging. Mediated experience has come to replace participation in events beyond the proximal realm. Computer researchers have evoked the transformative power of images ever since they began to develop visual displays for the computer in the 1960s. In a paper presented in 1965 to the International Federation of Information Processing, Ivan Sutherland envisioned the "ultimate" computer display. He argued that "the screen is a window through which one sees a virtual world. The challenge is to make that world look real, act real, sound real, feel real."[45]

The technological power to transform the senses underpins the history of virtual reality. Myron Kreuger characterizes the development of virtual reality as the fulfilment of a Western desire to dominate Nature:

The world described in Genesis, created by mysterious cosmic forces, was a volatile and dangerous place. It molded human life through incomprehensible caprice. Natural beneficence tempered by natural disaster defined reality. For centuries, the goal of human effort was to tap Nature's terrible power. Our success has been so complete, that a new world has emerged. Created by human intelligence, it is an artificial reality.[46]

Virtual realities offer a Faustian promise – control over nature. For Kreuger, artificial reality is desirable because it is more easily controlled than external reality and because it creates a realm of imagination or mind through science. Kreuger's new world arises out of a symbiosis of human and machine achieved through the mediation of audiovisual technology and replaces Nature with a humanly constructed environment in which "humans will be able to increase the power of [their] most important, innate tools for dealing with the world – [their] ability to perceive, think, analyze, reason, communicate."[47] Not only will science unlock the secrets of nature, but it will mimic creation.

McLuhan's description of how, as communications networks have spread across the globe, the human being becomes "an organism that now wears its brain outside its skull and its nerves outside its hide,"[48] prefigures Kreuger's claim about the symbiosis between person and machine. Once again we encounter a Platonic view of body as a trap from which the mind must escape to fulfil human potential.

Photography at one time represented, so it was claimed, a real world. Now cyberspace builds worlds with imagery. We interact; we can do things we can do in the "real" world. But we can also do some things that are not possible for us to do outside the device. I have already suggested that computer programming involves a particular set of language practices. Virtual reality also involves particular sets of image practices. Virtual reality allows the television viewer a way to move inside the box, to act and interact with images. The dichotomy between television as a technology of images and perception and the computer as a technology of literacy and semiosis breaks down. In fact, the computer extends beyond television to create an immersive experience in which television viewers (now computer users) are able to interact with the images on the screen. The extreme-proximal so distrusted by J. David Bolter, becomes the experiential field of cyberspace. Virtual reality extends the ends of the visual screen so that a technical framing of vision replaces the natural field of vision.

Recall that Michael Heim argues that the computer creates "a new relationship to symbols, to language, and, by extension, to reality."[49] He argues that the phenomenological engagement we experience in virtual environments, coupled with the technical possibilities of ever-increasing fidelity and resolution that provide sensory input for virtual reality systems, instigates "a change in the world under our feet, in the whole context in which our knowledge and awareness are rooted."[50] In essence, he argues that virtual reality creates an ontological shift that suggests that the model of the world codified through digital symbols becomes a "full-fledged, aggressive, surrogate reality." His view of "surrogate" realities has two sources: Plato's problematizing of the relationship between the real and the unreal and the so-called argument from illusion.

Plato's view of images echoes his distrust of written language. The painter is the artist who "represents" the objects made by the carpenter or by God. Painting does not aim to reproduce any actual object as it is but only as it appears. The painting is a representation not of a truth but of a semblance at some distance from the real. Practices that privilege representations, like programming, are developed based on their presumed homomorphism with reality.

Plato dramatizes the problem of appearances and reality most explicitly in his myth of the cave.[51] In the cave, which is open at one end to the outside world, a group of people are chained by their necks and feet, facing an inner wall. Trapped in this underground den since childhood, they experience the world only as "the shadows of the images which the fire throws on the wall of the den." If a group of the prisoners are turned towards the light or are dragged up to the surface, writes Plato, they will slowly "get the habit of perceiving" as their eyes become accustomed to the light of the moon, stars, and sun. Upon returning to the cave, this group will be hard-pressed to compete with their former companions in the perception of shadows on the wall. The inhabitants of the cave, in turn, will steadfastly refuse to believe in a world beyond the shadows in the cave.

The problem of appearance versus reality has two facets for Plato. First, we can be deceived about the true nature of things by their appearances alone. Our senses are not always sufficient to discern the properties of things. Second, appearances are surfaces, while realities have greater depth. The senses must be trained to be subservient to intellect, which alone is able to plumb through the depths of perception to the true nature of things. For Plato, we are all captives in the cave. He argues that it is possible to learn to see beyond the shadows of images to the "true" nature of things if one learns "the relation of the shadow to the substance," a connection that most of us fail to grasp.

Heim, in his celebration of virtual reality, posits an ontological continuity between the cave and our global information systems. Platonism, according to Heim, is often taken to imply, in principle, or metaphysically, a separation of the mind from physical existence. The computer recycles ancient Platonism; the computer clothes the details of empirical experience so that they "seem to share the ideality of the stable knowledge of the Forms."[52] Further, at the computer interface, the spirit migrates from the body to a world of total representation. Information and images float through the Platonic mind without a necessary grounding in bodily experience.[53] This lack of grounding forms the basis of a perceptual scepticism characterized in philosophical terms by the argument from illusion.

The argument from illusion maintains that perception of the appearance of things varies from person to person, depending on their physical point of view in relation to the object observed, on their physical and psychological condition while observing, or on contextual or environmental circumstances such as the presence or absence of light.[54] Because we have no reliable criteria to decide whether a hallucination is real, we cannot tell if reality is a hallucination. Since different appearances can be mutually incompatible, they cannot all really characterize the material object. Thus, none of the competing appearances can be said to be "in the thing." Rather, they are all "in the mind."

An argument like this suggests that a person cannot distinguish between objects that exist and those that do not. James J. Gibson argues that this doctrine rests on the assumption that because a percept and an image both occur in the brain, the one can pass over to the other by gradual steps. While this assumption is consistent with the cognitivist approach to describing vision, Gibson claims that it is based on a confusion between sensation and image. He challenges the idea that reality testing is an intellectual (or second-order) process and suggests that a surface becomes clearer when we fixate on it, while an image does not.[55]

For Gibson the most decisive test for reality is whether you can discover new features and details in an object by the act of scrutiny. Reality testing is not a logical or formal process but an activity that requires embodied engagement with the world. Thus, the kind of perceptual scepticism implicit in the argument from illusion is unnecessary if we consider cyberspace in terms of embodied perception.

As I have argued, much of the discourse of cyberspace rejects or ignores the embodied nature of perception, even though as a medium, virtual reality takes advantage of perceptual embodiment to achieve its effects. The issue concerns the role of imagination in social construction. The technological utopians and the technological pessimists have no place for imagination, playfulness, or ambiguity.

The implicit value judgement in Heim's Platonism chooses the realm of ideal forms as an escape from the messy complications of the world of the flesh. However, even Heim is aware of the problems of uncritically accepting the model of disembodied communication. He suggests that without a body to ground experience, you can lose your humanity.[56]

Heim maintains that bodily existence stands at the front of personal identity and individuality. Both law and morality recognize the physical body as an absolute boundary establishing and protecting any privacy. The computer network, he suggests, simply brackets the physical presence of the participants by either omitting or simulating corporeal immediacy. In one sense, this frees us from the restrictions imposed by our physical identity. We are more equal on the net because we can either ignore or create the body that appears in cyberspace. Members of the community need never stand face-to-face. However, in another sense, the quality of human encounter narrows because the stand-in can never fully represent us. "The more we mistake our cyberbodies for ourselves," Heim argues, "the more the machine twists ourselves into the prostheses we are wearing."[57] In this way, Heim creates a moral issue in the adoption of cyber-bodies. For Heim the living, nonrepresentable face is the primal source of responsibility, and the direct, warm link between private bodies. He worries that without directly meeting others physically, our ethics languishes. Face-to-face communication supports a long-term warmth and loyalty, as well as a sense of obligation. This is something for which computer-mediated communities have yet to be tested.[58]

Heim's metaphorical substitution of the virtual for reality echoes the cybernetic substitution of one formal symbol system with another. It also resonates with a Platonic and Hobbesian distrust of the ornamental nature of metaphor. Heim's dualism appears to support the Platonic distrust of images. Both the Platonic and the digital approaches to cognition first extend, then ultimately renounce the physical embodiment of knowledge. As in the promise of Kreuger's artificial reality, cyberspace for Heim supplants physical space.

Thus, the virtual environment of cyberspace is "as good as" the world of everyday reality. More importantly, if there is a "true" representation of things, it appears within the world of forms. Heim emphasizes an idealist preference for mind over body, the mental origin of appearances, and the Platonic notion of Ideal Forms that are beyond the evidence of the senses.

In familiar disembodiments of communication such as telephone calls, electronic mail, and on-line newsgroups, we may have the experience of breaking free from bodily existence, but for Heim this experience is illusory. He argues that the body is seduced by appearances but that the mind can attain knowledge of essences, of pure Forms. This emancipation of the mind is at the heart of Heim's fascination with computers and expresses the technological utopian assumption, shared by Kreuger, that a constructed world can be better than the one in which we live. For Heim, "Cyberspace is Platonism as a work-ing product. The cybernaut seated before us, strapped into sensory-input devices, appears to be, and is indeed, lost to this world. Sus-pended in computer space, the cybernaut leaves the *prison of the body* and emerges in a world of digital sensation."[59]

The ultimate goal of virtual environments from this perspective is "to outrun the drag of the 'meat' – the flesh – by attaching human attention to what formally attracts the mind."[60] Cyberspace is thus considered better than previous media because it creates worlds that promise the stability of Platonic Forms. Mirror worlds are built using the "essence" of reality – its code – creating radical simulations that serve as operative images of aspects of the phenomenal world.

THE SPIRITLESS REALM

I have argued throughout this book that the body is the "carnal ground" of our perception and knowledge. From embodied experi-ence we make metaphoric associations, some of which come to serve as cognitive models. This idea counters a number of dominant assumptions about the world that I have connected to objectivism, the transformative view of technology, and the "transcendental inti-macy" of language and reality. To what extent can we substitute "vir-tual" actions for those we take in the off-line world? I challenge Heim's Platonic version of cyberspace as a realm of pure spirit with an example of how the disembodied realm of communication can empty a spiritual quest – a pilgrimage – of its human significance. The following example illustrates in a telling way the problems of inhabiting cyberspace.

There is a site on the World Wide Web where people can send electronic messages to be placed in the Wailing Wall. The site, called *Virtual Jerusalem*, raises a metaphysical question about cyberspace: if we send messages to the Wailing Wall, what is the nature of the activity in which we engage? The *Virtual Jerusalem* home page reads:

Placing notes in the cracks of the Kotel (the Western Wall) is an age old custom. These notes traditionally contain personal prayers or the names of ill relatives and friends. Placing a note in the Kotel lends a permanence to your prayer; even after you leave, your prayer remains at one of the world's holiest sites. But not everyone can go to the Kotel and place his or her note.

We will be taking prayers which are e-mailed to us to the Kotel daily –
allowing those who cannot go there themselves to send their special prayers
through Virtual Jerusalem.[61]

The designers of the *Virtual Jerusalem* web site even offer a template
for a prayer for the sick. Another option on the site is the *Kotel-Kam*,
a "round the clock camera at the Western Wall." *Virtual Jerusalem* illustrates the paradox of distance in digital communication. The person
who writes a prayer is separated from the message that has been sent
to the home page, printed, and placed on the Wall. Presumably the
content of the message, the prayer, will someday reach its intended
reader. However, at which steps in the process of separation does a
supplicant participate in the ritual? Which elements of the process
carry meaning, if any? Does the metaphor of the Wailing Wall as a
dead-letter office cause us to reevaluate the experience of the religious
pilgrimage or to reject the whole experience as devoid of meaning?

In sending a message to *Virtual Jerusalem* the significant act is no
longer the pilgrimage to the Wailing Wall (the body is no longer
important); the significance lies in the message. Between the sender
and the ultimate receiver of a *Kotel* message is a huge gap. We can
ask ourselves what the significance is of the prayer composed by the
supplicant, the codification of the prayer into an electronic message,
the space through which the e-mail travels, the recipient at *Virtual
Jerusalem* as mediator, the printed paper, the act of transporting the
message to the Wailing Wall, and the Wall itself. Is there a degradation
in the content of the message as it passes through these many steps;
is there a degradation in the prayer's meaning? Activities that have
no connection to the human body, in the end, have no human meaning. If we have already won the battle of the spirit over the flesh in
cyberspace, then we no longer have need for the pilgrimage to holy
sites; we have no need for intercession if we can inhabit the spirit-
space of virtual reality.

This leads to another alternative method for characterizing virtual
places, based on the point made earlier in this chapter about place as
an iconographic setting for ongoing activity. Places take many shapes,
serve many functions, and contribute to the complex assemblage of
experience in both virtual and external reality. Instead of a contest to
see which version of reality becomes the "nature of reality," we can
look at cyberspace as a multiplicity of coextant domains.

6

From Public Image to Public Memory: Building Heterotopia

In this chapter a third approach to building the iconic landscapes of cyberspace will be presented in the heterotopic attitude (in which multiple places of interaction coexist without being necessarily reducible to one another). This last attitude toward spatial organization might best characterize environments that would allow for social experiment and creativity. Spatial constructions can be self-consciously manufactured and can allow for metaphoric playfulness, although constructed spaces are also influenced and constrained by underlying assumptions about technology, space, and social organization.

Using the method of interactive realism, we can look at constructions that take the body into account and that characterize digital experience as heterogeneous and supportive of a kind of selfhood comprised of complex assemblages of interactive skills and experience. Michel Foucault has described such constructions as heterotopian.

Heterotopia is not simply an alternative to utopian or dystopian space but is a way of describing multiple domains and their coexistence. Heterotopian spaces are playful and metaphoric. By accepting the constructed *as* construction we need not assume an underlying social program. Instead, looking at heterotopias is a way of examining the boundaries of significant symbolic sites.

Mark Poster observes that computerized communication transforms the relationship between ideas and the artifacts created through writing. He argues that compared to the pen, the typewriter, or the printing press, the computer dematerializes the written trace. Poster's dematerialization holds important consequences for the writer, who "thus confronts a representation that is similar in its spatial fragility and temporal simultaneity to the contents of the mind or to the spoken word. Writer and writing, subject and object have a similarity that approaches identity, a simulation of identity that subverts the expectation of the Cartesian subject that the world is composed of *res extensa*, beings completely different from the mind."[1]

Advocates and critics of digital culture draw many conclusions from this line of reasoning: with the advent of digital technology communication has become dematerialized; the dot-com world is both volatile and insubstantial; community has become temporary, voluntary, ephemeral, and transient. In the face of such chaotic insubstantiality, what better call to social and psychological stability could there be than Plato's notion of the Ideal Form? Plato's assertion of an eternal substratum to reality, combined with a persistent faith in human ingenuity, characterizes the utopian dream that justifies perpetual high-tech progress. This assumption is unsatisfactory. If it were true that digitization dematerializes writing and thought, then it might make sense to talk about digitization as the ultimate victory of spirit or mind over the flesh. Instead, digitization signifies a new materialization of communication. This new materialization is neither universalizing nor abstract. It recalibrates, rather than replaces, the human body in relation to communication.

Social construction is at a significant level about creating and maintaining a sense of common reality – a social narrative of text, image, audio, and video collected in a vast interactive transcript. The social transcript in technological society is about the perpetual innovation of technological society, as opposed to structures of thought more concerned with tradition. The problem of permanence in digital culture, according to Mark Poster, can be addressed by examining the ways we construct virtual environments. In the last chapter it was shown how these constructions are guided by utopian desires. The question addressed in this final chapter is how we create and preserve a variety of coextant virtual environments and social transcripts.

MAPPING THE VIRTUAL

When Gelernter suggests that we can change our attitude to software and grant our software tools the power to engineer mirror worlds, he objectifies the information landscape, granting it the greatest validity of the image in rationalist thought – a correspondence to reality. Cartography and architecture become the dominant metaphoric structures for his investigation of the informational landscape, and while he does not use it to its best advantage, the map is a fruitful metaphor for thinking about virtual places.

By way of example, the computer network might be thought of as an artifact that connects the material to the symbolic. A map also makes such a connection. Cartographers study communication theory as part of their training, and most models for cartography illustrate a dynamic system for communicating information via maps. The communicative system in which a map operates includes four essential components. First, the real world provides the context from which the cartographer samples information. The second component is the cartographer herself, who is responsible for representing the information. Third is the map, created to convey the information and message. The final component is the map reader who passively or actively responds to the stimuli presented and then decodes or interprets it. And yet the map, like the metaphor, makes no reductive claim to scientific representation. The map's symbolic language, its ability to depict the landscape on a one-to-one scale, and the mapping of abstract ideas all require more than simply recording or translating. As the creator of an image, the cartographer interprets the place and its characteristics, determines how to represent them on a two- or three-dimensional surface, and provides one perspective on the project (her own).[2] The map is a complex communicative artifact; it is a construction shared by a number of users. The map is also a vehicle for metaphoric double awareness in that it points to lived spaces but also to narrative spaces that embody their viewer.

Set the image of the map aside for the time being so that we might ask a question: is cyberspace radically different from earlier utopian spaces? In the previous chapter it was suggested that utopian ideals drive the construction of mirror worlds. The goal of utopian projects is to correct the wrongs of a current social or moral order by devising a plan for a future community. Similar claims have been made about the potential of cyberspace as a realm of "pure" communication: the digitopian impulse. Digitopia embodies the myth of pure communication without the mess of bodies in conflict. By way of contrast, the complexity of our experience of the world has been consistently emphasized throughout the book. Thus, from the perspective of interactive realism, any theory that denies the role of the body in generating experience or that reduces human experience to a code is unsatisfactory. Similarly, any theory that professes the perfectibility of human society, by technological or any other means, is also suspect. To understand the iconic landscapes of cyberspace, we need a more complex theory.

THE SOCIAL TRANSCRIPT AND THE MONOPOLY OF KNOWLEDGE

To articulate such a theory, I propose we return to an image taken from the social cybernetics of Kenneth Boulding – the public image. Boulding tells us that a public image almost invariably produces a "transcript," that is, a record in more or less permanent form that can be handed down from generation to generation.[3] Unlike the passing on of rituals, legend, ceremony, and the like in nonliterate societies, Boulding argues that the invention of writing marks the beginning of the "disassociated transcript" – a transcript that is in some sense independent of the transcriber, a communication independent of the communicator.[4] Here, once again, we are confronted with the transformative view that drives the work of writers like Mark Poster half a century later. However, we cannot simply dismiss Boulding's public image or Poster's mode of information, because they do provide pertinent insights into the socially constructed nature of reality. The social imaginary is a composite of common experiences to a large degree influenced by mass media, new technologies, and global culture. Where writers like Boulding, and to a lesser extent Poster, err is in their assumption that a single culture is represented by the social imaginary. In fact, there are many coextant and incommensurable "public" images.

Harold Innis's work helps one understand the cultural or societal influence of communications media on the social imaginary. Although for Boulding the medium influences the nature of the social transcript, which, in turn, influences the nature of the society, for Innis the driving force behind technological change (and, consequently, behind cultural change) is the quest for power. Power is understood in this context as the attempt on the part of emerging social groups to erode previous monopolies of knowledge. It is by placing the quest for power at the centre of his analysis that Innis breaks with previous economic analyses of staples, resources, and commodities. Further, it is by equating power with knowledge that he offers a conceptualization of social change that will appeal both to the social cybernetics of thinkers like Boulding and the media determinists like McLuhan to follow.

But what happens when the spread of information technologies so weakens the ability of a social order to control the forms and flows of information that the very idea of a "monopoly" of knowledge becomes untenable? In other words, how can we discuss a social transcript when it becomes increasingly difficult to distinguish the dominant from the oppositional or emergent forms of social practice even within our own society?

The Italian philosopher Gianni Vattimo examines precisely this question. For Vattimo a universal notion of history (characteristic of Enlightenment culture) is simply no longer useful. Instead, history must come to terms with many localized rationalities, as well as with many temporal locations that, paradoxically, seem to coexist in public memory.[5] Our culture's fascination with virtual realities and re-creations of historical moments of our past contributes to what Jean Baudrillard has called the "undoing of history." According to Baudrillard, the marking of a significant event like the countdown to the millennium "extends in both directions: not only does it put an end to time in the future, but it also extends itself in the obsessive revival of the events of the past."[6] For Baudrillard, history is illusory; any attempt to relive moments in history launders their memory. But what if we do not launder but create public memory? What if our historical awareness involves processes of interactive realism?

Philosopher Paul Ricœur is particularly concerned with the intangibility of history. He asserts a view of history as narrative and as transcript. Such a view has been discussed in chapter 1 in relation to metaphor and poetics. Ricœur, in a sense, articulates a poetics of history. History involves the construction of particular kinds of narrative. Ricœur cites the similarity between the painter and the historian, who are both seeking to *render* (in the first case a landscape, in the second, a course of events). The historian's work then consists in making the narrative structure a model, an icon of the past, capable of representing it. In this there are similarities between the writing of history and the writing of other kinds of narrative, including the novel. But unlike the work of the novelist, the activity of the historian is constrained by what once was. This is the conviction that is expressed by the notion of the trace; inasmuch as it is left by the past, the trace stands for the past; it represents the past.[7]

In Ricœur's historical method, we must inevitably fall back on the authority of *preuve documentaire*; evidence is, in the end, always textual. But if we open our field of investigation to other traces of the past, it may be possible to recreate more than the thoughts of historical actors. For example, it may be possible to gain a sense of the artifacts they created and the places they occupied. In this endeavour, we attempt to excavate the materialities of history (the wrappings of experience) in the artifacts used to construct public memories.

Even in our understanding of space we must consider patterns of use, representations of space, psychological space, and the symbolic nature of physical artifacts. These are elements of physical and spatial organization that reflect the characteristics of social order.

Historian David Lowenthal claims that three sources provide signposts or aides-mémoire when reconstructing past events for analysis and in considering how culture is constructed in the present.[8] These signposts include, first, the notion of presence of the past as manifested in personal memories. Memories are not ready-made reflections of the past but eclectic, selective reconstructions of past events based on subsequent actions and perceptions. Memories are also based on ever-changing codes by which we delineate, symbolize, and classify the world around us. The prime function of memory, then, is not to preserve the past but to adapt it so as to enrich and manipulate the present. Memory is the process of internalizing what a society deems worthy of recall. Legal scholar H. Patrick Glenn discusses how the instruction of law in the Middle Ages was bound to the process of teaching the process of internalizing the law.[9] Far from simply storing previous experiences, memory helps us to understand them by making them useful to us in some way.

Next, the notion of public memory extends personal recollections by understanding them as material for the creation of a shared consciousness. If we accept memory as a premise of knowledge, we can infer history from evidence that includes other people's memories. History is contingent, based on empirical sources that we can decide to accept or reject, building and replacing competing versions of the past.[10] Public or collective memory can be defined as consisting of the perceptions and uses of the past by the public.[11] Such public memory emerges from the intersection of official and vernacular cultural expressions.[12] It is not simply the creation of a cultural elite whose versions of events are imposed upon the rest of society, nor is it the result of political discussion concentrated on moral or economic problems. Instead, public memory emerges from fundamental issues about the society, such as the very meaning of its past and present.[13] This description of history as a kind of public memory concurs with Ricœur's view of history as a construction.

Finally, and of particular value to this study, is Lowenthal's third source: the relic. Tangible relics survive in two forms: as natural features and as human artifacts. Lowenthal suggests that awareness of such relics enhances knowledge gained through memory and history. For our purposes, Lowenthal's concept of the relic ties neatly with Feibleman's category of the tool – the artifact constructed through human agency for human use – even when this use is symbolic (see chapter 1). Further, there is a sense of double awareness in the concept of the relic that in turn brings to mind the moebius strip of metaphoricity. Each relic exists simultaneously in the past and in the present; we identify objects as ancient depending on environment and history, individual and culture, historical awareness or inclination.[14] Lowenthal suggests that we apprehend the past in its surviving relics in a variety of ways.

For example, the apparent antiquity of things around us arouses a sense of the past. This felt past is a function of atmosphere, as well as locale. Lowenthal also emphasizes the constructed character of relics. Like memories, relics, once abandoned or forgotten, may become more treasured than those in continual use, because we enter into a dialogue with antiquity when we rediscover particular relics. Yesterday's relics thus enlarge today's landscapes as they hand down their stored-up past.

Iconic landscapes like the ones we construct in cyberspace provide repositories for the social transcript Boulding describes. Yet, iconic landscapes are not just transcripts but serve more as maps or archives. As Lowenthal argues, "artifacts are simultaneously past and present; their historical connotations coincide with their modern roles ... The tangible past is in continual flux, altering, ageing, and always interacting with the present."[15] Here they may provide the method we adopt to pass on our cultural heritage (the reproximation or re-oralization McLuhan and Ong described in hopes of re-enchanting technological society). In this case, we would pass traces of cultural heritage from desktop to desktop. The question is how to make permanent what is inherently ephemeral (electronic bits and bytes).

HETEROTOPIA

Cyberspace, with utopian and dystopian potentials, can perhaps be understood as an experimental environment, yet set apart from everyday life, addressing what philosopher Michel Foucault calls "the anxiety of our era" regarding space.[16] Our anxieties about space manifest themselves in a number of fundamental oppositions, including the opposition between private space and public space, family space and social space, cultural space and useful space, and the space of leisure and that of work.

All these spaces are instances of what Foucault calls "heterotopia," the impossible space in which fragments of disparate discursive orders are merely juxtaposed, without any attempt to reduce them to a common order. To visualize this, think of a computer screen running Windows or MAC OS in which a number of boxes, each running different applications, are open at the same time.

Foucault's notion of heterotopias, the characteristic spaces of the modern world, supersedes the hierarchic ensemble of places of the Middle Ages and the enveloping space of emplacement opened up by Galileo. They are present in an early-modern, infinitely unfolding space of extension and measurement. There are important cultural spaces that are removed from the space of everyday life. Further, for Foucault, "we do not live in a kind of void, inside of which we could place individuals and things. We do not live inside a void that could be colored with diverse shades of light, we live inside a set of relations that delineates sites which are irreducible to one another and absolutely not superimposible on one another."[17]

Foucault strengthens the link between ideology and utopia in his argument that utopias are sites related to the real space of society through direct or inverted analogy. They present society itself in a perfected form or turned upside down. In any case, these utopias are fundamentally unreal spaces. The real places are Foucault's heterotopias, to be contrasted to utopias. A heterotopia is, like a utopia, apart from the everyday, but it still remains a real space. Examples of heterotopias include museums, where the total past of a culture is collapsed and contained within the walls of the institution and, at the other extreme, the festival, in which all historical time is dissipated, creating a space that exists only for the moment. However, a heterotopia can arguably exist in many everyday instances as well. For example, a mirror functions as a heterotopic space: "It makes this place that I occupy at the moment when I look at myself in the glass at once absolutely real, connected with all the space that surrounds it, and absolutely unreal, since in order to be perceived it has to pass through this virtual point which is over there."[18] This image returns us to our starting point – the magic mirror of transformative technology. The crucial difference is the implicit suggestion that the world looks different only when we gaze in the mirror, or, in other words, the world appears different only so long as we interact with the technology of transformation.

Heterotopias function in relation to all the space that remains; they are capable of juxtaposing in a single real place several spaces or sites that are in themselves incompatible. Foucault claims that heterotopias function in one of two ways: they either create a space of illusion that exposes every real space as even more illusory (recall the goal of cinema – to create illusion), or they serve as a manifestation of the utopian ideal of a particular social group. In this second function, the heterotopia "create[s] a space that is other, another real space, as perfect, meticulous, as well arranged as ours is messy, ill constructed, and jumbled."[19]

Some writers have tried to discuss the construction of new social spaces without using the complicated concept of the heterotopia at all. For example, Benjamin Genocchio (1995) argues that the term overemphasizes the discursive nature of Foucault's construction.[20] More recently, McBeath and Web (2000) link the virtual to the utopian by attempting to differentiate between stable-state and flexible utopias. The stable-state utopia refers to the traditional understanding of the utopia as a blueprint for a perfect society. The flexible utopia, on the other hand, involves an endless reconfiguration of virtual spaces. The goal in creating the flexible utopia is not to create immersive, game-like environments but rather to account for the creative process of interaction as the computer user continually interacts upon a virtual environment. The flexible utopia is a kind of guiding metaphor for those concerned with the design and use of virtual environments.[21] This idea is useful but limited. Not all spaces are constantly changed by interactions, even in cyberspace. Nor are all spaces utopian. Finally, as shown in the last chapter, utopian spaces carry a lot of baggage. As Foucault implies and others argue more explicitly, the built environment understood as a heterotopian construct allows us to spatialize history by looking at geography as a materialization of social interactions.[22]

The concept of the heterotopian space does not solve the tensions between utopian and dystopian visions of society. It offers, instead, a description of the complexity of spatial representations that returns to the Renaissance image drawn with the conventions of linear perspective. Heterotopia is a conceptual metaphor for the Renaissance image. In Renaissance art, the represented space is formed by a combination of several microspaces, each structured according to the laws of linear perspective with its own independent organization (that is, with its own horizon line). The background space often has its own special frame, often a doorway or a windowpane, which exemplifies the concept of the painting as "a view through a window."[23]

It would be tempting to argue that in virtual reality we see (à la McLuhan) a re-medievalizing of perspective as distance is erased; the so-called end of history in post-structuralism and the end-of-geography metaphor of cyberspace. In medieval perspective the artist places herself within the field of representation. This is a creative potential inherent in any virtual reality as a medium of artistic expression: audiences are immersed in an experience that places them within the work. Based on our sense of the opacity or transparency of the medium intervening between ourselves and the world we perceive, we can escape the circular trap of trying to reach a nonmediated state of human interaction. Indeed, cyberspace fosters a multiple, rather than double, awareness that reflects the complexity of human experience in social interactions. Cyberspace may be a museum *and* a carnival; a market and an archive. Like the great expositions of the past, cyberspace can become a permanent exhibition of cultural traditions in which our predecessors speak to us.[24]

THE PROBLEM OF PERMANENCE
ON THE INTERNET

The task of the archivist is to manage the public transcript. In the digital society we each engage in activities of selection, reproduction, and storage that were once the province of a professional elite charged with the task of creating and maintaining monopolies of knowledge. At the micro-level, the importance of the archivist is demonstrated by the frequent crashes of the Ultima Online servers described in chapter 4. The problem for the game-playing community was that once the servers came back on-line, character experience, accumulated possessions, user profiles (all of the characteristics of digital identity within the game space) were forgotten – in what was described rather tellingly as a kind of social amnesia. The work of the archivist institutionalizes the process of creating and maintaining the integrity of the social transcript in Boulding's sense of the term and also demonstrates the creation and maintenance of Innissian monopolies of knowledge. Cultural hegemony regarding the social transcript is constructed and perpetuated by bureaucratizing and institutionalizing the collection and preservation of documents and by controlling their provenance as a marker of origin and authority. Of particular interest is the fact that professional archivists have been concerned with the provenance of electronic documents far longer than the general public.

To cast records managers as business administrators and archivists as historians does not hold up to historical analysis. For example, in his study *Archives in the Ancient World* (1972) Ernst Posner describes archiving activities as early as 4000 BC that were concerned with what would have been "current" records.[25] Conversely, there is an undeniably archival quality to records management in antiquity.[26] A variety of organizational practices associated with the creation of records, the planned selection of records for preservation (such as the selection of baked clay tablets over unbaked clay tablets), and their systematic arrangement for easy retrieval correspond to the same kinds of activities that are inherent in the preservation of records about actions and transactions.[27]

New communications media, such as electronic mail and web pages, offer expanded opportunities to document the personal lives of individuals. However, societal problems and implications exist for the archival retention of personal electronic records in such an everchanging medium.[28] One problem is record integrity, which ensures that evidence of actions and transactions has not been altered. This has traditionally been accomplished by placing records in a dedicated place, which now, superficially at least, seems very difficult to do, given the ubiquity of electronic records.

Protecting the provenance of electronic records presents challenges for archivists. Because they do not exist as physical entities, much of the contextual information about them is not visible to users or may not be routinely captured. For example, what guarantees do archivists and users have that no intentional or accidental changes have occurred? Furthermore, other traditional indicators of authenticity, such as signatures, watermarks, marginalia, and the like are not captured in many electronic documents. Archivists, therefore, cannot simply rely upon the original physical order of electronic records as a means of protecting their provenance and authority. They must also ensure that the context in which records were created and used is preserved (including the relations of documents with their creators, with the facts and acts that they are evidence of, and with other documents). Here, evidential value becomes less important than informational value.

Archivists and records managers must also consider the accessibility of such electronic documents over time; electronic archiving is one example of the process of creating and maintaining the provenance of both electronic records and electronic environments. Archival procedures create and maintain the social transcript. In fact, social transcripts are multiple; they are heterotopic landscapes. We can also think of heterotopic constellations of time to complement our understanding of hetrotopic landscapes.

HETEROTOPIC TEMPORALITY

Virtual environments draw our attention to new ways of creating heterotopic temporality. Okenagan artist Lawrence Paul Yuxweluptan's experiment in virtual reality creates the experience of an altered time scale, a responsively enigmatic environment, and a situation that allows an audience to witness a user making a spiritual journey. Yuxweluptan investigates the potential of virtual reality to communicate across cultural boundaries. He writes:

I approach [virtual reality] from the aspect of the fear others have of native people. Not understanding our spirit world. In it, the longhouse is a given space in time which I use to show a religious concept, to physically bring people into contact with a native worshipping aspect of life, praying indians – a way to bring others close to my heart so they can understand my belief system. What is it like being in a possessed state feeling rhythmic sounds in a longhouse, feeling sounds go through one's own self, feeling a spirit inside you?[29]

His strategy, like Haraway's metaphoric appropriation of the cyborg from scientific discourse, is to employ technology "that has in the past been used against native peoples."[30] To give his virtual space an ambience that did not seem overtly "computer-generated," Yuxweluptan scanned images from his notebooks into the computer.

In *Inherent Rights, Vision Rights* Yuxweluptan creates a mythic space that embodies the promise of a shared experience of an alternate reality. In the virtual experience of Yuxweluptan's sweat lodge, one can experience cyberspace as a spiritual no-place, though it is not a utopia. It is the promise of utopia that enables us to stand outside our own society to see its faults and rebuild it in the image of the promised place. Yuxweluptan creates, instead, an environment where one can undergo an imaginative journey. He creates a virtual sweat lodge.

While Yuxweluptan disdained the limitations of the technology, he created a powerful and evocative sensory experience. I saw this work at the National Gallery of Canada in 1993. The virtual reality engine was a crude assemblage of television monitors and a MacIntosh computer. The contraption resembled a home-made arcade video game. Two small television monitors were mounted at eye level in front of a bench. The screens could be seen through a metal frame that was similar to an old-fashioned stereoscopic viewer. Once a viewer sat in front of the screens, a joystick controlled the motion in the simulation, and a pair of headphones provided sound. Of particular interest to me was a long bench set back from the installation. Headsets were plugged into the bench. Across from the bench were mounted four video displays, so that observers could watch what the user was experiencing "inside" the simulation. I preferred to watch other people run the program but still experienced a sense of immersion by wearing headphones and watching the action on a bank of monitors to the side of the virtual-reality engine. I remember the experience as one in which I felt part of a ritual, drawn for a while outside quotidien reality in a strange, shared experience with a group of strangers in an art gallery. The compelling aspect of the exhibit was the sense of engagement with both the technologically created environment and the other people who viewed the exhibit with me. The virtual sweat lodge did not replace anything in the everyday world; it offered an additional place to experience something radically different.

HETEROTOPIC SPATIALITY

Virtual reality highlights the constructedness of the world. Therefore, we can take everyday reality as less ontologically fixed than we might have thought. But this means we must investigate the particularities of different constructed realities, emphasizing the constraints and opportunities common to and different in each. Computers are technological artifacts based on rationalism, internal representations corresponding to reality and objectivism. Yet, as maps and as metaphors they also allow for a creative, interactive exploration of reality. As models of utopian order, artifacts, like the Internet, acquire the characteristics of reified spaces.

For example, cyberspace, according to Benedikt, is more than a hardware system or a simulation or sensorium production system or a software graphics application. "It is a place, and a mode of being."[31] Such an assertion exemplifies the utopian reductionism or substitution of the cyberspatial for the actual world. This conflates the map with the territory by confusing linear perspective (a system for representing three-dimensional information on a two-dimensional picture plane) with a natural phenomenon (visual perception). Regarding this reification of linear perspective, it has been said that the image has come to precede the reality it is supposed to represent.[32] However, the conflation of map and territory does not adequately describe the functions of the iconic landscapes of cyberspace.

As physical objects continue to serve as the location for repeated social situations, those very activities come over time to be viewed as structural. The places come to stand as icons that facilitate the recall and renewal of social relationships. Changing the icons helps to foster social change.[33] The built environment and the natural landscape serve as repositories of cultural meaning. Thus, architectural and environmental sites are cultural markers that emphasize the on-going construction and reconstruction of physical sites, as well as the "meanings" each structured landscape (material or symbolic) carries.

Consider a nondigital example. The old British Museum Reading Room was a large, slow version of a database server: once a request was mediated through the reference librarian, items of stored information were delivered to the end-user. The development of both the architectural form of the building and the interactive processes of requesting, searching, storing, and delivering materials was the result of a long historical process.[34] Architectural theorist William Mitchell argues that this very analogy between the reading room and a database allows us to consider a new kind of library that would exist only in virtual space. For Mitchell,

Popular graphical user interfaces of personal computers function in much the same way as [the British Museum stacks designed by Sydney Smirke]. Icons are arranged on the screen, like doorways along a street, to make visible the available access points. Clicking on an icon (like knocking on a door) puts the user in a space – in this case a rectangular "window" on the screen – from which files of information can be requested. In response to user requests, software routines retrieve files from the disk, display them on the screen for inspection and manipulation, and, perhaps eventually rewrite them back to the disk.

   Now extrapolate from this small-scale example and imagine a 10-million-volume, digital, online, humanities research library ... The catalogue would be available on the network ... It matters little where the digital volumes physically reside – just that they can be accessed efficiently ... The collection's existence would not be celebrated architecturally.[35]

Mitchell draws upon two concepts I have already discussed. First, the reading room and the database are operative images of one another: the process of requesting and receiving stored information is key to each. Second, once the procedures of the physical library are sufficiently abstracted, the library can exist on one or even a hundred computers as long as they share a common index. Display of the collection as well as its readiness for use become issues of interface, rather than of architecture and storage.

   Here we return to the image of the map as a kind of performative artifact. It is not that we exchange places or procedures in the real world for digital simulacra. Indeed, our understanding of those very processes becomes more complicated when we abstract them into digital form. Philosopher Gianni Vattimo argues that even in a world where the norm is the exact reproduction of reality – perfect objectivity, the complete identity of map and territory – the result is, paradoxically, a world where it becomes "increasingly difficult to conceive of a single reality."[36]

   Further, the identification between the map and the territory is fallacious. Why is this the case? Maps are not simple reflections of the territories they describe. Maps are invitations to explore. The logic of geometry that makes linear perspective possible establishes a hierarchy of tracings, each tracing attempting to stand in for what it represents. By making maps instead of images, the role of representation shifts toward the task of establishing contact with the real experimentally. Describing the "maps" of psychoanalysis, Deleuze and Guattari argue that the map does not reproduce an unconscious closed on itself; it constructs it.[37]

Cyberspace thus provides a map of the world that can be experienced, after a fashion, through a technologically mediated kind of perceptual experience. The question is whether the environments we experience are offered as substitutes for reality (characteristic of both the utopian drive and the dystopian fear) or as invitations to linger in experiential domains outside our quotidian experience.

A final metaphor that emphasizes the heterotopic spatiality of cyberspace is the metaphor of the postmodern city. Utopian views of the urban environment characterize it as a place of order, a place where technocratic management creates a balance of order and nature. The archetypal images of the technological utopian urban landscape are the garden cities and the Grecian revival in late-nineteenth-century civic architecture. Dystopian images of the city invoke Burton's chaotic Gotham City, the factories of Fritz Lang's *Metropolis*, or the decayed, nocturnal confusion of Los Angeles in Ridley Scott's *Blade Runner*. Another postmodern view of the city reflects a view of cyberspace as a dream landscape where moving through the city is like opening a jewel box filled with phantasmagoric images. Cyberspace as heterotopia is a globalized collection of cyberhoods where one can continually search for the "villages" in the city. Such an attitude towards virtual place stands as an alternative to the technocratic, rationalist city.

Utopias were, in effect, circumscribed, planned communities. Cyberspace, on the other hand, acknowledges the urban experience of much of our cultural reality, not in the sense that traditional development theory valorized the urban technological society, but simply by acknowledging that this is where many of us live.

The temporal and spatial differentiation that marks the physical environment of the city produces an experience of aesthetic inexhaustibility. Iris Marion Young (1990) describes how buildings, squares, and the twists and turns of streets and alleys offer an inexhaustible store of individual spaces and things, each with unique aesthetic characteristics. For Young, the modern city is not planned and coherent. Instead, she argues, dwelling in the city means having "a sense of beyond, that there is much human life beyond my experience."[38] The city can never be grasped as a whole. Indeed, perhaps the view of the city life expressed here provides the corrective to Cass Sunstein's understanding of the Internet as a democratically threatening force. The urban image of the city provides an image not only of community but also of an environment where we are confronted with perspectives and opinions that challenge our own. It is a fruitful image to bear in mind.

City life also, for Young, embodies difference as the contrary of the face-to-face ideal expressed by most assertions of community. City life is the "being-together" of strangers who encounter one another, either face to face or through the media, often remaining strangers and yet acknowledging their contiguity in living and the contributions each makes to the others. Is this not the image of heterotopic places?

In the end, by characterizing spatial construction in cyberspace as heterotopic, we acknowledge the creative energy involved in constructing and maintaining symbolic environments. At the same time, by thinking of such constructions collectively as a cityscape, we emphasize the volume of activity already taking place, the irreducibility of this phantasmagoria to a single, all-encompassing logic, and the flexibility that allows us to change aspects of digital cultures as we desire. Cyberspace is a city of dreams, fantasies, and creativity that serves as an example of the more general creative construction of social reality.

The Fortunes of Invention

Returning to our original metaphor, we come full circle in this examination of cyberspace. Looking at the process of invention (or construction) underlying the stories of cyberspace, we see that an evolutionary view of media ecology misses something of the rich interactions involved in social construction. Themes and images persist, are transformed, and raise broad questions about the relationship between communication, mediation, and reality. I want here, in this brief conclusion, to reclaim the idea of the *inventio fortunata*, in order to show what we learn from interactive realism and how we might use the method in media and cultural studies.

Recall the reason for juxtaposing the ghost books of exploration with John Perry Barlow's disenchantment with Internet culture. Barlow has blamed the failure of the Internet as a restorative to democracy on governmental attacks on free speech in the United States and on the coopting of virtual community by market forces. A decade ago Michael Benedikt argued for the need to spatialize cyberspace – to think of it in architectural terms. He laments that to date spatialization has yet to happen. Like Barlow, Benedikt is concerned that the Internet has not given rise to a new utopia.

The fact that the world has not developed into the world Barlow and Benedikt hoped for does not negate the insight that through acts and processes of communication we create the real in the social sense. That is the insight of interactive realism as demonstrated by the development of cyberspace. Columbus pieced together a picture of the world using maps and earlier accounts of the New World. We do the same as we construct models of the social world using representations, metaphors, and models.

THE LESSONS OF INTERACTIVE REALISM

There is a persistent tendency to understand "the Internet" and "cyberspace" as synonyms. The focus in this book has been on the distinction between the Internet (as a technological infrastructure and as an information delivery system) and cyberspace (as a communicative environment). Cyberspace is a psychological space that develops through our use of technology to mediate our communications and our interactions.

The transformative turn chronicled in the preceding pages shows how we have become used to thinking that technology creates new identities, new forms of citizenship, and new worlds. I have characterized this relationship between metaphor, artifact, and experience in terms of a poetics of cyberspace. The dominant characteristics of an Internet-biased understanding of cyberspace can be expressed in what I have called a poetics of "e." The poetics of "e" attributes an evolutionary power to digital technology. It reinforces a Platonic essentialism based on the presumed intimacy between language and reality. From this perspective computer code is the latest, and perhaps ultimate, expression of the world made through language. Finally, the poetics of "e" perpetuates the desire to escape the body through participation in virtual communities. Cyberspace becomes, in this heuristic, a realm of "pure" communication. Instead, I have argued that cyberspace is best understood as a new communicative environment using digital technologies to create new experience.

Benedikt's digitopia is based on an optimistic attitude toward technology and a view of the perfectibility of social order combined with a Platonic rationalism – the perfect social order is the outcome of a disembodied community. Dystopian writing attacks the utopian fantasy of perfect order by challenging the utopian as ideological or by expressing disappointment in a particular utopian project's ultimate failure. Utopianism and dystopianism alike carry traces of the transformative view of technology.

Heterotopian constructions, by contrast, emphasize the symbolic nature of place as an iconic landscape (reproximating space in relation to ongoing, embodied activities). Heterotopian places create safety zones that are set apart from the normal constraints of societal interactions. Cyberspace can be understood as involving a double awareness of displaced, detached, and disembodied communication, as well as a sense of emplacement in a virtual, iconic landscape. Cyberspace as an urban landscape is a reflection of our times, providing dreamlike visions of new identities and communities. It is also like the city, a crowded environment of chance encounters and an unexpected mix of culture and commerce wherein we must be prepared to adapt to rapid change as we negotiate communal and personal space for ourselves. Cyberspace conceived in this way also provides maps for exploring the boundaries of symbolic and perceptual experience.

This is the allure of Plato – that we can engage in some pure and essential form of communication (commercial activity, learning, falling in love) without the mess of bodies. In fact, precisely because this is not the case, cyberspace remains a useful metaphor. It is spatial – we create spaces and opportunities to engage in acts of communication. Through these, we can think more reflexively about issues pertaining to personal and collective identity, society, and mediation.

The concern of this book has been to shift the terms of debate from technological evolutionism and the linguistic determination of subjectivity and reality to the kinds of worlds we construct using the tools at our disposal – metaphors and technologies of representation. I have characterized this dimension of the poetics of cyberspace as a poetics of "mediation." The method of interactive realism looks at the metaphors we use in relation to embodied experience; to the devices, buildings, and artifacts; and to the skills we acquire that affect selfhood and community.

We do live, to a degree, in a world transformed by digital technology. Its ubiquity makes it seem mundane. The frontier has been settled as industries and governments have moved in to codify property rights. Yet are there chinks in the walls surrounding the emerging gated communities of e-commerce? Legal, security, and privacy issues facing the regulation of Internet communication suggest that policymakers do not believe that identity is flexible or dispersed through the communication networks of the world. Governments, financial institutions, and media companies are spending considerable time, energy, and money to link on-line identities to off-line individuals as precisely as possible.

INTERACTIVE REALISM
AND A NEW MEDIA ECOLOGY

What are the possibilities for interactive realism as an approach to media studies? As with weather prediction, we can map the possible terrains of cyberspace, but our predictions about what will actually happen are only educated guesses. In the end, we have no scientific or mystical abilities to bring about desired results. Predictions are dangerous, mainly because they almost inevitably prove embarrassing for their authors in the long run.

I can, however, identify two areas of further research that arise from our discussion of interactive realism and the poetics of cyberspace. First, I have focused the discussion in this book on cyberspace, rather than the Internet. This begs for a complementary analysis of the Internet. There have been several shocks in the development of the Internet since the late 1990s – the rash of media mergers under the clarion call of convergence, followed by the dot-com crash in 1999 and the increased efforts to establish security on the Internet in the wake of September 11. The mergers and crash have created a New Media Economy and an accompanying shift from thinking of the Internet as an unregulatable zone to a new environment where information is considered property and copyright has become a contested regulatory tool. As corporations look for stricter rules regarding Internet content, governments have used September 11 and the emerging New Media Economy to introduce potentially repressive legislation about Internet use. I have begun work on this subject, and a volume accompanying this one is forthcoming.

A second area of research arising from the present study is based on the observation that place, identity, and memory will become sites of emerging and ongoing debate. There is a new materiality of communication – we create spaces of expression and interaction using digital technology. These spaces allow for new forms of shared experience (networked games, personal web pages, commercial and governmental web sites). Further, they have the potential to foster interactions between individuals, cultures, and systems of informal and formal governance that intersect with and extend beyond the new communicative spaces. The aspect of virtuality in communities I am interested in exploring further has to do with how communities negotiate a sense of belonging and participation through mediated interactions. For example, global social movements have developed sophisticated communicative skills for sharing information, mobilizing protests, and creating new forms of protest. Less obvious is the effect that technologies have had on local cultures, "traditional" groups and forms of heritage, and cultural and musical activity. In particular, how do such communities interact with outside communities? How are cultural forms changed as group members adopt new tools of expression? I intend to apply the method of interactive realism to these questions in the future.

Futurist Alvin Toffler once wrote that we experience the future in a perpetual state of culture shock. Yet social change occurs when we foreground the human-constructedness of the social world. This is, ultimately, a creative act, since our tendency seems to be to reify (naturalize through a process of habituation or sedimentation) the conditions of the social world in order to live in it as a sustainable environment. Such a process is what we witness as cyberspace is transformed into the commercial space of the New Media Economy.

In cyberspace we construct interactive maps of possible iconic landscapes; we build places where we might live part of our lives. The crucial point to remember is the creative energy involved in this, as in all social construction. As John O'Neill puts it, the ordinary person needs to remember that society and its future technologies of the mind, body, and political economy "have not really come a long way without the enormous legacy of past human efforts."[1]

The digital is not a separate realm – it is a conceptual suit we put on, a house we enter, an arcade we visit for a while, a poem we recite in our play at culture. To argue a new model of the self that is a break with the past passes judgment that is unnecessary and falls into a reductive will to erase. Digitopia can never completely erase the past – our activities "carry over" traces of where we have been, what we have done, and who we have been, to enrich the present and to serve as material with which to actively build the future. Permanence and temporality take on a human scale.

Cyberspace seen as an artifact like the built environment emphasizes the understanding of media as tools that allow us to create meaning in the world. We play *inside* Plato's Cave, yet we can take pride and pleasure in the fact that we can actively participate in its construction in the first place. If we ignore the "real" world, it is because we assume our images preclude the kind of introspection or retrospection that reminds us of their fabrication. Stated in this way, technology could serve as a kind of forgetting (on the psychological level) and as a manifestation of the will to erase traces of past human effort (at the social level). However, these acts of forgetting are not inevitable. Instead, reification of the technological elements of social life involves social projects to make us forget. Images and representations do not distance us from the true nature of reality. They expand our horizons.

The worlds created through digital technology are real to the extent that we choose to play their games. The question is to consider the value of the game among other possibilities. Interpretation, since it depends on the historical and social circumstances that drive the "need" to interpret, is a never-ending process. This leaves many questions unresolved, but the quest to understand persists. In the end, even John Perry Barlow may come around. I find that hopeful.

Notes

INTRODUCTION

1 Hakluyt, *Principal Navigations*, 301–4; see also Holand, *Explorations in America before Columbus*, 282–5.
2 Such a view is clearly expressed by communications scholar James Carey, who identifies communications as the instrument by which we construct reality. For Carey, "to speak or to write or to program ... is not merely to pick up a tool or to exercise a skill. It is to constitute a world, to bring a world into existence, and to simultaneously constitute a self." Carey, "The Language of Technology," 23, 25.
3 Barlow, "Declaration of Independence of Cyberspace."
4 Sanders, "Mr Wrong," F4.
5 Ibid.

CHAPTER ONE

1 Gibson, *Neuromancer*.
2 Silver, "Looking Backwards, Looking Forwards," 19–30.
3 IBM started using the word "virtual" in the late 1960s to refer to any nonphysical link between processes or machines, such as virtual memory (random-access memory being simulated using disk drives). Pimentel and Teixeira, *Virtual Reality,* 288.
4 Burke, "Auscultation, Creation, and Revision," 66. Alfred Schutz and others have argued that we *experience* multiple realities – virtual worlds. See Schutz, "On Multiple Realities," 533–76.
5 Krol, *The Whole Internet*.
6 *Canadian Technology,* May 2000, 12.

7 Statistics Canada, *Household Internet Survey.*

8 Samoriski, *Issues in Cyberspace.*

9 Witherford, *CyberMarx*. See also Shade, "A Gendered Perspective on Access to the Information Infrastructure."

10 Rheingold, *The Virtual Community.*

11 Murray, *Hamlet on the Holodeck*, 72–85. Brenda Laurel (1992) discusses computer and virtual reality as an opportunity for a new kind of drama. Laurel, *Computers as Theatre*. Designer Mark Stephen Meadows (2003) urges designers of online media to think of web sites using the organizing metaphor of "interactive narrative." Meadows, *Pause and Effect.*

12 Rucker, Sirius, and Mu, *Mondo 2000*, 264.

13 Benedikt, *Cyberspace: First Steps*, 14–16. See also Rushkoff, *Cyberia*, 2.

14 See Strate, Jacobson, and Gibson, "Surveying the Electronic Landscape," 4.

15 A similar view has been articulated by philosopher James K. Feibleman (1982), who defines technology as "the production and use of artifacts, and artifacts as materials altered through human agency for human uses." Feibleman, *Technology and Reality*, 4.

16 Ibid.

17 In what follows I will explore the social constructivist position on the nature of social being, a position that claims that "people and what they do are artifacts." See Harré, *Social Being*, 2, 3.

18 Von Glasersfeld, "Radical Constructivism," 20. For a discussion of objectivist epistemology as contrasted with experientialism, see Lakoff *Women, Fire and Dangerous Things*, 266–7, and Johnson, *Body in the Mind*, x–xvii.

19 Rorty, *Consequences of Pragmatism*, xviii.

20 Harré and Gillett, *Discursive Mind*. For a brief history of constructivism in the social sciences, see Sarkin and Kitsuse, "Prologue to *Constructing the Social*," 1–18.

21 Sarkin and Kitsuse, "Prologue to *Constructing the Social*," 18.

22 On this subject, Lynn Hoffman's (1990) view goes beyond conventional "constructivism" or "constructionism." She argues that societies construct the lenses through which their members experience the world. Hoffman, "Constructing Social Realities," 1–12. On the shift from an experiential to a social epistemology, Freedman and Combs (1996) emphasize "a shift from focussing on how an individual person constructs a model of reality from individual experience to focus on how people interact to construct modify and maintain what their society holds to be true." Freedman and Combs, *Narrative Therapy*, 26–7.

23 Weingarten, "The Discourses of Intimacy," 289.

24 A text can function as an object for decoding or as a script for performance. See Collins, *Poetics of the Mind's Eye.*

25 Kelly, "The Language of Hypothesis," 147–62.

26 Black, "More about Metaphor," 28. George Lakoff and Mark Turner (1989) call this the "Literal Theory Position." See Lakoff and Turner, *More than Cool Reason.* The preference for the literal over the figurative use of language is evident in Bacon, Locke, Hobbes, Mill, and Bentham, all of whom call for an austere precision and plainness of language. Hobbes and Locke both argue that metaphor is an abuse of ordinary language and that reason and science are separate from art and imagination.

27 See Johnson, *The Body in the Mind,* 67. For the objectivist position (Johnson calls this the "literal core" theory), metaphors assert cross-categorical identities that do not exist objectively in reality. Thus, for the objectivist there is no usefulness in metaphor.

28 See Black, *Models and Metaphors,* 44–5. See also Richards, *Philosophy of Rhetoric,* and Davidson, *Inquiries into Truth and Interpretation,* 245–64. See Lakoff and Johnson, *Metaphors We Live By;* Lakoff, *Women, Fire, and Dangerous Things;* and Johnson, *Body in the Mind,* for the development of an experiential basis for meaning.

29 See Watzlawick, Beavin, and Jackson, *Pragmatics of Human Communication,* 61, 66–7. See also Wilden, *System and Structure,* 155.

30 Fiurama, *The Metaphoric Process,* 67.

31 Ibid., 64–5.

32 Others have explored the relationship between poetics and knowledge. For example, Richard Brown develops a constructivist argument that claims a good sociological account has internal coherence, is aesthetically pleasing, and is a good fit in the corpus of other texts and in describing a situation. Paul Atkinson, elaborating on Brown's work, suggests that sociology is as much about writing accounts as about discovering truths about an objective world. For Brown, all ways of knowing the world are symbolic and perspectival. One implication of this view is that different symbolic forms create their own domains of application. Arguing that science and art are symbolic forms makes possible a reinterpretation of both correspondence theories (theories of how symbolic forms copy or resemble some reality external to them) and cogency theories (theories about the internal properties of a scientific theory or work of art). Brown argues that the artist and the scientist are both involved in the same activity of making paradigms

through which experience becomes intelligible. Brown, *Poetic for Sociology*, 24–5. See also Atkinson, *The Ethnographic Imagination*.

CHAPTER TWO

1 Gore, "A National Vision," 188–9. See also Johnson, *Getting Canada Online*.
2 McQuail, *Mass Communication Theory*, 61.
3 Carey, "The Language of Technology," 19. Examples of the media ecology position include Ong's oral, literate, or electronic culture, Mazlish's four discontinuities, and Beniger's agrarian, industrial, and control revolutions. Ong, *Orality and Literacy*; Mazlish, "Fourth Discontinuity," 217–19. See also Mazlish, *Fourth Discontinuity: The Co-evolution of Humans and Machines*, and Beniger, *Control Revolution*.
4 Ong, *Orality and Literacy*, 105. See also Havelock, *Preface to Plato*.
5 McLuhan, *Understanding Media*. The insight was McLuhan's but has remained part of the discourse of technological development, particularly the development of computers as a communications medium.
6 Innis, *Bias of Communication*, 134.
7 McLuhan and Fiore, *War and Peace in the Global Village*, 55. McLuhan's view is common in assessments of the social impact of computers. Frederick Williams, for example, compares earlier communications technologies, which extended the range of human messages, with the computer, which allows us to extend our capability to act upon messages. Williams, *Communications Revolution*.
8 Miller, "Technology as a Form of Consciousness," 229.
9 Noam, "Media Concentration in the United States."
10 Diebert, *Parchment, Printing, and Hypermedia*, 17–18.
11 Bell, *Post-Industrial Society*. See also Fuller, *Critical Path*, and Toffler, *Future Shock; The Third Wave*; and *Powershift*.
12 Pacey, *Culture of Technology*, 2.
13 Cooper, "Technology: Liberation or Enslavement?" 10.
14 Turkle, *The Second Self*, 14. See also Suchman, *Plans and Situated Actions*, 7.
15 See Appadurai, "Disjuncture and Difference," and Vattimo, *The End of Modernity*.
16 Cairncross, *The Death of Distance*.
17 Dizard, *The Coming Information Age*, xiii.
18 See, for example, Carey, "Technology and Ideology," and Mattelart, *Networking the World, 1794–2000*.

19 Martin-Barbero, *Communication, Culture and Hegemony.*
20 Kroker and Weinstein, *Data Trash*, 7. See also Doheny-Farina, *The Wired Neighborhood.*
21 This view of technology is what Albert Borgmann calls the *substantive* view, in which technology appears as a force in its own right and shapes societies and values from the ground up. Its proponents are usually antitechnologists like Jacques Ellul or Martin Heidegger. David E. Cooper calls this view technology as enslavement, or the Frankenstein thesis. Technology should control nature but rises against us. See Borgman, *Technology and Everyday Life.* Lewis Mumford argued that technology is inimical to human development and fulfilment. While Mumford's early work predicted a humane evolution based on establishing equilibrium between technological and social development, in later works he saw instead an information-based bureaucracy running a military-industrial complex. Mumford, *Technics and Civilization.* For a taste of Mumford's early optimism, see 431–5. For examples of his later pessimism see *Pentagon of Power*, 293–9, and *The Myth of the Machine.* Jacques Ellul made the case that technology is out of control because it proceeds according to a logic that is independent of human needs and concerns. For Ellul, technology is an autonomous and uncontrollable force. Langdon Winner, expanding on Ellul's technological determinism, argues that technology is not a neutral means to human ends but that it creates an all-encompassing system that imposes its patterns on every aspect of life and thought. Ellul, *Technological Society.* See also Winner, *Autonomous Technology.*
22 Pacey, *Culture of Technology*, 172.
23 Robins, "Cyberspace and the World We Live In," 136, 139.
24 See Witherford, *CyberMarx*, 237.
25 Eisenstein, *Global Obscenities*, 13, 17.
26 See also Saco, *Cybering Democracy.*
27 See Wood, *Post-Intellectualism and the Decline of Democracy* for a clear expression of the culturalist perspective.
28 Postman, *Amusing Ourselves to Death.*
29 Heidegger, "The Question concerning Technology," 318.
30 Grant, *Philosophy in the Mass Age*, and *Technology and Empire.* For an introduction to the existentially based thought of this Canadian philosopher see Kroker, *Technology and the Canadian Mind*, and Angus, *A Border Within.*
31 Both are also, according to Bruce Gronbeck, interpretations of life set out purposively by rhetors "who want to control the way we envisage

ourselves and the world." Gronbeck, "Communication Technology, Consciousness, and Culture," 14.

32 For contemporary proponents of media ecologies see Heim, *Electric Language*, and *Metaphysics of Virtual Reality* and Bolter, *Writing Space*.

33 Heim, *Electric Language*, 59.

34 Stamps, *Unthinking Modernity*.

35 For an extended discussion of the relationship between digital technologies, romanticism, and language, see Coyne, *Technoromanticism*.

36 Poster's version of postmodernism does not lie far outside the mainstream of American communications theory. For example, Chesebro and Bertelsen (1996) valorize communications technology in terms similar to the mode of information concept. For them, the mode of communication (traditionally the channel) offers a perspective for examining the entire communication process. Communication technologies are also types of symbolic action. Technological processes can change power relations, material outcomes, and the human environment. Realignments in these areas create new languages for describing changes and suggest new priorities or values and recommendations for action. New technology can also create an aesthetic unique and appropriate to it. See Chesebro and Bertelsen, *Analyzing Media*, 187.

37 Poster, *Second Media Age*, 3.

38 Ibid., 7–8.

39 Poster, *Mode of Information*, 6.

40 Ibid., 111.

41 Sociologist Sherry Turkle also claims that subjectivity becomes fluid through interaction with technology. She argues that in computer-mediated communication, "the self is multiple, fluid, and constituted in interaction with machine connections; it is made and transformed by language; sexual congress is an exchange of signifiers; and understanding follows from navigation and tinkering rather than analysis." Turkle, *Life on the Screen*, 15.

42 Poster, *Foucault, Marxism, and History,* 166–7.

43 Marx's view of language as practical consciousness is implicit in Poster's mode of information. For Marx, "Language is as old as consciousness, language is practical consciousness ... for language, like consciousness, only arises from the need, the necessity, of intercourse with other men." Thus, for Marx and Engels language is material, as it arises as an instrument to satisfy a human need – the need for social intercourse and consciousness is from the very beginning a social product. Marx and Engels, *The German Ideology*, 19.

44　Poster, *Mode of Information*, 8.

45　See Lévi-Strauss, *Structural Anthropology*. See also Althusser, *For Marx*.

46　Poster, *Mode of Information*, 3.

47　Poster, "Cyberdemocracy."

48　Poster, *What's the Matter with the Internet*.

49　Poster, *Second Media Age*, 30.

50　Vattimo, *End of Modernity*, 9.

51　Appadurai, *Modernity at Large*, 9–10.

52　Suspicion of the body appears as a form of neoplatonism in St Augustine and St Paul. See Campbell, *Masks of God*, 148. Campbell detects in St Augustine a Gnostic-Manichean revulsion towards the flesh. For Augustine God is concerned not with the body but with the "life of souls." *Confessions*, book 3, chapter 6. The tension between flesh and Spirit is a consequence of the corruption of human nature after the fall. He writes, "the soul revelling in its own liberty, and scorning to serve God, was itself deprived of the command it had formerly maintained over the body." *City of God*, book 13, chapter 13. According to Charles Levin, the Christian view of the body as flesh continues today as an ontological suspicion of embodiment unwittingly maintained by the social sciences. Levin, "Entre la chair et l'esprit," 67. The Christian legacy of aestheticism, Levin argues, laid the foundation for the nature-culture split, which has been the conceptual basis of industrial and postindustrial culture. The body is seen as the embodiment of random natural forces that must be domesticated and socialized by the artificial order we have created out of "pure" mind or spirit (76–7).

53　See Roszak, *The Cult of Information*. See also Franklin, *Real World of Technology*. Franklin argues that the danger of technology lies in the creation of a "culture of compliance" wherein society no longer challenges the values of rationalism and instrumentality.

54　Writing from a different perspective than Roszak, Jean Baudrillard comes to a similar conclusion. Baudrillard argues that the entire prosthetic and protective environment becomes a substitute for the natural, biological body. Baudrillard writes, "The increasingly cerebral capacities of machines would normally lead to a *technological purification* of the body." Baudrillard, *Ecstasy of Communication*.

55　A more optimistic appropriation of Heidegger's *Gestell* appears in Don Ihde's concept of *instrumental reason*. Simply put, Ihde argues that our technologies shape what we know about the world. Technology is part of the equipment we use in our engagement with the world. For Heim and Bolter, and Poster, as well, our symbolic system and its materialization in electronic form shapes the way the world is revealed. See Ihde, *Technology and the Lifeworld*, 26.

CHAPTER THREE

1 Black, *Models and Metaphors*, 41–2.
2 See Bettelheim, "Joey," *The Informed Heart*, and *The Empty Fortress*. Since his death in 1990 Bettelheim has been a subject of controversy. Three months after his death particularly vitriolic accounts of verbal and physical abuse were given by several former students of the Sonia Shankman Orthogenic School, the institution Bettelheim ran for over twenty years. In response, equally intense letters by former colleagues began to appear in his defence, leaving the issue unresolved. The controversy does not alter the usefulness of Bettelheim's work for this project, since he represents a common and pessimistic attitude towards the alienating power of technology. He addresses common concerns about the fear of technology in a practical setting. The alienation he perceives in society is in the case of Joey a symptom of his psychosis. In spite of a general evenhandedness in his case studies, Bettelheim tends to cast the human and the mechanical in terms of his concentration camp experience (the prisoner and the guard). Ultimately, his treatment of the mechanical angst involves fostering the humanity of the patient – a fact that is most clearly apparent in the Joey's "cure" through a symbolic rebirth. For a balanced account of Bettelheim's life and the controversy following his death, see Sutton, *Bettelheim*.
3 O'Neill, *Five Bodies*.
4 Turkle, *The Second Self*, 29–63.
5 Bettelheim, *Informed Heart*, 51–65.
6 Bettelheim, *Empty Fortress*, 234.
7 Bettelheim, "Joey," 438.
8 See Sutton, *Bettelheim*, 234.
9 Bettelheim, *Empty Fortress*, 13–49.
10 Ibid., 25.
11 Ibid., 37.
12 Bettelheim does not use the term "skill set," nor does he emphasize, as do I, that there are self-constituting skills other than linguistic communication.
13 Bettelheim, *Empty Fortress*, 233–9.
14 Bettelheim, "Joey," 438.
15 Bettelheim, *Empty Fortress*, 238, emphasis added.

16 Bertalanffy, *General System Theory*, 188.

17 As Fodor (1994) puts it, "There is no computation without representation." Fodor, "The Mind-Body Problem," 38.

18 Rucker, *Mind Tools*.

19 Newell and Simon, "Computer Science as Empirical Enquiry."

20 Simon, "Patterned Matter."

21 21. Turkle, *Second Self*, 247.

22 Two systems that seem quite different can be essentially the same if there is formal equivalence. Equivalent systems can be very different on the surface, so long as appropriate correspondences can be found. If one structure produces a certain effect and an entirely different structure generates the same event, the two structures are said to be isomorphic. See Newell and Simon, *Human Problem Solving*.

23 Lupton, "The Embodied Computer/User," 100.

24 Ibid.

25 Ibid.

26 Hockenberry, "Fearless Entrepreneur," 105.

27 Plant, *Zeros + Ones*, 36.

28 Technological evolutionary theories are common to cyberpunk fiction about new technologies and to what might be termed the folk psychology of cyberspace. See Sponsler, "Cyberpunk"; Hollinger, "Cybernetic Deconstructions."

29 Lanier and Biocca, "Future of Virtual Reality," 162.

30 Freud, *Civilization and its Discontents*.

31 Tomas, "Old Rituals for New Space," 32. See also Howes, *Varieties of Sensory Experience*, 170.

32 Tomas, "Old Rituals for New Space," 32–6.

33 See also Levy, *Collective Intelligence*.

34 La Barre, *Human Animal*, 89–90.

35 Hall, *Hidden Dimension*, 3–4.

36 Jastrow, *Enchanted Loom*, 162.

37 Hardison, *Disappearing through the Skylight*, 685.

38 Sontag (1977) argues that the sense of presence is weakened by a false sense that the mediated world is available to us. Meyrowitz (1985) similarly argues that there is a weakening of the sense of place in the face of mediated culture. See Sontag, *On Photography*, and Meyrowitz, *No Sense of Place*.

39 Locke, *Essay concerning Human Understandin*, 23.

40 Ibid., 228.

41 Newell, "The Knowledge Level," 88.

42 Newell and Simon, "Computer Science as Empirical Enquiry," 121.

43 Merleau-Ponty, *Phenomenology of Perception*, xxi.

44 Merleau-Ponty, *Primacy of Perception*, 4–5.

45 O'Neill, *Five Bodies*, 16–17. See also O'Neill, *Perception, Expression, and History.*

46 O'Neill writes, "We seek out other bodies in society as mirrors of ourselves ... Our own bodies are the permeable ground of all social behavior ... Here is *the incarnate bond between self and society*" (*Five Bodies*, 22–3).

47 Lingis, "The Phantom Equator," 234–5.

48 Hunt, *Nature of Consciousness*, 64.

49 Ibid., 183–4, 111–26.

50 Gibson, *The Ecological Approach*, 200 (emphasis in original). Concerning the activity of the observer, Gibson was chiefly interested in overt activity: in eye movement, head movements, body movements, and any form of action that made it possible to sample new aspects of the optical array. Others, including Neisser, have been more concerned with covert activity, that is, with what the nervous system does when we perceive. Neisser points out that it is often assumed that the ecological approach is incompatible with neuroscience. "That assumption," he writes, "is quite unjustified: the brain is just as real as the environment, and there is every reason to be interested in how it works. Neisser, "Without Perception," 158.

51 Neisser, *Cognition and Reality*, 20–1. See Harré and Gillet, *The Discursive Mind*, 166–70, for a critical discussion of the role of direct perception in cognition.

52 Neisser, "Without Perception," 152.

53 Ibid., 151.

54 Ibid., 158.

55 Ibid., 148. Dreyfus criticizes Neisser for claiming that perception has gestalt qualities and then making the further claim that it involves "a plan as a description of a response." In other words, claims Dreyfus, Neisser slides from gestalt perception to plan. Neisser argues that the brain makes use of two independent systems of perception, which provides a way out of such criticism – there is not a *single* mode of visual perception.

56 Searle, "Minds, Brains and Programs," 304–5. Like Searle, Hubert Dreyfus places cognitive science in the Platonic and Cartesian tradition, in which the body is perceived to get in the way of intelligence

and reason, rather than being in any way indispensable for it. Dreyfus, *What Computers Can't Do*, 147.

57 Rosenfield, *Strange, Familiar, and Forgotten*.

58 Edelman, *Bright Air, Brilliant Fire*.

59 Ibid., 234.

60 Neisser, "Without Perception," 161.

61 Varella, Thompson, and Rosch, *Embodied Mind*, 172–3. There is much here in common with Edelman's contention that the brain gets wired after repeated action. There is also much in common with Gibson's ecological perception. But in the end, Varella, Thompson, and Rosch distance themselves from any notion of direct perception. Whereas Gibson claims that the environment is independent (we can all see the same things) and that perception is direct detection, the authors claim that the environment is enacted (we create it) and that perception is sensorimotor enactment. Ibid., 203–4.

62 Johnson, *Body in the Mind*, 75–9, 98.

63 See Varella, Thompson, and Rosch, *Embodied Mind*, 147–8.

64 Ibid., 148.

65 Ibid., 164.

66 Papert, *Children's Machine*, 197.

67 Ibid., 198.

68 Ibid., 199.

69 Uspensky, *Poetics of Composition*, 135n.

70 The metaphor of the artist at work has been used to describe the task of the historian. See Ricœur, *Reality of the Historical Past*, 1–2. The modern system of perspective, based on the realization of a fixed distance between the eye and the object, enables the artist to build up comprehensive and consistent images of visible things. The modern idea of history is based on an intellectual distance between the present and the past that enables the scholar to build up comprehensive and consistent pictures of bygone periods. Panofsky, *Meaning in the Visual Arts*, 51.

71 See Bourdieu, *In Other Words*. In *Electric Language* Michael Heim discusses the posture of scientific detachment in the context of transformative media (60). However, something new occurs with electronic media: these media reawaken impulses of the oral culture. The personal distance and individualism fostered by the print culture seem to be overcome by a further elaboration of communication technology (ibid., 67).

72 Romanyshyn, *Technology as Symptom and Dream*, 31.

73 Crary, *Techniques of the Observer*.

74 Cook, *Movement in Two Dimensions*, 31.

75 Here is a description of the spectacle of the diorama as viewed by an English visitor:

> The visitors, after passing through a gloomy anteroom, were ushered into a circular chamber, apparently quite dark. One or two small shrouded lamps placed on the floor served dimly to light the way to a few descending steps and the voice of an invisible guide gave directions to walk forward. The eye soon became sufficiently accustomed to the darkness to distinguish the objects around and to perceive that there were several persons seated on benches opposite an open space resembling a large window. Through the window was seen the interior of Canterbury Cathedral undergoing partial repair with the figures of two or three workmen resting from their labours. The pillars, the arches, the stone floor and steps, stained with damp, and the planks of wood strewn on the ground, all seemed to stand out in bold relief, so solidly as not to admit a doubt of their substantiality, whilst the floor extended to the distant pillars, temptingly inviting the tread of exploring footsteps. Few could be persuaded that what they saw was a mere painting on a flat surface. The impression was strengthened by perceiving the light and shadows change, as if clouds were passing over the sun, the rays of which occasionally shone through the windows, casting coloured shadows on the floor. Then shortly the lightness would disappear and the former gloom again obscure the objects that had been momentarily illumined. The illusion was rendered more perfect by the sensitive condition of the eye in the darkness of the surrounding chamber.
>
> While gazing in rapt admiration at the architectural beauties of the cathedral the spectator's attention was disturbed by sounds underground. He became conscious that the scene before him was slowly moving away and he obtained a glimpse of another and very difficult prospect, which gradually advanced until it was completely developed and the cathedral had disappeared. What he now saw was a valley surrounded by high mountains capped with snow.
> (Quoted in Cook, *Movement in Two Dimensions*, 35–7)

76 Friedberg, *Window Shopping*, 17.

77 Foucault, *Discipline and Punish*, 195–228. A number of scholars have used the panopticon as the model of the global information system. See Menzies, *Fast Forward and Out of Control*; Mosco, *The Pay-Per*

Society; and Wilson, *Technologies of Control*. Mark Poster (in conversation with the author) also invokes the panopticon as an example of the totalizing power of the virtual. Because we never know when someone may be watching, we eventually come to assume that someone is watching all the time.

78 Friedberg, *Window Shopping*, 22.

79 See Sobchack, "Scene of the Screen," 84.

80 Bazin, "Total Cinema," 21.

81 Bazin, "Ontology of the Photographic Image," 13.

82 Rudolph Arnheim bases his view of photography squarely on automatism. Because in photography physical objects print their image by means of the optical and chemical action of light, Arnheim argues that photographs have "an authenticity from which painting is banned from birth." See Arnheim "Nature of Photography," 154.

83 Bazin, "Ontology," 14.

84 Sontag, *On Photography*, 22. To see how this attitude fits with the "cybernetic" view described in earlier chapters, recall that the goal of cybernetics is control of systems by controlling information. See Beniger, *Control Revolution*. See also Cavell, *The World Viewed*, 23.

85 Metz, "Photography and Fetish," 156.

86 Willis,"Digitization and Photography," 201–2.

87 *The Crow* (Independent, Alex Proyas, U.S., 1994). The film was produced by Paramount Studios, who pulled out of production after the death of star Brandon Lee. Only the efforts of producer Ed Pressman to find distributors led to the film's release on 13 May 1994.

88 Interview on *Entertainment Tonight*, Monday, 16 May 1994.

89 George Lucas, in Magid, "Master of His Own Universe," 27.

90 Pollock, "Missing Women."

91 Bourdieu, *Photography*, 77.

92 Goodman, *Languages of Art*, 5, 38. See also Gombrich, *Art and Illusion*.

93 Michotte, "Character of 'Reality,'" 209.

94 A number of feminist scholars have discussed the relationship between power, language, and social construction. See Hunt, "Law Confronts Postmodernism"; Halley, "Politics of the Closet"; and Minow, *Making All the Difference*.

95 Lauretis, *Alice Doesn't*.

96 Clynes and Kline, "Cyborgs and Space."

97 Levidow and Robins, "Military Information Society," 172–3.

98 Erik Davis describes our fascination with technology in terms of a "secret history" of the mystical impulse to use technology as a means

past the body to the sacred. He suggests that the first cyborgs were probably the shamans. Davis, *Techgnosis*.

99   Bailey, "Virtual Skin." See also Turkle, *Life on the Screen*.
100 Haraway, "A Manifesto for Cyborgs," 82–3.
101 Ibid., 95.
102 Poster, *What's the Matter*, 181.
103 "In their play children substitute actions (which were the original precursors of thoughts) for words. *Acting* plays a prominent part." Klein, *Selected Melanie Klein*, 65.
104 Ibid., 98.
105 Haraway, "Actors are Cyborg," 21–2. See also Haraway, *Simians, Cyborgs, and Woman*.
106 Haraway, "Cyborg Manifesto," 73.
107 Bruce Sterling, quoted in Hollinger, "Cybernetic Deconstructions," 31.
108 A similar rhetorical strategy appears in the discourse of deep ecology, which reinforces metaphysical realism even as it appears radical. Van Wyck, *Primitives in the Wilderness*.
109 Foucault, *Foucault Live*, 313.

CHAPTER FOUR

1   Roszak, *Cult of Information*, 70.
2   Robinett, "Synthetic Experience."
3   Anthropologist and communication researcher Gregory Bateson asks a similar question about the boundary between the self and the outside world. Bateson writes, "what about 'me'? Suppose I am a blind man, and I use a stick. I go tap, tap, tap. Where do *I* start? Is my mental system bounded at the handle of the stick? Is it bounded by my skin? Does it start halfway up the stick? Does it start at the tip of the stick?" Bateson, *Ecology of Mind*, 458–9.
4   Poster, *Second Media Age*, 59.
5   Steuer, "Defining Virtual Reality." Frank Biocca suggests that virtual reality can be defined as a psychological variable, "as the environment created by a computer or other media, an environment in which the user feels *present*." Biocca, "Communication within Virtual Reality."
6   Akin et al., "Space applications of Automation." See also Johnsen and Corliss, *Teleoperators*.
7   Loomis, "Distal Attribution," 117.
8   Ibid., 116.
9   Ibid.

10 Held and Durlach, "Telepresence."

11 Hector, "Being There," 262.

12 Ibid., 262, 264.

13 Ibid., 265.

14 Hall, *Hidden Dimension*, 188.

15 Hall, *Silent Language*, 28, 37–8.

16 Duplantier, "Archetypal Communication," 34.

17 Ibid., 36.

18 Beniger, "Growth of Pseudo-community," 369. Earlier, John Dewey argued that the major obstacles to creating a public sphere (a discursive and dialogic social space in which various social groups could find common ground) were the mass media, which diverted public concern from political concerns; the bureaucratization of politics; the geographical mobility of people; and the cultural lag in ideas, ideals, and symbols, which results in dysfunctional communication. Dewey, *Public and Its Problems*, 137.

19 Saco, *Cybering Democracy*, 74.

20 Poster, *Second Media Age*, 60.

21 As Jarvie argues, by confronting ourselves, playfully, with the seemingly real and thereby "limning the boundary-line between the real and the unreal," we thus continually test our sense of reality. Jarvie, *Philosophy of the Film*, 55.

22 Bettelheim, *Freud's Vienna*, 115–16.

23 Clover, *Her Body, Himself.*

24 See Barney, *Prometheus Wired.*

25 Bolter, *Writing Space.*

26 Bolter and Grusin, "Re-mediation," 340. See Poster, *What's the Matter with the Internet*, chapter 3, for a similar critique of Bolter's concept of re-mediation.

27 Bolter, *Writing Space*, 224–6.

28 Roscoe, "Construction of the Audience," 680.

29 Downes, "The Medium Vanishes?"

30 Bolter, *Writing Space*, 227–8.

31 Cooper and Berdayes, "Information Highway," 104.

32 Bormann, "Symbolic Convergence Theory," 129–30.

33 Fiske, *Postmodernism and Television*, 54.

34 Bromberg, "Contradiction in Cyberspace," 125.

35 Giddens, *Consequences of Modernity.*

36 Appadurai, *Modernity at Large*, 54. Harold Lasswell has also argued that an effective information and communications system has an

important role to play in the creation (a convergence) of global values. Lasswell actually promotes the desirability of a differentiated yet unified global culture supported by media images. See Lasswell, *Communications in a Divided World*, and "Future of World Communication and Propaganda," 528.

37 MacKinnon, "Searching for the Leviathan in Usenet."
38 Ibid., 114–15.
39 Rheingold, "Slice of Life," 62.
40 Poster, "Cyberdemocracy."
41 Jones, *CyberSociety*, 11.
42 Ibid., 31.
43 Ibid., 10.
44 Jones, *Virtual Culture*, 9.
45 Licklider and Taylor, "Computer as a Communication Device," 30.
46 Rheingold, "Slice of Life," 61.
47 Finn, "Helping Processes," 222.
48 Snydnes, "Internet as Social Medium."
49 Finn, "Helping Processes," 222.
50 Kolko, "Representing Bodies," 181.
51 Ibid., 177.
52 Healy, "Cyberspace and Place," 62.
53 Ibid., 63.
54 Ayers, "Comparing Collective Identity."
55 Selnow, *Electronic Whistle-Stops*.
56 Sunstein, *Republic.com*.
57 Curran, "Mass Media and Democracy Revisited," 92.
58 See, for example, Conor Cruise O'Brien's attack on the role of media in diluting the democratic functioning of Western politics. O'Brien blames the media for creating politics in the image of a spectacle. Thus, our political processes are beyond our control and become little more than myth understood as deception of the masses by powerful industrial and political elites. See O'Brien, *Eve of Millenium*.
59 Robins, "Cyberspace and the World We Live In," 151.
60 There is a thick tradition on the relationships between a particular mode of communication (characterized by the dominance of a particular medium) and forms of social organization. Usually, this literature takes a technologically deterministic view that is either critical of mass society or nostalgic for some form of premodern social grouping. See Meyrowitz, *No Sense of Place*.
61 Habermas, *Structural Transformation*.

62 See van Wyck, *Primitives in the Wilderness*, for a critique of the foundationalist fallacy characteristic of the deep ecology movement's rhetoric.

63 Cited in Damer, *Avatars!* 12.

64 Dibble, "Rape in Cyberspace," 36.

65 Ibid., 38.

66 Ibid.

67 Ibid., 40, 42.

68 Nancy, "Virtual Rape Consequences."

69 Dibble, "Rape in Cyberspace," 40.

70 Lessig, *Code*, 20.

71 Miller, "Game Addict."

72 Huizinga, *Homo Ludens.*

73 Ibid., 9.

74 Ibid., 10.

75 MacKinnon, "Punishing the Persona."

76 Mnookin, "Virtual(ly) Law."

77 Rheingold, "Community Development," 173–4.

78 I wish to thank my friend and colleague Richard Janda for this insight.

79 Warner, *Letters of the Republic,* 9.

80 Human Rights Watch, "Electrifying Speech."

81 The visits to Kapor and Barlow had nothing to do with the larger hacker crackdown. See Quittner, "The Merry Pranksters."

82 Barlow, "Law Comes to Cyberspace," 332.

83 Maloney, "Does Digital Equal Free," 34.

84 Kapor and Barlow, "Across the Electronic Frontier."

85 Ibid.

86 Ibid.

87 Quoted in Meyer, "Fascism in the Cyberstate," 41.

88 Quittner, "The Merry Pranksters."

89 For Barlow, as well, Internet culture must be protected by "physical governments." See Barlow, "Is There a There in Cyberspace?"

90 Rose, "Cyberspace and the Legal Matrix."

91 See Poster, "Cyberdemocracy."

92 Kline, Witherford, and de Peuter, *Digital Play,* 186.

93 Kim, "Killers Have More Fun," 197.

94 Kline, Dyer-Witherford, and de Peuter, *Digital Play,* 162.

95 Raph Koster, lead designer for *Ultima Online*, interviewed by Meadows, in *Pause and Effect,* 198.

96 Ibid., 198.

97 Quoted in Kline, Dyer-Witherford, and de Peuter, *Digital Play*, 162.

98 Ibid., 163.

CHAPTER FIVE

1 Jakle, "Social Stereotypes and Place Images," 83.

2 Foucault, "Questions of Geography," 70.

3 See Castells, *The Informational City*, 124.

4 Harvey, *The Limits to Capital*; Massey, *Geography Matters!* One of the most influential collections of social theory and spatial concerns from the period is Gregory and Urry, *Social Relations and Spatial Structures*.

5 Janelle, "Global Interdependence," 67.

6 Dyck, "Notes on Feminist Research," 237.

7 Zukin, *Landscapes of Power*, 268.

8 See Jakle, "Small Towns as Historical Places," 82–3.

9 Williams, "Constructing Economic Space."

10 Lefebvre, *Production of Space*, 46–8.

11 Williams, *Materialism and Culture*, 32.

12 Mattelart, *Networking the World*, viii.

13 Winner, *Autonomous Technology*, 26.

14 Ibid., 26.

15 Bell, "Social Framework," 40.

16 According to philosopher Paul Ricœur, ideologies accommodate themselves to a reality that they justify and dissimulate, whereas utopias directly attack and explode reality. Ricœur, *From Text to Action*, 264.

17 Klaic, *Plot of The Future*, 32.

18 Winner, *Autonomous Technology*, 45. For Patrick Geddes, electricity was the key to a great transformation, a future utopia in which politics and ideologies pass away and humans and nature enter into a new partnership in "a world redesigned to resemble a garden." Quoted in Carey and Quirk, "History of the Future," 184–5. Lewis Mumford, following Geddes, predicted a future where a final balance could be achieved between town and country, industry and agriculture. Mumford's early optimistic forecasts were popularized by later writers such as Alvin Toffler for whom the new society has "broken irretrievably with the past," surpassing geography and history. The future is envisioned as a new realm of dispensation from the consequences of the Industrial Revolution.

19 Slade, "American Writers and American Invention," 38. This classification calls to mind Marx's concept of dead labour.

20 Carey and Quirk, "History of the Future," 181.

21 Howard Segal expresses the technological utopian view, which in contrast to its optimistic tone, also echoes the totalizing nature of Heidegger's *gestell*: "Technology tames both nature and itself, subduing the wind, water, fire, and climate, purifying its own wastes, staunching its own excesses, and replanting the gardens it has trampled underfoot. Utopian man aspires to similar control over human nature." Segal, *Technological Utopianism*, 24, 31.

22 Mosco, "Mything Links," 58.

23 Ibid., 58–9.

24 McHale, *Constructing Postmodernism*, 250–1.

25 Gibson, *Count Zero*, 16.

26 According to Burton, "For Gotham City we looked at pictures of New York ... We just said, 'This is what's happening to New York at the moment. Things are being added and built on and design is getting all over the place.' We decided to darken everything and build vertically and cram things together and then just go further with it in a more cartoon way. It has an operatic feel, and an almost timeless quality." Burton, *Burton on Burton*, 75, 76.

27 Gibson, *Count Zero*, 7.

28 Sibley, "The Unreal World of Virtual Reality," B3.

29 See chapter 1, note 54.

30 Benedikt, *Cyberspace: First Steps*, 9.

31 Becker, *Heavenly City*, 29.

32 Ibid., 6.

33 Ibid., 48–9.

34 Ibid., 122, 130.

35 Campion, *The Great Year*.

36 Benedikt, *Cyberspace: First Steps*, 15.

37 Ibid., 18.

38 Ibid., 22.

39 Gelernter, *Mirror Worlds*, 3.

40 Intellectual property law agrees. Computer software is protected by the same body of law that protects other forms of creative expression like poems, plays, or novels. For an overview of copyright and intellectual property issues pertaining to cyberspace, see Samoriski, *Issues in Cyberspace*, and Downes, "Intellectual Property and Copyright Issues."

41 Gelernter, *Mirror Worlds*, 40.

42 Ibid., 39.

43 Ibid., 40–1.

44 Ibid., 40–5.

45 Sutherland, "The Ultimate Display," 506–8.

46 Kreuger, *Artificial Reality*, 2.

47 Rheingold, *Virtual Reality*, 23.

48 McLuhan, *Understanding Media*, 64.

49 Heim, *Metaphysics of Virtual Reality*.

50 Ibid., xiii.

51 Plato, *Republic of Plato*, 25–7.

52 Heim, *Metaphysics of Virtual Reality*, 89.

53 Ibid., 101.

54 Ayer, *Language, Truth and Logic*, 188.

55 Gibson, *Ecological Approrach to Visual Perception*, 257.

56 Heim, *Metaphysics of Virtual Reality*, 101.

57 Ibid., 100–1.

58 Ibid., 102.

59 Ibid., 89 (emphasis added).

60 Ibid., 88.

61 See http://virtualjerusalem.com. The Kotel cam can be accessed through http://kotelcam.tv (accessed 13 December 2002). Prayers can be sent to the Wall via http://www.westernwall.co.il.

CHAPTER SIX

1 Poster, *Mode of Information*, 111.

2 Andrews, "Cartographer's Choice," 64, 66.

3 "An enormous part of the activity of each society is concerned with the transmission and protection of its public image; that set of images regarding space, time, relation, evaluation, etc., which is shared by the mass of its people." Boulding, *The Image*, 64.

4 Ibid., 64–5.

5 Vattimo argues that "with the demise of the idea of a central rationality of history, the world of generalized communication explodes like a multiplicity of 'local' rationalities – ethnic, sexual, religious, cultural, or aesthetic minorities – that finally speak for themselves." See Vattimo, *Transparent Society*, 9.

6 Baudrillard, "The End of the Millennium," 449.

7 Ricœur, *Reality of the Historical Past*, 1–2.

8 Lowenthal, *Past Is a Foreign Country.*

9 Glenn, *Legal Traditions of the World,* 10.

10 Lowenthal, *Past Is a Foreign Country,* 212–13.

11 Cox, "Concept of Public Memory," 122.

12 Bodnar, *Remaking America,* 13.

13 Cox, "Concept of Public Memory," 125.

14 Lowenthal, *Past Is a Foreign Country,* 241.

15 Ibid., 248.

16 Foucault, "Of Other Spaces," 23.

17 Ibid., 23.

18 Ibid.

19 Ibid., 27.

20 Genocchio, "Discourse, Discontinuity, Difference."

21 McBeath and Web, "On the Nature of Future Worlds?"

22 See, for example, Soja, "Heterotopias."

23 Uspensky, *Poetics of Composition,* 157.

24 See Glenn, *Legal Traditions of the World,* 3.

25 Posner, *Archives in the Ancient World.*

26 Dollar, "Archivists and Records Managers in the Information Age."

27 Ibid., 38.

28 Hyry and Onuf, "The Personality of Electronic Records."

29 Yuxweluptan, "Inherent Rights, Inherent Visions," 316.

30 Ibid.

31 Benedikt, *Cyberspace: First Steps,* 130.

32 Howes, *Varieties of Sensory Experience,* 4.

33 Jakle, "Small Towns as Historical Places," 81–2.

34 Markus, "Visible Knowledge."

35 Mitchell, *City of Bits,* 55–6.

36 Vattimo, *End of Modernity,* 6–7.

37 Deleuze and Guattari, *On the Line,* 25–6. Deleuze and Guattari's discussion of the performative nature of the map is reminiscent of George Kelly's concept of the invitational mode of language (see chapter 1).

38 Young, "The Ideal of Community."

CONCLUSION

1 O'Neill, *Five Bodies,* 45.

Bibliography

* Texts so identified are available only in electronic form.

Akin, D.L., M.L. Minsky, E.D. Thiel, and C.R. Kurtzman. "Space Applications of Automation, Robotics, and Machine Intelligence Systems (ARAMIS)," phase 2, vol. 3. Executive Summary, MIT, Contract NASA 8-34381, Marshall Space Flight Center: NASA, 1983.

Althusser, Louis. *For Marx.* Translated by Ben Brewster. London: Verso 1986.

Andrews, Sona Karentz. "The Cartographer's Choice: Decisions Affecting Tactual Map Design." In Leo Zonn, ed., *Place Images in Media: Portrayal, Experience, and Meaning,* 63–79. Rowan and Littlefield Publishers 1990.

Angus, Ian. *A Border Within: National Identity, Cultural Plurality, and Wilderness.* Montreal: McGill-Queen's University Press 1999.

Appadurai, Arjun. *Modernity at Large: Cultural Dimensions of Globalization.* Minneapolis, MN: University of Minnesota Press 1996.

– "Disjuncture and Difference in the Global and Cultural Economy." *Public Culture* 2, no. 2 (spring 1990): 1–24.

Arnheim, Rudolph. "On the Nature of Photography." *Critical Inquiry* 1 (1974): 154–7.

Atkinson, Paul. *The Ethnographic Imagination: Textual Constructions of Reality.* London: Routledge 1990.

Attallah, Paul, and Leslie Regan Shade, eds. *Mediascapes.* Toronto: Nelson Thomson Learning 2002.

Augustine. *City of God.* Harmondsworth, England: Penguin 1972.

– *Confessions.* Oxford: Clarendon Press 1992.

Ayer, A.J. *Language, Truth and Logic.* Markham, ON: Pelican Books 1971.

Bailey, Cameron. "Virtual Skin: Articulating Race in Cyberspace." In Mary Anne Moser, ed., 29–50. *Immersed in Technology: Art and Virtual Environments.* Cambridge: MIT Press 1996.

Barlow, John Perry. "The Law Comes to Cyberspace." *Byte* 16, no. 10 (October 1991): 332.

– "The Great Work." *Communications of the ACM* (January 1992): 25–8.

– "Is There a There in Cyberspace?" *Utne Reader* (March–April 1995): 53–6.

– "Declaring Independence." *Wired* (June 1996): 121–2.

– "Declaration of Independence of Cyberspace." http://www.eff.org/~barlow/Declaration-Final.html. Accessed on 21 October 2002.

Barney, Darrin. *Prometheus Wired: The Hope for Democracy in the Age of Networked Technology.* Vancouver: University of British Columbia Press 2000.

Bates, John. "Burning Man." *Websight* (November–December 1996): 16–17.

Bateson, Gregory. *Steps to an Ecology of Mind.* New York: Ballantine Books 1972.

Baudrillard, Jean. *The Ecstacy of Communication.* Translated by Bernard and Caroline Schutze. Edited by Sylvère Lotringer. New York: Semiotext(e) 1987.

– "The End of the Millennium or the Countdown," translated by Chris Turner. *Economy and Society* 26, no. 4 (November 1997): 447–56.

Bazin, André. "The Myth of Total Cinema." In *What is Cinema?* translated by Hugh Gray, 17–22. Berkeley: University of California Press 1967.

– "The Ontology of the Photographic Image." In *What is Cinema?* translated by Hugh Gray, 9–16. Berkeley: University of California Press 1967.

Becker, Carl L. *The Heavenly City of the Eighteenth-Century Philosophers.* New Haven, CT: Yale University Press 1932.

Bell, Daniel. *The Coming Post-Industrial Society: A Venture in Social Forecasting.* New York: Basic Colophon 1976.

– "The Social Framework of the Information Society." In Michael L. Dertouzas and Joel Moses, eds., *The Computer Age: A Twenty Year View,* 163–211. Cambridge: MIT 1979.

Benedikt, Michael, ed. *Cyberspace: First Steps.* Cambridge: MIT Press 1992.

Beniger, James. *The Control Revolution: Technological and Economic Origins of the Information Society.* Cambridge: Harvard University Press 1986.

– "Personalization of Mass Media and the Growth of Pseudo-community." *Communications Research* 14, NO. 3 (1987): 312–71.

Bertalanffy, Ludwig von. *General System Theory: Foundations, Development, Applications.* New York: George Braziller 1968.

Bettelheim, Bruno. *The Informed Heart: Autonomy in the Mass Age.* New York: Avon 1960.

– "Joey the Mechanical Boy." *Scientific American,* March 1959. Reprinted in Eric and Mary Josephson, eds. *Man Alone: Alienation in Modern Society,* 437–46. New York: Dell 1962.

- *The Empty Fortress: Infantile Autism and the Birth of the Self.* New York: The Free Press 1967.
- *Freud's Vienna and Other Essays.* New York: Knopf 1990.

Biocca, Frank. "Communication within Virtual Reality: Creating a Space for Research." *Journal of Communication* 42, no. 4 (autumn 1992): 5–19.

Black, Max. *Models and Metaphors.* Ithaca, NY.: Cornell University Press 1962.
- "More about Metaphor." In Andrew Ortony, ed., *Metaphor and Thought*, 19–43. Cambridge: Cambridge University Press 1979.

Bodnar, John. *Remaking America: Public Memory, Commemoration, and Patriotism in the Twentieth Century.* Princeton, NJ: Princeton University Press 1992.

Bolter, Jay David. *Writing Space: The Computer, Hypertext, and the History of Writing.* Hillsdale, NJ: Lawrence Erlbaum Associates 1991.

Bolter, Jay David, and Richard Grusin. "Re-mediation." *Configurations* 4, no. 3 (1996): 311–58.

Borgman, Albert. *Technology and the Character of Everyday Life: A Philosophical Inquiry.* Chicago: University of Chicago Press 1984.

Bormann, Ernest G. "Symbolic Convergence Theory: A Communication Formulation." *Journal of Communication* 35, no. 4 (autumn 1985): 128–38.

Bourdieu, Pierre. *Distinction.* Cambridge: Harvard University Press 1984.
- *In Other Words: Essays towards a Reflexive Sociology.* Translated by Matthew Adamson. Cambridge: Polity Press 1990.
- *Photography: A Middle-Brow Art.* Translated by Susan Whiteside. Stanford, CA: Stanford University Press 1990.

Bromberg, John M. "Contradiction in Cyberspace." In Rob Shields, ed., *Cultures of the Internet*, 99–124. London: Sage 1996.

Brown, Richard. *A Poetic for Sociology: Toward a Logic of Discovery for the Human Sciences.* New York: Cambridge University Press 1977.

Brunn, Stanley D., and Thomas Leinbach, eds. *Collapsing Space and Time: Geographical Aspects of Communication and Information.* London: Harper Collins 1991.

Burke, Kenneth. *Permanence and Change: An Anatomy of Purpose.* 2d rev. ed. New York: New Republic 1965. (Original work published 1935.)
- "Auscultation, Creation, and Revision." In James Chesebro, ed., *Extensions of the Burkeian System*, 42–172. Tuscaloosa, AL: University of Alabama Press 1993.

Burton, Tim. *Burton on Burton.* Edited by Mark Salisbury. London: Faber and Faber 1995.

Busch, Thomas W., and Shaun Gallagher, eds. *Merleau-Ponty, Hermeneutics, and Postmodernism.* Albany, NY: State University of New York Press 1992.

Cairncross, Frances. *The Death of Distance: How the Communications Revolution Will Change Our Lives.* Boston: Harvard Business School Press 1997.

Campbell, Joseph. *Masks of God: Creative Mythology.* Harmondsworth, England: Penguin 1968.

Campion, N. *The Great Year: Astrology, Millennarianism, History in the Western Tradition.* Harmondsworth, England: Penguin 1994.

Carey, James W. *Communications as Culture: Essays on Media and Society.* Boston: Unwin Hyman 1989.

– "The Language of Technology: Talk, Text, and Template as Metaphors for Communication." In Martin J. Medhurst, Alberto Gonzalez, and Tarla Rai Peterson, eds., *Communication and the Culture of Technology,* 19–39. Pullman, WA: Washington State University Press 1990.

Carey, James, and John Q. Quirk. "The History of the Future." In James Carey, *Communications as Culture: Essays on Media and Society,* 173–200. Boston: Unwin Hyman 1989.

– "The Mythos of the Electronic Revolution." In James Carey, *Communications as Culture: Essays on Media and Society,* 113–41. Boston: Unwin Hyman 1989.

Castells, Manuel. *The Informational City: A New Framework for Social Change.* Toronto: Centre for Urban and Community Studies, University of Toronto 1991.

Cavell, Stanley. *The World Viewed: Reflections on the Ontology of Film.* Enlarged Edition. Cambridge, MA: Harvard University Press 1979.

Chesebro, James, ed. *Extensions of the Burkeian System.* Tuscaloosa, AL: University of Alabama Press 1993.

Chesebro, James, and Dale A. Bertelsen. *Analyzing Media: Communication Technologies as Symbolic and Cognitive Systems.* New York: Guilford Press 1996.

Claydon, Tony, and Ian MacBride. *Protestantism and National Identity.* Cambridge: Cambridge University Press 1998.

Clover, Carol J. *Her Body, Himself: Gender in the Slasher Film.* London: Verso 1995.

Clynes, Manfred E., and Nathan Kline. "Cyborgs and Space." *Aeronautics* (September 1960). Reprinted in Chris Hables Gray, ed., *The Cyborg Handbook,* 29–33. New York: Routledge 1995.

Collins, Christopher. *Poetics of the Mind's Eye: Literature and the Psychology of the Imagination.* Philadelphia: University of Pennsylvania Press 1991.

Cook, Olive. *Movement in Two Dimensions: A Study of the Animated and Projected Pictures Which Preceded the Invention of Cinematography.* London: Hutchinson 1963.

Cooper, David E. "Technology: Liberation or Enslavement?" In Roger Fellows, ed., *Philosophy and Technology,* 7–18. Cambridge: Cambridge University Press 1995.

Cooper, Linda, and Vincent Berdayes. "The Information Highway in Contemporary Magazine Narrative." *Journal of Communication* 48, no. 2 (1998): 109–24.

Coyne, Richard. *Technoromanticism, Digital Narrative, Holism and the Romance of the Real.* Cambridge, MA: MIT Press 1999.

Cox, Richard J. "The Concept of Public Memory and Its Impact on Archival Public Programming." *Archiveria* 36 (autumn 1993).

Crary, Jonathan. *Techniques of the Observer.* Cambridge, MA: MIT Press 1982.

Curran, James. "Mass Media and Democracy Revisited." In James Curran and Michael Gurevitch, eds., *Mass Media and Society.* 2d ed. New York: Arnold 1996.

Damer, B. *Avatars! Exploring and Building Virtual Worlds on the Internet.* Berkeley, CA: Peachpit Press 1997.

Davidson, Donald. *Inquiries into Truth and Interpretation.* Oxford: Clarendon Press 1984.

Davis, Erik. *Techgnosis: Myth, Magic and Mysticism in the Age of Information.* New York: Harmony 1998.

de Lauretis, Teresa, Andreas Huyssen, and Kathleen Woodward, eds. *The Technological Imagination: Theories and Fictions.* Madison, WI: Coda Press 1980.

Deleuze, Gilles, and Felix Guattari. *On The Line.* New York: Semiotext(e) 1983.

Dertouzas, Michael L., and Joel Moses, eds. *The Computer Age: A Twenty Year View.* Cambridge: MIT 1979.

Dewey, John. *The American Intellectual Frontier: Characters and Events.* New York: Henry Holt 1929.

– *The Public and Its Problems.* Chicago: Swallow Press 1954.

Dibble, Julian. "A Rape in Cyberspace: How an Evil Clown, a Haitan Trickster Spirit, Two Wizards and a Cast of Dozens Turned a Database into a Society." *The Village Voice,* 21 December 1993, 36–43.

Diebert, Ronald J. *Parchment, Printing, and Hypermedia: Communication in World Order Transformation.* New York: Columbia University Press 1998.

Dizard, Wilson. *The Coming Information Age: An Overview of Technology, Economics, and Politics.* New York: Longman 1982.

Doheny-Farina, Stephen. *The Wired Neighborhood.* New Haven, CT: Yale University Press 1996.

Dollar, Charles M. "Archivists and Records Managers in the Information Age." *Archiveria* 36 (autumn 1993): 37–52.

Downes, Daniel M. "The Medium Vanishes? The Resurrection of the Mass Audience in the New Media Economy. " *M/C: A Journal of Media and Culture* 3, no. 1 (2000). http://www.uq.edu.au/mc/0003/mass.html.

- "Intellectual Property and Copyright Issues in the Global Economy." In Paul Attallah and Leslie Regan Shade, eds., *Mediascapes: New Patterns in Canadian Communication*. Toronto: Nelson Thomson Learning 2002.

Downes, Daniel M., and Richard Janda. "Virtual Citizenship." *Canadian Journal of Law and Society* 13, no. 2 (fall 1998): 27–61.

Dreyfus, Hubert L. *What Computers Can't Do: A Critique of Artificial Reason*. New York: Harper & Row 1972.

Duplantier, Stephen. "Archetypal Communication: Ecology, Psyche and Utopia in a Teleproxemic World: Essays for Harold A. Innis and James W. Carey." PHD diss., University of Southern Mississippi, 1992.

Dyck, Isabel, "Further Notes on Feminist Research." In Pamela Ross, ed., *Feminist Geography in Practice: Research and Methods*, 234–44. Oxford: Blackwell 2002.

Edelman, Gerald M. *Bright Air, Brilliant Fire: On the Matter of the Mind*. New York: Basic Books 1992.

Eisenstein, Zilla. *Global Obscenities: Patriarchy, Capitalism and the Lure of Cyberfantasy*. New York: New York University Press 1998.

Ellul, Jacques. *The Technological Society*. New York: Vintage Books 1964.

Featherstone, Mike, and Roger Burrows, eds. *Cyberspace/Cyberbodies/Cyberpunk – Cultures of Technological Embodiment*. London: Sage 1995.

Feibleman, James K. *Technology and Reality*. The Hague: Nijhoff 1982.

Fellows, Roger, ed. *Philosophy and Technology*. Cambridge: Cambridge University Press 1995.

Finn, Jerry. "An Exploration of Helping Processes in an Online Self-help Group Focusing on Issues of Disability." *Health and Social Work* 24, no. 3 (August 1999): 320–31.

Fiske, John. "Postmodernism and Television." In James Curran and Michael Gurevitch, eds., *Mass Media and Society*. 2d ed., 53–65. New York: Arnold 1996.

Fiurama, Gemma Corradi. *The Metaphoric Process: Connections between Language and Life*. New York: Routledge 1995.

Fodor, Jerry A. "The Mind-Body Problem." In Richard Warner and Tadeusz Szubka, eds., *The Mind-Body Problem: A Guide to the Current Debate*, 24–40. Oxford: Blackwell 1994.

Foucault, Michel. *The Archaeology of Knowledge*. New York: Harper & Row 1972.

- *Discipline and Punish: The Birth of the Prison*. Translated by Alan Sheridan. New York: Vintage 1977.

- "Questions of Geography." In C. Gordon, ed., *Power/Knowledge: Selected Interviews and Other Writings, 1972–1977*, 63–77. New York: Pantheon 1980.

- "Of Other Spaces." *Diacritics*. 16 (spring 1986): 22–7.

– *Foucault Live: Interviews, 1966–1984.* Sylvère Lotringer, ed., and John Johnson, trans. New York: Semiotext(e) 1990.

Franklin, Ursula. *The Real World of Technology.* Toronto: CBC Enterprises 1990.

Freedman, Jill, and Gene Combs. *Narrative Therapy: The Social Construction of Preferred Realities.* New York: Norton 1996.

Freud, Sigmund. *Civilization and its Discontents.* James Strachey, ed. and trans. New York: Norton 1962.

Friedberg, Anne. *Window Shopping: Cinema and the Postmodern.* Berkeley, CA: University of California Press 1993.

Fuller, R. Buckminster. *Critical Path.* New York: St Martin's Press 1981.

Gauntlett, David, ed. *Web.studies: Rewiring Media Studies for the Digital Age.* London: Arnold 2000.

Geddes, Patrick. *Ideas at War.* London: Williams and Norgate.

Gelernter, David. *Mirror Worlds: Or the Day Software Puts the Universe in a Shoebox ... How It Will Happen and What It Will Mean.* New York: Oxford University Press 1991.

Genocchio, Benjamin. "Discourse, Discontinuity, Difference: The Question of 'Other' Spaces." In Sophie Watson and Katherine Gibson, eds., 35–46. *Postmodern Cities and Spaces.* Oxford: Blackwell 1995.

Gernsheim, M., and A. Gernsheim. *J.M. Daguerre.* New York: Dover 1968.

Gibson, James J. *The Ecological Approach to Visual Perception.* Boston: Houghton Mifflin 1979.

Gibson, William. *Neuromancer.* New York: Ace 1984.

– *Count Zero.* New York: Ace 1986.

– *Mona Lisa Overdrive.* New York: Bantam 1988.

Giddens, Anthony. *The Consequences of Modernity.* Stanford, CA: Stanford University Press 1990.

Glenn, H. Patrick. *Legal traditions of the World: Sustainable Diversity in Law.* Oxford: Oxford University Press 2000.

Goodman, Nelson. *Languages of Art: An Approach to a Theory of Symbols.* Indianapolis, IN: Bobbs-Merrill 1968.

Gore, Al. "A National Vision." *Byte* 16, no. 7 (July 1991): 188–9.

Grant, George. *Philosophy in the Mass Age.* Edited and with an introduction by William Christian. Toronto: University of Toronto Press 1995.

– *Technology and Empire: Perspectives on North America.* Toronto: Anansi 1969.

Gray, Chris Hables, ed. *The Cyborg Handbook.* New York: Routledge 1995.

Gregory, D., and J. Urry, eds. *Social Relations and Spatial Structures.* London: MacMillan 1985.

Gronbeck, Bruce E. "Communication Technology, Consciousness, and Culture: Supplementing FM-2030's View of Transhumanity." In Martin J.

Medhurst, Alberto Gonzalez, and Tarla Rai Peterson, eds., *Communication and the Culture of Technology*, 3–18. Pullman, WA: Washington State University Press 1990.

Guattari, Felix. *Chaosmosis: An Ethico-Aesthetic Paradigm*. Translated by Paul Bains and Julian Pefanis. Bloomington, IN: Indiana University Press 1995.

Gumbrecht, Hans Ulrich, and K. Ludwig Pfeiffer, eds. *Materialities of Communication*. Stanford, CA: Stanford University Press 1994.

Habermas, Jürgen. *The Structural Transformation of the Public Sphere*. Trans. Thomas Burger. Cambridge, MA: MIT Press 1989.

Hakluyt, Richard. *The Principal Navigations Voyages Traffiques and Discoveries of the English Nation*. Vol. 1. New York: AMS Press 1965.

Hall, Edward T. *The Silent Language*. Garden City, NY: Doubleday 1959.

– *The Hidden Dimension*. New York: Anchor Books 1969.

Halley, Janet E. "The Politics of the Closet: Legal Articulation of Sexual Orientation Identity." In Dan Danielson and Engle, eds., *After Identity: A Reader in Law and Culture*, 326. New York: Routledge 1995.

Haraway, Donna. "A Manifesto for Cyborgs." *Socialist Review* 80 (1985): 65–108.

– "The Actors Are Cyborg, Nature is Coyote, and the Geography is Elsewhere: Postscript to 'Cyborgs at Large.'" In Constance Penley and Andrew Ross, eds., *Technoculture*, 21–6. Minneapolis, MN: University of Minnesota Press 1991.

– *Simians, Cyborgs, and Woman: The Reinvention of Nature*. New York: Routledge 1991.

Hardison, O.B. *Disappearing through the Skylight: Culture and Technology in the Twentieth Century*. New York: Viking 1990.

Harré, Rom. "Man the Rhetorician." In Anthony Chapman and Dylan M. Jones, eds., *Models of Man*, 201–13. Leicester: British Psychological Society 1980.

– *Social Being*. 2d ed. Oxford: Blackwell 1993.

Harré, Rom, and Grant Gillett. *The Discursive Mind*. Thousand Oaks, CA: Sage 1994.

Harvey, David. *The Limits to Capital*. Oxford: Blackwell 1982.

Havelock, Eric A. *Preface to Plato*. Cambridge: Belknap Press of Harvard University Press 1963.

Hayward, Philip, ed. *Culture, Technology and Creativity in the Late Twentieth Century*. London: John Libbey 1990.

Healy, Dave. "Cyberspace and Place." In David Porter, ed. *Internet Culture*, 55–67. New York: Routledge 1997.

Hector, Carrie, "Being There: The Subjective Experience of Presence." *Presence* 1, no. 2 (spring 1992): 262–71.

Heidegger, Martin. "The Question Concerning Technology." In *Basic Writings: Ten Key Essays*. Revised and expanded edition. Edited by David Farrell Krell, 311–41. San Francisco: Harper Collins 1993.

Heim, Michael. *Electric Language: A Philosophical Study of Word Processing*. New Haven, CT: Yale University Press 1987.

– "The Erotic Ontology of Cyberspace." In Michael Benedikt, ed., *Cyberspace: First Steps*. Cambridge: MIT Press 1992.

– *The Metaphysics of Virtual Reality.* New York: Oxford University Press 1993.

Held, Richard, and Nathaniel J. Durlach. "Telepresence." *Presence* 1, no. 1 (1992): 69–112.

Hockenberry, John. "This Is the Story of the Most Fearless Entrepreneur Ever: The Human Brain." *Wired* (August 2001): 94–105.

Hoffman, Lynn. "Constructing Social Realities: An Art of Lenses." *Family Process* 29 (1990): 1–12.

Holand, Hjalmar R. *Explorations in America before Columbus*. 2d ed. New York: Twayne Publishers 1958.

Hollinger, Veronica. "Cybernetic Deconstructions: Cyberpunk and Postmodern Fiction." *Mosaic* (spring 1990).

Howes, David. *The Varieties of Sensory Experience: A Sourcebook in the Anthropology of the Senses*. Toronto: University of Toronto Press 1991.

Huizinga, Johan. *Homo Ludens: A Study of the Play-Element in Culture*. Boston: Beacon Press 1950.

Human Rights Watch. "Electrifying Speech: New Communications Technologies and Traditional Civil Liberties." Vol. 4, no. 5 (July 1992). Internet address: ftp.eff.org/pub/EFF.*

Hunt, A. "The Big Fear: Law Confronts Postmodernism." (1990) 35 *McGill Law Journal* at 507.

Hunt, Harry T. *On the Nature of Consciousness: Cognitive, Phenomenological, and Transpersonal Perspectives*. New Haven, CT: Yale University Press 1995.

Hyry, Tom, and Rachel Onuf. "The Personality of Electronic Records: The Impact of New Information Technology on Personal Papers." *Archival Issues: Journal of the Midwest Archives Conference* (1997): 37–44.

Ihde, Don. *Technology and the Lifeworld: From Garden to Earth*. Bloomington, IN: Indiana University Press 1990.

– "Image Technologies and Traditional Culture." In *Postphenomenology: Essays in the Postmodern Context*, 43–55. Evanston, IL: Northwestern University Press 1993.

Innis, Harold. *The Bias of Communication*. Toronto: University of Toronto Press 1951.

– *Empire and Communications*. Victoria: Press Porcepic 1986.

Jakle, John A. "Social Stereotypes and Place Images: People on the Trans-Appalachian Frontier As Viewed by Travellers." In Leo Zonn, ed., *Place Images in Media: Portrayal, Experience and Meaning*, 83–103. Rowan and Littlefield 1990.

– "Small Towns as Historical Places: A Symbolic Interactionist Approach to Structuration Theory through the Study of Landscape." In David Wilson and James O. Huff, eds., *Marginalized Places and Populations: A Structurationist Agenda*, 61–83. Westport, CT: Praeger Publishers 1994.

Janelle, Donald G. "Global Interdependence and its Consequences." In Stanley D. Brunn and Thomas Leinbach, eds., *Collapsing Space and Time: Geographical Aspects of Communication and Information*, 49–81. London: Harper Collins 1991.

Jarvie, Ian. *Philosophy of the Film: Epistemology, Ontology, Aesthetics*. New York: Routledge and Kegan Paul 1987.

Jastrow, Robert. *The Enchanted Loom: Mind in the Universe*. New York: Simon and Schuster 1981.

Johnsen, Edwin G., and William R. Corliss. *Teleoperators and Human Augmentation* (Washington, DC: NASA 1967). In Chris Hables Gray, ed. *The Cyborg Handbook*, 84–92. New York: Routledge 1995.

Johnson, David. *Getting Canada Online: Understanding the Information Highway.* Toronto: Stoddart 1995.

Johnson, Mark. *The Body in the Mind: The Bodily Basis of Meaning, Imagination and Reason*. Chicago: University of Chicago Press 1987.

Jones, Steven G., ed. *CyberSociety: Computer-Mediated Communication and Community*. Thousand Oaks, CA: Sage 1995.

– *Virtual Culture: Identity and Communication in Cyberspace*. London: Sage 1997.

Josephson, Eric, and Mary Josephson, eds. *Man Alone: Alienation in Modern Society*. New York: Dell 1962.

Kapor, Mitchell, and John Perry Barlow. "Across the Electronic Frontier" (1990). Internet address: ftp.eff.org/pub/EFF.*

Kelly, George. *Clinical Psychology and Personality: The Selected Papers of George Kelly*, edited by Brendan Maher. New York: John Wiley and Sons 1969.

– "The Language of Hypothesis: Man's Psychological Instrument." In *Clinical Psychology and Personality: The Selected Papers of George Kelly*, edited by Brendan Maher, 147–62. New York: John Wiley and Sons 1969.

Kim, Amy Jo. "Killers Have More Fun." *Wired* (May 1998): 140–7, 197.

King, R., ed. *Computers and Controversy*. 2d ed. San Diego: Academic Press 1996.

Klaic, Dragan. *The Plot of The Future: Utopia and Dystopia in Modern Drama.* Ann Arbor, MI: University of Michigan Press 1991.

Klein, Melanie. *The Selected Melanie Klein.* Edited by Juliet Mitchell. Harmondsworth, England: Penguin 1986.

Kline, Stephen, Nick Dyer-Witherford, and Greg de Peuter. *Digital Play: The Interaction of Technology, Culture and Marketing.* Montreal: McGill-Queen's University Press 2003.

Kolko, Beth. "Representing Bodies in Virtual Space: The Rhetoric of Avatar Design." *Information Society* 15 (1999): 177–86.

Kranzberg, Melvin, and William Davenport, eds. *Technology and Culture.* New York: New American Library 1972.

Kreuger, Myron. *Artifical Reality 2.* Reading, MA: Addison Wesley 1991.

Kroker, Arthur. *Technology and the Canadian Mind: Innis/McLuhan/Grant.* Montreal: New World Perspectives 1984.

Kroker, Arthur, and Michael A. Weinstein. *Data Trash.* New York: St Martin's Press 1994.

Krol, Ed. *The Whole Internet.* Sebastopol, CA: O'Reilly and Associates 1992.

La Barre, Weston. *The Human Animal.* Chicago: University of Chicago Press 1954.

Lakoff, George. *Women, Fire, and Dangerous Things: What Categories Reveal about the Mind.* Chicago: University of Chicago Press 1987.

Lakoff, George, and Mark Johnson. *Metaphors We Live By.* Chicago: University of Chicago Press 1980.

Lakoff, George, and Mark Turner. *More than Cool Reason: A Field Guide to Poetic Reason.* Chicago: University of Chicago Press 1989.

Lanier, Jaron, and Frank Biocca. "An Insider's View of the Future of Virtual Reality." *Journal of Communication* 42, no. 4 (1992): 150–72.

Lasswell, Harold. "Communications in a Divided World." Louis G. Cowen Lecture. London: International Broadcast Institute 1977.

– "Future of World Communication and Propaganda." In Harold Lasswell, Daniel Lerner, and Hans Speine, eds., *Propaganda and Communication in World History.* Vol. 3, 516–34. Honolulu: University of Hawaii Press 1980.

Laurel, Brenda. *Computers as Theatre.* Reading, MA: Addison-Wesley 1992.

Lauretis, Teresa de. *Alice Doesn't.* Bloomington, IN: Indiana University Press 1984.

Lefebvre, Henri. *The Production of Space.* Translated by Donald Nicholson-Smith. Oxford: Blackwell 1991.

Lessig, Lawrence. *Code and Other Laws of Cyberspace.* New York: Basic Books 1999.

Levidow, Les, and Kevin Robins. "Towards a Military Information Society." In Levidow and Robins, eds., *Cyborg Worlds: The Military Information Society*, 159–77. London: Free Association Press 1989.

– eds. *Cyborg Worlds: The Military Information Society*. London: Free Association Press 1989.

Levin, Charles. "Entre la chair et l'esprit: Le corps social du nouveau-né." *Sociologies et sociétés* 24, no. 1 (spring 1992): 67–79.

Lévi-Strauss, Claude. *Structural Anthropology*. Trans. Claire Jacobson and Brooke Grundfest Schoepf. New York: Basic Books 1963.

Levy, Pierre. *Collective Intelligence: Mankind's Emerging World in Cyberspace*. New York: Plenum Trade 1997.

Licklider, J.C.R., and Robert Taylor. "The Computer as Communication Device." *Sci-Tech* (April 1968): 21–31.

Lingis, Alphonso. "The Phantom Equator." In Thomas W. Busch and Shaun Gallagher, eds., *Merleau-Ponty, Hermeneutics, and Postmodernism*, 227–39. Albany, NY: State University of New York Press 1992.

Lipton, Mark. "Forgetting the Body: Cybersex and Identity." In Lance Strate, Ron Jacobson, and Stephanie B. Gibson, eds., *Communication and Cyberspace: Social Interaction in an Electronic Environment*, 335–49. Cresskill, NJ: Hapton Press 1996.

Locke, John. *Essay concerning Human Understanding*. New York: Dover 1959.

Loomis, Jack M. "Distal Attribution and Presence." *Presence* 1, no. 1 (winter 1992): 113–19.

Lowenthal, David. *The Past is a Foreign Country*. Cambridge: Cambridge University Press 1985.

Lupton, Deborah. "The Embodied Computer/User." In Mike Featherstone and Roger Burrows, eds., *Cyberspace/Cyberbodies/Cyberpunk – Cultures of Technological Embodiment*, 97–112. London: Sage 1995.

MacKinnon, Richard C. "Searching for the Leviathan in Usenet." In Steven G. Jones, ed., *CyberSociety: Computer-Mediated Communication and Community*, 112–37. Thousand Oaks, CA: Sage 1995.

– "Punishing the Persona: Correctional Strategies for the Virtual Offender." In Steven G. Jones, ed., *Virtual Culture: Identity and Communication in Cyberspace*, 206–35. London: Sage 1997.

Magid, Ron. "Master of His Universe." In *American Cinematographer* (September 1999): 26–7, 30–5.

Maloney, Janice. "Does Digital Equal Free? The Intellectual Property Debate Ties Itself in Knots." *Digital Media: A Seybold Report* 2, no. 2 (22 July 1992).

Markus, Thomas A. *Buildings and Power*. London: Routledge 1993.

Martin-Barbero, J. *Communication, Culture and Hegemony*. London: Sage 1993.

Marx, Karl, and Frederick Engels. *The German Ideology.* New York: International Publishers 1947.

Massey, Doreen. *Geography Matters!* Cambridge: Cambridge University Press 1989.

Mattelart, Armand. *Networking the World 1794–2000.* Translated by Liz Carey-Libbrecht and James A. Cohen. Minneapolis, MN: University of Minnesota Press 2000.

Mazlish, Bruce. "The Fourth Discontinuity." In Melvin Kranzberg and William Davenport, eds., *Technology and Culture,* 217–19. New York: New American Library 1972.

– *The Fourth Discontinuity: The Co-evolution of Humans and Machines.* New Haven, CT: Yale University Press 1993.

McBeath, G., and S.A. Web. "On the Nature of Future Worlds? Considerations of Virtuality and Utopia." *Information, Communication and Society* 13, no. 1 (1 March 2000): 1–96.

McCaughey, Martha, and Michael D. Ayers, eds. *Cyberactivism: Online Activism in Theory and Practice.* London: Routledge 2003.

McHale, Brian. *Constructing Postmodernism.* London: Routledge 1990.

McLaughlin, Margaret C., Kerry K. Osborne, and Christine B. Smith. "Standards of Conduct on Usenet." In Steven G. Jones, ed., *CyberSociety: Computer-Mediated Communication and Community,* 90–111. Thousand Oaks, CA: Sage 1995.

McLuhan, Marshall. *The Gutenberg Galaxy.* Toronto: University of Toronto Press 1962.

– *Understanding Media.* New York: Mentor 1964.

McLuhan, Marshall, and Quentin Fiore. *War and Peace in the Global Village.* New York: Bantam Books 1968.

McQuail, Denis. *Mass Communication Theory.* 2d ed. London: Sage 1987.

Meadows, Mark Stephen. *Pause and Effect: The Art of Interactive Narrative.* Indianapolis, IN: New Riders 2003.

Medhurst, Martin J., Alberto Gonzalez, and Tarla Rai Peterson, eds. *Communication and the Culture of Technology.* Pullman, WA: Washington State University Press 1990.

Menzies, Heather. *Fast Forward and Out of Control: How Technology Is Changing Your Life.* Toronto: Macmillan 1989.

Merleau-Ponty, Maurice. *The Phenomenology of Perception.* London: Routledge and Kegan Paul 1962.

– *The Primacy of Perception.* Evanston, IL: Northwestern University Press 1964.

Metz, Christian. "Photography and Fetish." In Carol Squires, ed., *The Critical Image: Essays on Contemporary Photography,* 155–64. Seattle: Bay Press 1990.

Meyer, Gary. "Fascism in the Cyberstate." *High Performance* (spring 1992): 39–41.

Meyrowitz, Joshua. *No Sense of Place: The Impact of Electronic Media on Social Behavior.* Oxford: Oxford University Press 1985.

Michotte, Albert. "The Real and the Irreal in the Image." Translated by Alan Costalls from "Le réel et l'irréel dans l'image," *Bulletin de la classe des Lettres de l'Académie royale de Belgique.* 5th series, 1960, 46, 330–44. In Georges Thinés, Alan Costall, and George Butterworth, eds., *Michotte's Experimental Phenomenology of Perception,* 187–97. Hillsdale, NJ: Lawrence Erlbaum Associates 1991.

– "The Character of 'Reality' of Cinematic Projections." Translated by Alan Costall from "Le caractère de 'réalité' des projections cinématographiques," *Revue internationale de filmologie,* 1948, 1, 249–61. In Georges Thinés, Alan Costall, and George Butterworth, eds., *Michotte's Experimental Phenomenology of Perception,* 197–209. Hillsdale, NJ: Lawrence Erlbaum Associates 1991.

Miller, Carolyn R. "Technology as a Form of Consciousness: A Study of Contemporary Ethos." *Central States Speech Journal* 29 (1978): 228–36.

Miller III, Stanley A. "Death of a Game Addict" *Milwaukee Journal Sentinel,* 20 March 2002. http://www.jsonline.com/news/State/Mar02/31536.asp, accessed 11 December 2002.

Minow, Martha. *Making All the Difference.* Cornell University Press 1990.

Mnookin, Jennifer L. "Virtual(ly) Law: The Emergence of Law in LambdaMoo." *Journal of Computer-Mediated Communication* (June 1996). http://jcmc.huji.ac.il/vol2/issue1/lambda.html.

Mosco, Vincent. *The Pay-Per Society: Computers and Communication in the Information Age.* Toronto: Garamond Press 1989.

– "Mything Links: Power and Community on the Information Highway." *Information Society* (January–March 1998): 57–62.

Moser, Mary Anne, and D. MacLeod, eds. *Immersed in Technology: Art and Virtual Environments.* Cambridge: MIT Press 1996.

Mumford, Lewis. *Technics and Civilization.* New York: Harcourt, Brace 1934.

– *The Myth of the Machine: Technics and Human Development.* New York: Harcourt, Brace and World 1967.

– *The Pentagon of Power.* New York: Harcourt Brace 1970.

Murray, Janet H. *Hamlet on the Holodeck: The Future of Narrative in Cyberspace.* Cambridge, MA: MIT Press 1998.

Nakamura, Lisa. "Race in/for Cyberspace: Identity Tourism and Racial Passing on the Internet: The Resurrection of the Corpus in Text-Based vr." *Works and Days* 13, nos. 1–2: 245–60.

Nancy. "Virtual Rape Consequences." Electronic Ballot 57980. Available at lamda@xerox.parc.com.

Neisser, Ulric. *Cognition and Reality: Principles and Implications of Cognitive Psychology.* San Francisco: W.H. Freeman 1976.

- *The Perceived Self: Ecological and Interpersonal Sources of Self Knowledge.* Cambridge: Cambridge University Press 1993.

- "Without Perception, There Is No Knowledge: Implications for Artificial Intelligence." In Robert G. Burton, ed., *Natural and Artificial Minds,* 147–64. Albany, NY: SUNY 1993.

Newell, Allen. "The Knowledge Level." *Artificial Intelligence* 18 (1982): 87–127.

Newell, Allen, and Herbert A. Simon. *Human Problem Solving.* Englewood Cliffs, NJ: Prentice-Hall 1972.

- "Computer Science as Empirical Enquiry: Symbols and Search." *Communications of the ACM* 19 (March 1976): 113–26. Reprinted in John Haughland, ed., *Mind Design,* 35–66. Cambridge, MA: MIT Press 1981.

Noam, Eli M. "Media Concentration in the United States: Industry Trends and Regulatory Responses." http://www.vii.org/papers/medconc.htm.*

O'Brien, Conor Cruise. *On the Eve of the Millennium.* Toronto: Anansi 1994.

O'Neill, John. *Perception, Expression and History.* Evanston, IL: Northwestern University Press 1970.

- *Five Bodies: The Human Shape of Modern Society.* Ithaca, NY: Cornell University Press 1985.

Ong, Walter J. *Orality and Literacy: The Technologizing of the World.* New York: Methuen 1982.

Pacey, Arnold. *The Culture of Technology.* Cambridge: MIT Press 1983.

Panofsky, Erwin. *Meaning in the Visual Arts: Papers in and on Art History.* New York: Doubleday 1955.

Papert, Seymour. *The Children's Machine: Rethinking School in the Age of the Computer.* New York: Basic Books 1993.

Pavlik, John V., and Everette E. Dennis, eds. *Demystifying Media Technology.* London: Mayfield Publishing 1993.

Penley, Constance, and Andrew Ross, eds. *Technoculture.* Minneapolis, MN: University of Minnesota Press 1991.

Pimentel, K., and K. Teixeira. *Virtual Reality: Through the New Looking Glass.* New York: Intel/Windcrest/McGraw-Hill 1993.

Plant, Sadie. *Zeros + Ones.* New York: Doubleday 1997.

Plato. *The Republic of Plato,* 3d ed., vol. 2. Translated by Benjamin Jowett. Oxford: Clarendon Press.

Pollock, Griselda. "Missing Women: Rethinking Early Thoughts on Images of Women." In Carol Squires, ed., *The Critical Image: Essays on Contemporary Photography,* 202–19. Seattle, WA: Bay Press 1990.

Posner, Ernst. *Archives in the Ancient World.* Cambridge: Harvard University Press 1972.

Poster, Mark. *Foucault, Marxism and History: Mode of Production versus Mode of Information.* Cambridge: Polity Press 1984.

– *The Mode of Information: Poststructuralism and Social Context.* Chicago: University of Chicago Press 1990.

– "Cyberdemocracy: Internet and the Public Sphere." *Difference Engine* 2 (December 1995). Available at http://www.gold.ac.uk/difference/papers/poster.html or at Mark Poster's home page: http://www.hnet.uci.edu/mposter/writings/democ.html.*

– *The Second Media Age.* Chicago: Polity Press 1995.

– *What's the Matter with the Internet.* Minneapolis, MN: University of Minnesota Press 2001.

Postman, Neil. *Amusing Ourselves to Death: Public Discourse in the Age of Show Business.* New York: Viking 1985.

Pribram, Karl. "From Metaphors to Models: The Use of Analogy in Neurophysiology." In David E. Leary, ed., *Metaphors in the History of Psychology,* 79–103. Cambridge: Cambridge University Press 1990.

Quittner, Joshua. "The Merry Pranksters Go to Washington." *Wired* (June 1994): 77–81, 128–31.

Rheingold, Howard. *Virtual Reality.* New York: Summit Books 1991.

– "A Slice of Life in My Virtual Community." In L.M. Harrison, ed., *Global Networks: Computers and International Communication,* 57–80. Cambridge: MIT Press 1993.

– *The Virtual Community: Homesteading on the Electronic Frontier.* Reading, MA: Addison-Wesley 1993.

– "Community Development in the Cybersociety of the Future." In David Gauntlett, ed., *Web.studies: Rewiring Media Studies for the Digital Age,* 170–7. London: Arnold 2000.

Richards, I.A. *Philosophy of Rhetoric.* London: Oxford University Press 1936.

Ricœur, Paul. *The Reality of the Historical Past.* Milwaukee, WI: Marquette University Press 1984.

– *From Text to Action: Essays in Hermeneutics II.* Translated by Kathleen Blamey and John B. Thompson. Evanston, IL: Northwestern University Press 1991.

Robinett, Warren. "Synthetic Experience: A Proposed Taxonomy." In *Presence* 1, no. 2 (spring 1992): 229–47.

Robins, Kevin. "Cyberspace and the World We Live In." In Mike Featherstone and Roger Burrows, eds., *Cyberspace/Cyberbodies/Cyberpunk – Cultures of Technological Embodiment*, 135–55. London: Sage 1995.

Romanyshyn, Robert. *Technology as Symptom and Dream*. London: Routledge 1989.

Rorty, Richard. *Consequences of Pragmatism*. Minneapolis, MN: University of Minnesota Press 1982.

Roscoe, Timothy. "The Construction of the World Wide Web Audience." In *Media, Culture and Society*, 673–84. London: Sage 1999.

Rose, Lance. "Cyberspace and the Legal Matrix: Laws or Confusion?" 1991. Internet address: elrose@well.sf.ca.us.*

Rosenfield, Isreal. *The Strange, Familiar, and Forgotten: An Anatomy of Consciousness*. New York: Vintage 1993.

Ross, Pamela, ed. *Feminist Geography in Practice: Research and Methods*. Oxford: Blackwell 2002.

Roszak, Theodore. *The Cult of Information: The Folklore of Computers and the Truth of Thinking*. New York: Pantheon 1986.

Rucker, Rudy. *Mind Tools: The Five Levels of Mathematical Reality*. Boston: Houghton Mifflin Company 1987.

Rucker, Rudy, R.U. Sirius, and Queen Mu, eds. *Mondo 2000: A User's Guide to the New Edge*. New York: Harper Collins 1992.

Rushkoff, D. *Cyberia: Life in the Trenches of Hyperspace*. San Francisco: Harper-Collins 1994.

Saco, Diana. *Cybering Democracy: Public Space and the Internet*. Minneapolis, MN: University of Minnesota Press 2002.

Salisbury, Mark, ed. *Burton on Burton*. London: Faber and Faber 1995.

Salter, Lee. "Comparing Collective Identity in Online and Offline Feminist Activities." In Michael D. Ayers, ed., *Cyberactivism: Online Activism in Theory and Practice*, 145–64. London: Routledge 2003.

Samoriski, Jan. *Issues in Cyberspace: Communication, Technology, Law and Society on the Internet Frontier*. Boston: Allyn and Bacon 2002.

Sanders, Doug. "Mr. Wrong." *Globe and Mail*, Saturday, 10 August 2002, F4.

Sarkin, Theodore R., and John I. Kitsuse. "A Prologue to *Constructing the Social*." In Theodore R. Sarkin and John I. Kitsuse, eds., *Constructing the Social*, 1–18. London: Sage 1994.

– eds. *Constructing the Social*. London: Sage 1994.

Schutz, Alfred. "On Multiple Realities." *Philosophy and Phenomenological Research* 5, no. 4 (1945): 533–76.

– *Collected Papers: The Problem with Social Reality*. Vol. 1. Edited by Maurice Natanson. The Hague: Martinus Nijhoff 1971.

Searle, John. "Minds, Brains and Programs." In John Haugeland, ed., *Mind Design: Philosophy, Psychology, Artificial Intelligence*, 287–306. Cambridge: MIT Press 1981.

Segal, Howard P. *Technological Utopianism in American Culture.* Chicago: University of Chicago Press 1985.

Selnow, Gary W. *Electronic Whistle-Stops: The Impact of the Internet on American Politics.* Westport, CT: Praeger 1998.

Shade, Leslie Regan. "A Gendered Perspective on Access to the Information Infrastructure." *Information Society* 14, no. 1 (January–March 1998).

Sibley, Robert. "The Unreal World of Virtual Reality." *Ottawa Citizen*, 19 January 1992, B3.

Silver, David. "Looking Backwards, Looking Forwards: Cyberculture Studies, 1990–2000." In David Gauntlett, ed., *Web.studies: Rewiring Media Studies for the Digital Age*, 19–30. London: Arnold 2000.

Simon, Herbert A. "The Patterned Matter That Is Mind." In David Steier and Tom M. Mitchell, eds., *Mind Matters: A Tribute to Allen Newell*, 407–31. Mahwah, NJ: Lawrence Erlbaum Associates 1996.

Slade, Joseph W. "American Writers and American Invention: Cybernetic Discontinuity in pre-World War II Literature." In Teresa de Lauretis, Anreas Huyssen, and Kathleen Woodward, eds., *The Technological Imagination: Theories and Fictions*, 27–47. Madison, WI: Coda Press 1980.

Snydnes, Jennifer. "The Internet as Social Medium." In R. King, ed., *Computers and Controversy.* 2d ed., 433–568. San Diego: Academic Press 1996.

Sobchack, Vivian. "The Scene of the Screen: Envisioning Cinematic and Electronic 'Presence.'" In Hans Ulrich Gumbrecht and K. Ludwig Pfeiffer, eds., *Materialities of Communication*, translated by William Whobrey, 83–106. Stanford, CA: Stanford University Press 1994.

Soja, Edward W. "Heterotopias: A Remembrance of Other Spaces in the Citadel – LA." In Sophie Watson and Katherine Gibson, eds., *Postmodern Cities and Spaces*, 13–34. Oxford: Blackwell 1995.

Sontag, Susan. *On Photography.* New York: Farrar, Strauss and Giroux 1977.

Sponsler, Claire. "Cyberpunk and the Dilemma of Postmodern Narrative: The Example of William Gibson." *Contemporary Literature* 3, no. 4 (winter 1993): 625–44.

Squires, Carol, ed. *The Critical Image: Essays on Contemporary Photography.* Seattle: Bay Press 1990.

Stamps, Judith. *Unthinking Modernity: Innis, McLuhan and the Frankfurt School.* Montreal: McGill-Queen's University Press 1995.

Statistics Canada, *Household Internet Survey* http://www.statcan.ca/Daily/ English/020725/d020725.htm. Accessed 21 October 2002.*

Steier, David, and Tom M. Mitchell, eds. *Mind Matters: A Tribute to Allen Newell*. Mahwah, NJ: Lawrence Erlbaum Associates 1996.

Sterling, Bruce. "Greetings from Burning Man." *Wired* (November 1996): 196–206, 274.

Steuer, Jonathan. "Defining Virtual Reality: Dimensions Determining Telepresence." *Journal of Communication* 42, no. 4 (1992): 73–93.

Strate, Lance, Ron Jacobson, and Stephanie B. Gibson. "Surveying the Electronic Landscape: An Introduction to *Communication in Cyberspace*." In Lance Strate, Ron Jacobson, and Stephanie B. Gibson, eds., *Communication and Cyberspace: Social Interaction in an Electronic Environment*, 1–22. Cresskill, NJ: Hapton Press 1996.

– eds. *Communication and Cyberspace: Social Interaction in an Electronic Environment*. Cresskill, NJ: Hapton Press 1996.

Suchman, Lucy A. *Plans and Situated Actions: The Problem of Human Machine Communication*. Cambridge: Cambridge University Press 1987.

Sunstein, Cass. *Republic.com*. Princeton: Princeton University Press 2001.

Sutherland, Ivan. "The Ultimate Display." *Proceedings of the International Federation of Information Processing Congress* (1965): 506–8.

Sutton, Nina. *Bettelheim: A Life and a Legacy*. Translated by David Sharp and the author. New York: Basic Books 1996.

Thinés, Georges, Alan Costall, and George Butterworth, eds. *Michotte's Experimental Phenomenology of Perception*. Hillsdale, NJ: Lawrence Erlbaum Associates 1991.

Toffler, Alvin. *Future Shock*. New York: Random House 1970.

– *The Third Wave*. New York: Morrow 1980.

– *Powershift: Knowledge, Wealth and Values at the End of the Twenty-first Century*. New York: Bantam 1990.

Tomas, David. "Old Rituals for New Space: Rites de Passage and William Gibson's Cultural Model of Cyberspace." In Michael Benedikt, ed., *Cyberspace: First Steps*. Cambridge: MIT Press 1992.

Turkle, Sherry. *The Second Self: Computers and the Human Spirit*. New York: Simon and Schuster 1984.

– *Life on the Screen: Identity in the Age of the Internet*. New York: Simon and Schuster 1996.

Uspensky, Boris. *A Poetics of Composition: The Structure of the Artistic Text and Typology of a Compositional Form*. Translated by Valentina Zavarin and Susan Wittig. Berkeley: University of California Press 1973.

Van Wyck, Peter C. *Primitives in the Wilderness*. Albany, NY: SUNY Press 1997.

Varella, Francisca J., Evan Thompson, and Eleanor Rosch. *The Embodied Mind: Cognitive Science and Human Experience*. Cambridge: MIT Press 1993.

Vattimo, Gianni. *The End of Modernity.* Translated and with an introduction by Jon R. Snyder. Baltimore, MD: Johns Hopkins University Press 1988.

– *The Transparent Society.* Trans. David Webb. Baltimore, MD: Johns Hopkins University Press 1992.

Von Glasersfeld, Ernst. "An Introduction to Radical Constructivism." In Paul Watzlawick, ed., *The Invented Reality,* 17–40. New York: Norton 1984.

Warner, Michael. *The Letters of the Republic: Publication and the Public Sphere in Eighteenth-Century America.* Cambridge, MA: Harvard University Press 1992.

Warner, Richard, and Tadeusz Szubka, eds. *The Mind-Body Problem: A Guide to the Current Debate.* Oxford: Blackwell 1994.

Watson, Sophie, and Katherine Gibson, eds. *Postmodern Cities and Spaces.* Oxford: Blackwell 1995.

Watzlawick, Paul, ed. *The Invented Reality.* New York: Norton 1984.

Watzlawick, Paul, Janet Helmick Beavin, and Don D. Jackson. *Pragmatics of Human Communication: A Study of Interactional Patterns, Pathologies, and Paradoxes.* New York: Norton 1967.

Weingarten, Kathy. "The Discourses of Intimacy: Adding a Social Constructionist and Feminist View." *Family Process* 30 (1991): 285–305.

Wilden, Anthony. *System and Structure: Essays in Communication and Exchange.* 2d ed. London: Tavistock Publications 1979.

Williams, David. "Constructing Economic Space: The World Bank and the Making of Homo Oeconomicus." *Journal of International Studies* 28, no. 1 (1999): 79–99.

Williams, Frederick. *The Communications Revolution.* Beverly Hills: Sage 1982.

Willis, Anne-Marie. "Digitization and the Living Death of Photography." In Philip Hayward, ed., *Culture, Technology and Creativity in the Late Twentieth Century.* London: John Libbey 1990.

Wilson, David, and James O. Huff, eds. *Marginalized Places and Populations: A Structurationist Agenda.* Westport, CT: Praeger Publishers 1994.

Wilson, Kevin G. *Technologies of Control: The New Interactive Media for the Home.* Madison, WI: University of Wisconsin Press 1988.

Winner, Langdon. *Autonomous Technology.* Cambridge: MIT Press 1977.

Witherford, Nick Dyer. *CyberMarx – Cycles and Circuits of Struggle in High-Technology Capitalism.* Urbana, IL: University of Illinois Press 1999.

Wood, Donald. *Post-Intellectualism and the Decline of Democracy.* Wesport, CT: Praeger 1996.

Young, Iris Marion. "The Ideal of Community and the Politics of Difference." In Linda J. Nicholson, ed., *Feminism/Postmodernism,* 300–23. London: Routledge 1990.

Yuxweluptan, Lawrence Paul. "Inherent Rights, Inherent Visions." In Mary
    Anne Moser, ed., *Immersed in Technology: Art and Virtual Environments*, 316–
    18. Cambridge: MIT Press 1996.

Zonn, Leo, ed. *Place Images in Media: Portrayal, Experience, and Meaning.*
    Rowan and Littlefield Publishers 1990.

Zukin, Sharon. *Landscapes of Power: From Detroit to Disney World.* Berkeley:
    University of Califormia Press 1991.

Index